EASTWOOD FOOD SERVICES LIMITED
61 SIGNET DRIVE
WESTON, ONTARIO   M9L 2W5

D1535715

The
Banquet
Business

The Banquet Business

Arno B. Schmidt

CBI Publishing Company, Inc.
51 Sleeper Street
Boston, MA 02210

Production Editor: Linda Dunn McCue
Text Designer: Jack Schwartz
Compositor: Trade Composition
Cover Designer: Betsy Franklin

Library of Congress Cataloging in Publication Data

Schmidt, Arno, 1937-
    The banquet business.

    1. Caterers and catering.   I. Title.
TX943.S35   642′.4   80-39641
ISBN 0-8436-2147-8

Printed in the United States of America.

Printing (last digit): **9 8 7 6 5 4 3 2 1**

CONTENTS

Special Luncheon
$3.00 PER PERSON

Clam Broth, Savarin

———

Poached Egg, Bonne-Femme

———

Mixed Grill à l'Américaine

———

Asparagus Salad

———

Biscuit Tortoni

Petits Fours

———

Coffee

———

October 27, 1928

ACKNOWLEDGMENTS

My gratitude goes to my wife, Agnes, and my teenage children, Stephanie and Christopher, who grumbled yet allowed me to work on this book when I came home after a long day's work. My thanks to my many friends and colleagues in the kitchen, in service, and in banquet sales for the advice they gave. In particular I want to thank Mr. Kurt Erman, Executive Sous Chef of the Waldorf-Astoria, and Mr. Jean Nicolas, private chef, for their expert help with chapter 14. My thanks also go to the management of the Waldorf-Astoria for allowing me to use a variety of materials in this book. Last, but not least, I am indebted to Mrs. Jule Wilkinson, who can read my mind with never-ending patience.

Easter Sunday Dinner
MENU

Suprême de Fruits Maraschino

———

Tortue Claire à l'Anglaise
Cœur de Céleri   Olives Verts et Noirs   Noix Salées

———

Truite de Rivière Meunière
Concombres Vernon

———

Poussin de Serre en Casserole à la Mayfair
Petits Pois Nouveaux au Beurre

———

Asperges de Californie, Hollandaise

———

Nid aux Oeufs
Friandises

———

Moka

———

Pastilles de Menthe

———

The Plaza
April 8, 1928

INTRODUCTION

Banquet business can be big business. Unfortunately, it is not growing consistently everywhere. Some hotels have seen a steady decrease in banquet covers. Other hotels have seen only a very modest increase in banquet covers, while their room sales and restaurant sales have increased nicely.

The banquet market varies in the same way for restaurants, clubs, and other foodservice operations set up to serve banquets. Some conventions now prefer to spend money on an additional guest speaker or on another professional seminar rather than finance a closing banquet that might be boring. The wedding market, influenced by social fashion and monetary considerations, now includes informal weddings, ceremonies at home, and small celebrations on the lawn. These too have eaten into the traditional banquet market, where elegant weddings with large numbers of guests provided a staple business. Fund raisers have discovered that fun is important to people attending a fund-raising affair. Instead of scheduling the oft-repeated Chicken Breast Luncheon, in a big hall with many speakers, recent fund-raising events have been held successfully in skating rinks, museums, even in railroad stations.

To be successful in the banquet business today, one must offer fun, informal elegance, and value in food, beverages, and service. People are willing to spend money for value received, but dull, uninteresting formal dinners are considered a waste of money.

This book is about the mechanics of selling banquets: planning the meal, getting along with the chef, writing proper menus, using foreign words on menus, and making a profit despite all the problems that can occur. Numerous sample menus are included to set you on the track to success. The steps needed to back up a good banquet menu are discussed in detail. Banquet business is well worth cultivating. Presenting tested systems that will help a foodservice operation build a profitable banquet business is the purpose of this book.

Menu

Dinner Menu

Consomme Celestine

Reserve   Poached Striped Bass
Chevillot   Bonne Femme   Golden Fleurons

Cabernet   Sliced Filet of Beef Wellington
Sauvignon   Chinese Snow Peas

Salad of Bibb & Avocado

Frozen Chestnut   Souffle
Tuilles
Demi - Tasse

A Note on the Menus

I have a huge menu collection, and it took a number of winter evenings to select the menus for this book. Some menus I selected for beauty of language; other menus because the wine and food offered were unusually well matched. Some menus I chose because they were interesting; others because they were practical.

I selected menus for historical value: some of the menus in this book were prepared for dinners given by chefs' associations to honor chefs, often dear friends of mine. Some menus were brilliant, and others were tailor-made for specific occasions.

To my dismay I discovered that some of these menus were not well-written. Perfection is a goal not often reached. Menus written by prominent chefs with impeccable knowledge of menu French had spelling mistakes. Was it the fault of the printer? Of the person who typed the menu? Of the person who should have proofread the menu? Of the committee who paid for the menu? We will never know. Some Kosher menus frequently use the words cream and meat together. Most were written before truth-in-menus became an issue, and the attending guests as well as the caterer knew that cream on a kosher menu does not always mean dairy cream but would be "ersatz" cream which is perfectly kosher. Still this practice should be avoided. Some elaborate menus listed good wines, but not the all-important vintages. Who is to blame?

Such errors in the production of some of the menus chosen for this book are the chief reason why I did not mention the name of the writer of the menu. In addition, most menus are joint efforts; an idea was born, tossed around, perfected, rejected by the client, modified, and finally accepted. It would be grossly unfair to mention a single name as the author of a menu that resulted from such group effort.

Some menus carry the names of the people in charge of a dinner, in most cases the chef, the headwaiter, and the director of catering. That is fine because these people produced the menu. No claim is ever made, however, that the people given credit on a menu actually wrote the menu.

Please accept the menus in this book for what they are: attempts to please people. Before you copy one of these menus, make sure it fits the occasion you plan to use it for; and check the spelling!

Profitability

1

Banquets can and must be profitable to pay for the tremendous investment banquet space represents. When you look at a banquet room, think how much that space could bring in revenue if it were turned into office or rental space. Recognize that this could be done without the worry of a business as complex as the banquet business and you will understand why banquet space must bring in considerably more profit that its use as rental space would bring.

CALCULATING COSTS

To achieve the required profit, all costs must be controlled. The performance of the sales staff must be monitored; prices must be adjusted to reflect inflation, and profit goals must be set. While unused space represents lost revenue, there is also the problem of marginally profitable banquets: they must be identified and their price upgraded to yield an acceptable profit margin. This, of course, has another risk: increased prices may cause parties to go to another operation. However, since no business can exist for long when part of the business is unprofitable, it is better to avoid unprofitable business altogether, and instead leave the space available for other, profitable business.

Every function should be evaluated. As a first step, when the party is booked and before the contract is signed, the proposed menu should be costed out by the food controller or by the chef. The necessary banquet food cost percentage varies from place to place. Large city hotels need an average banquet food cost of 20 percent on luncheons and dinners to stay in business, while other operations require a banquet food cost of 25 to 30 percent. Whatever the food cost percentage, it should be determined by the management, not left up to the individual who sells banquets. Many banquet salespeople have no idea how much the potential food cost percentage is for a given menu. In smaller operations, the headwaiter, an office employee, or sometimes even the owner will sell a function and unwittingly "give away the house" because they just do not realize how much the merchandise will cost. (A banquet portion chart is included in my book, Notes from the Chef's Desk, CBI Publishing Co., Inc. Boston.)

In addition to the food cost, the liquor cost must be considered. An acceptable markup on liquor is much easier to calculate than is one for food. The wholesale cost of wine and liquor can be made available to the banquet sales personnel and therefore the cost can be calculated quickly. (Food preparation, on the other hand, requires many different ingredients, in various amounts, at varying prices: this makes food cost comparatively difficult to calculate precisely.) A drink cost of around 20 percent is acceptable; a wine and beer cost of 25 percent to 30 percent is often used as the basis for calculation.

Obviously, liquor costs can be calculated quickly. In contrast, a food cost of 20 percent cannot be achieved at all times, so many times exceptions must be made. It should be necessary for these exceptions to be approved each time. Some functions, like receptions and breakfasts, have lower food costs than luncheons and dinners; combining them makes it possible to achieve an overall food cost of 20 percent in some foodservice operations. In chapter 2, Figures 2.2 and 2.3 show how a large sales staff is monitored. Many operations add a section to these charts showing the food cost achieved on each event.

Labor Costs

After the food and liquor cost, the next big item is labor cost. This cost factor can be difficult to calculate. In most cases the kitchen payroll can be divided into a basic, or steady, payroll and extra payroll. The steady payroll covers all personnel in the back of the house, including the chef, the chef's staff, the storeroom staff, the steward, the cleaners, and similar personnel. When there is a heavy load, the kitchen staff is often augmented by extra employees or by regular employees working overtime; their wages covered by the extra payroll.

In small operations, such as a restaurant with only one or two function rooms, the kitchen staff is often able to prepare small banquets in addition to providing food for regular restaurant business. For such cases, the kitchen labor cost of banquet business is nil. On the other hand, if a restaurant is open for luncheon only and a kitchen staff must stay overtime to prepare a banquet, the cost can be considerable. When doing capacity business, an operation with large banquet facilities is normally able to produce banquet food in large volume and well ahead of time—providing the menus are made available—and, in such cases, the labor cost can be small. If there is a slow week, however, with only one function booked, the labor cost is naturally very high, even at such a well-equipped operation. To charge to one function the kitchen payroll for the whole week would be foolish, yet I have seen it done by over-eager systems analysts. Result: the hapless salesperson who sold that function was penalized because he booked the only party in the week!

Incidentally, when I talk about payroll, I refer to the gross payroll, which includes all fringe benefits. It would be misleading to consider only the cash payroll without calculating the payroll taxes, insurance, and contingency for vacations. Generally, bartenders, waiters, and waitresses work only when there is a function. But even when they do not work, in most cases certain fringe benefits, like vacations, holiday pay, and personal days, accumulate and must be paid to steady banquet service staff members.

When talking about back-of-the-house payroll, the question of allocations also comes up. Large hotels and other sizable operations divide payroll between food payroll and liquor payroll. In a smaller operation, a steward is in charge of receiving both food and beverages. Is part of his salary charged to beverages? Is the salary of a dishwasher who handles glasses along with dishes charged to beverages or food? In a small restaurant, the person who cleans the kitchen floor might also vacuum the dining room. Is part of his salary charged to the service payroll? Allocation of labor costs can involve great detail.

Controlling Labor Costs

No matter how the labor cost in the kitchen is allocated, it must be monitored. In large operations, the labor cost is forecasted one month ahead on a daily basis using available bookings. The labor cost is reviewed daily. The actual payroll is compared with the forecasted payroll in dollars as well in percentages, and also with the percentages of the prior year, if they are available. If the payroll is out of line, an adjustment must be made.

To reduce the payroll in a very large operation without undue hardship is difficult, but it can be done. Large operations often use extra employees in addition to their steady crew, and, when business is slow, the extras are just not called in. Where time off is not covered by the payroll, vacations can be scheduled during slow periods, or employees can be encouraged to take extra time off for personal reasons. Only in extreme cases should employees get laid off.

To adjust the payroll in a small operation is more difficult. It is most unfair and also unwise to lay off employees as soon as business slows down a little. Employees may well seek employment elsewhere and not come back when your business improves. Problems in finding competent employees for the kitchen staff easily result. Smaller places often solve this difficulty by using regular employees to prepare food for freezing during slow periods. This practice must be evaluated, however: merchandise tied up in storage really means cash tied up without producing any interest. The small-business manager must be sure that labor cost savings balance storage cost loss.

The key to managing a successful payroll is to know how much business to expect. The key to that is a realistic forecast of sales. (Chapter 4 discusses forecasting in more detail.) When you know what to expect, adjustments can be made. Better scheduling can eliminate some or all overtime. Time off can be given. Semi-retired employees can be offered a few days or weeks away from the job; younger members of the staff can be sent to a short season job for a few weeks. In a

Figure 1.1.   Special function services—sample information.

Check Rooms

Our check rooms are operated by a concessionaire. The owner of the concession is Mr(s). . . . .

It is our policy not to allow racks in meeting rooms, as our insurance company does not cover lost articles unless checked.

Check Room Charges:	$ . . . . . p.p.
Check Room and Washroom charges:	$ . . . . . p.p.

or

Tipping by each guest.

In case the check room and/or washroom charges are paid by the host, the check room will display a "No Tipping" sign.

Engineering Charges

Electrical

150-Watt Fixed Spotlight	$ . . . .
Outlets, 120 Volts	$ . . . . per 1000 Watts
Outlets, 208 Volts, single or triple phase	$ . . . . per 2000 Watts
Switchboard Operator	$ . . . . per hour, 4 hour minimum, Overtime after 1 AM
Spotlight Operator	$ . . . . per hour, 4 hours minimum
Electrician Labor	$ . . . . per hour

Radio Room

Microphones	First Microphone free, additional microphone rental and installation $ . . . . per day
Standing Microphone for Bank	$ . . . .

Carpentry

Banner Hanging 4x4 feet,	$ . . . .
over 4x4 feet	$ . . . .
Upholsterer, draping of Runway	$ . . . . per foot plus cost of material
Telephone Services:	To be discussed with Telephone Company

word, the payroll must be managed, regardless of how big the business is.

To suggest acceptable percentages here for the back-of-the-house payroll is very difficult because conditions vary widely. A payroll of 15 percent to 20 percent for the whole back of the house is often acceptable.

Effect of Union Contracts

In many places, the union contract describes precisely the duties and corresponding salaries for the service staff. In addition to salary, the service staff is usually paid a share of the banquet gratuities. Some banquet areas have one waiter or waitress for each table of ten covers. This ratio allows for good service, but it is also costly for the operation since the basic salary per employee the operation must pay is about the same. Other operations assign fifteen covers, while still others assign up to thirty covers to a service person. Naturally, the waiter or waitress makes much more money in these cases, since gratuities collected are based on the number of people served.

As stated, the basic salary for a waiter or waitress is about the same whatever the number served, but some union contracts set a special base salary for "splits," that is, the number of covers assigned in addition to the basic ten covers. In such cases, it is to the advantage of the service personnel to get as many covers as possible. However, it is also to the advantage of the operation to give each service person as many covers as possible, because a split is still cheaper than paying another person. Service to the guest, however, invariably suffers as the proportion of covers to service personnel is increased.

Further Payroll Costs

When calculating front-of-the-house payroll, miscellaneous personnel also must be considered. Large operations employ house personnel. These people set up a room for a function, placing the tables and chairs, rolling up the carpet when needed, or bringing in the piano. Large banquet houses whose banquet rooms are often sold for meeting set-ups employ many house personnel. Smaller operations can use the service staff or perhaps busboys for room set-up, but large establishments need special personnel. When house personnel are steady employees, their payroll must also be closely watched.

Another service payroll often overlooked is banquet housekeeping. It is a small payroll but still an important one. Banquet housekeeping staff keep the guest bathrooms in good order, tidy up the rooms, sweep up cigarette butts, and perform other small but important duties. Overall the front-of-the-house payroll often runs between 12 and 15 percent.

The next payroll factor is the cost of sales. This includes the salary of the sales staff and office staff in the sales office. Even in a small operation there must be somebody to answer the phones, type the letters, and to do the actual selling. Related to cost of sales in a banquet operation is the administrative cost. In small operations, the cost of sales and the administrative cost are often combined. There is, however, the cost of bookkeeping—the salary for the person who does the

Menu, the Tavern Club, reception and dinner, November 1977.

LE DINER

LA INA FINO SHERRY   LE CONSOMME GERMINY

*   *   *

BARTON AND GUESTIER
PULIGNY MONTRACHET
1973

LE BAR RAYE POCHE AU COURT-BOUILLON
SAUCE HOLLANDAISE
PARFUMEE AU BEURRE DE HOMARD

*   *   *

LE GRANITE AUX PRUNELLES

*   *   *

BEAULIEU VINEYARD
CABERNET SAUVIGNON
1973

LE MEDAILLON DE VENAISON
SAUCE GRAND-VENEUR
NAVETS ET MARRONS SAUTES

*   *   *

LA BIBB DU KENTUCKY
LE FROMAGE EXPLORATEUR

*   *   *

CHARLES HEIDSIECK,
BRUT
N.V.

LE ROCHER DE CASSIS

*   *   *

LES TUILES ET LES FLORENTINES

*   *   *

LIQUEURS   LE CAFE

buying and for the accountant who is on the staff or comes once a week. This payroll cost is small, but must be included.

Finally there is the cost of caring for the exterior of the building. Hotels usually do not charge the food department for the services of the plumbers, carpenters, and other craftsmen doing normal maintenance. However, if these services are required for a specific function, the guests must be charged (see Figure 1.1). This will be discussed in greater detail later in this chapter. Some operations employ people to take care of the garden, shovel snow, park cars, and do repairs on the premises. Some very successful businesses have been built little by little with only their own staff.

Clearly, it is not easy to calculate precisely the labor cost to be charged against every function. This figure will vary considerably according to volume. There should be, however, a basic payroll percentage figure set for each day. If this figure is exceeded, the danger signals must be recognized, and the payroll scrutinized. As pointed out earlier, this should be done weekly if possible; daily is better, but once a month is too late.

MISCELLANEOUS COSTS

When evaluating the profit potential of a function, other cost factors must be considered. Previously, the cost of heating or cooling a room has not been a major consideration for a banquet salesperson when selling a function. Today, attention must be paid to the rising cost of utilities. In many places, the various function rooms have separate heating and cooling units, not all operating with the same rate of efficiency. It behooves good management to make the banquet sales staff aware of the cost factors involved in heating and cooling each room.

In hotels, the question also must be asked as to how many free rooms are being given away by the banquet staff. On certain occasions, it is customary and good business to accommodate the partygiver, or, in case of a wedding, the bride and groom, with sleeping quarters. In a sellout situation, however, this is money thrown away on good will. Sometimes providing free rooms cannot be avoided, but banquet salespersons should not give rooms away without thought and awareness of the costs.

The cost of china, linen, and glassware constitute a percentage cost not under the control of the sales staff, though salespeople can and should charge for the use of special china. Certain menu items require the use of easily broken dishes and/or glassware. Laundry cost is also an operating expense not controlled by sales. The cost should be under one percent of gross sales. If special linens or lace are requested,

Figure 1.2.   Specialty items—flowers.

Flowers and Decorations

Lilac Tree Inc. is the official florist and decorator for our company. All inquiries and recommendations should be directed to them. Price list is provided below.

Price List for Flowers and Decorations

Corsages	$ . . . . .
Boutonnieres	$ . . . . .
Orchid Corsages	$ . . . . .

Table Centerpieces

Small	$ . . . . .
Special and up	$ . . . . .

Head Table Decorations

Center Pieces from	$ . . . . .
Special Selection	$ . . . . .
Hedge of Flowers	$ . . . . .
Smilax in front of head table, per foot	$ . . . . .
Minimum	$ . . . . .

Buffet Arrangements

Center Pieces, low	$ . . . . .
High Stanchion Arrangements	$ . . . . .
Fountains	$ . . . . .
Arbors	$ . . . . .
Other designs on request	

Lattice Work Screens Covered with Smilax

For partitions, etc., from	$ . . . . .

Stage Background

Large Ferns, on stands	$ . . . . .
Potted Palms, Large	$ . . . . .

Wedding Decorations, Bunting Work, and Rental of other Decorative Items on Request.

there should be an extra charge. Provisions for replacement of china, linen and glassware must be budgeted. Percentages vary from place to place; a figure of 3½ to 4½ percent of gross sales is often the norm.

Figure 1.3.   Specialty items—cakes.

Wedding and Birthday Cakes

Quotations should be by the cake and not by the number of persons to be served. The reason for this is that the final guarantee might drop after the cake is made.

List of Selling Prices for Birthday Cakes

6 x 3 in.	serves	3 to 6 guests	$ . . . . . .
9 x 3 in.	serves	6 to 8 guests	$ . . . . . .
10 x 3 in.	serves	8 to 12 guests	$ . . . . . .
12 x 3 in.	serves	12 to 20 guests	$ . . . . . .
16 x 3½ in.	serves	20 to 30 guests	$ . . . . . .

List of Selling Prices for Wedding Cakes

Tiers	Size	Serves	Price
One Tier	6 in.	6 to 8	$ . . . .
	8 in.	8 to 12	$ . . . .
	12 in.	12 to 20	$ . . . .
One Tier One Dummy Tier	6 in.	6 to 8	$ . . . .
	8 in.	8 to 12	$ . . . .
	10 in.	12 to 16	$ . . . .
Two Tiers One Dummy Tier	12 + 6 in.	16 to 20	$ . . . .
	13 + 10 in.	18 to 25	$ . . . .
	16 + 12 in.	15 to 35	$ . . . .
Three Tiers Two Dummy Tiers	16 + 12 + 8 + 6 + 4 in.	35 to 40	$ . . . .
	20 + 16 + 12 + 8 + 6 in.	40 to 45	$ . . . .
	24 + 20 + 16 + 12 + 8 in.	60 to 70	$ . . . .
Four Tiers One Dummy Tier	16 + 12 + 8 + 6 + 4 in.	50 to 60	$ . . . .
	20 + 16 + 12 + 8 + 6 in.	65 to 80	$ . . . .
	24 + 20 + 16 + 12 + 8 in.	80 to 110	$ . . . .

For prices for special cakes check with the chef.

Menu, testimonial dinner for the benefit of the Culinary Institute of America, February 1968. Note the formal titles for each course.

Escriteau

LE MENU DÉDIÉ A LA CULINARY INSTITUTE OF AMERICA

On dégustera:

Veuve Clicquot Brut 1961
Pommery and Greno Brut 1961
Piper Florens Louis 1961

Réception:

LES PERLES D'IRAN ROMANOFF
SAUMON FUMÉ NOUVELLE ECOSSE
LES FRIANDS

Première Assiette:

CONSOMMÉ EN GELÉE CARMEN

On boira:

Bollinger Brut 1961

Deuxième Assiette:

LE SUPRÊME DE POMPANO
ALBERT DU MAXIM
SURMONTÉ DE MOUSSE DE CRABE

On boira:

Moet and Chandon
Cuvée Dom Pérignon 1961

Troisième Assiette:

LA SELLE DE VEAU
DU
MAÎTRE CUISINIER JOSEPH CASTAYBERT
PURÉE DE CHAMPIGNONS
BOUQUET POINTS DES ASPERGES

Pour se Rafraichir:

LE GRANITÉ À LA PRUNELLE

On boira:

Taittinger
Blanc de Blanc Brut 1961

Quatrième Assiette:

MÉDAILLON DE FOIE GRAS
DES PETITS SOUPERS
DU REGENT

On boira:

Mercier
Réserve de l'Empereur 1959

On dégustera:

Hine's Triomphe
Grand Marnier
Otard V.S.O.P.
Crème de Menthe
Marie Brizard

Boutehors:

LA SURPRISE GLACÉE DU CENTENAIRE
DE LA SAINT MICHEL
—
LA TOQUE BLANCHE
AVEC SES FRIANDISES
—
LE CAFÉ NOIR

Herman R. Nerz
Directeur d'Alimentation

Herman Masini
Directeur des Banquets

Joseph J. Melz
Exécutif Chefs des Cuisines

Edward Soyer
Maître d'Hotel des Banquets

The cost of rented uniforms also can be great, especially when the event is a theme party that requires the service staff to work in special costumes. Costs for specialty items requested by the host or hostess, such as candles or flowers, should also be charged to the party giver as part of the cost of the event (see Figures 1.2 and 1.3).

Other considerations cannot be easily measured in dollars and cents. If a party requires an excessive amount of furniture to be moved, the wear and tear must be taken into consideration, especially if the room in question was rehabilitated at great expense a short time before. Some parties are traditionally very noisy, which requires that they be almost isolated to avoid inconveniencing other guests. Certain groups are souvenir-happy and take along whatever is around.

If a banquet is to be held away from the operation, it is well to remember that outside catering involves extra costs, such as transportation, tent rental, table rental, and breakage allotment. In addition, there may be business expenditures for licenses, permits, allocations for rehabilitation, mortgage payments, and taxes.

CHARTING THE TREND OF OPERATIONS

Even in a small restaurant that handles only occasional banquet business, it is essential to know how profitable that business is. Management can keep informed about the banquet profit by preparing the simple chart shown below. Similar charts are used in large operations to keep track of banquet profitability.

A quick glance at the Trend of Operation chart in Figure 1.4 shows that this operation is not very healthy. Banquet revenue did not increase to keep pace with inflation. The large increase in covers in 1974 over 1973 lowered the average check. Only a decline in the number of covers brought the average check up in 1975 and 1976. In 1977 and 1978, more business was booked, but the average check clearly shows that it did not pay enough. It is a dismal picture.

To find out exactly what happened, this chart must be expanded. The meal functions must be broken down. For example, perhaps many breakfast covers were served in 1974, 1977, and 1978. Breakfast functions are not as profitable as many people think. Breakfast requires almost as much labor, both in the kitchen and in the diningroom, as dinner, yet at a dinner the check would be as much as three times higher. Only the food cost is low when serving breakfasts.

In 1975, the average check increased while the number of covers decreased. Perhaps more dinners were served. If so, why did the dinner business decrease in 1977? It must have, because the number of covers went up, but the revenue did not increase in the same propor-

Figure 1.4.   Trend of operations chart.

Year	1973	1974	1975	1976	1977	1978
Banquet Revenue in Dollars	556,000	610,200	593,100	605,000	643,500	679,300
Covers*	64,312	71,502	66,910	64,120	69,290	72,629
Revenue Percentage Increase or Decrease	—	9.75	2.80	2.00	6.36	5.56
Covers Percentage Increase or Decrease	—	11.18	6.42	4.17	8.06	4.82
Average Food Check**	$8.64	$8.53	$8.86	$9.43	$9.29	$9.35

* Reception covers are not counted.

** Average food check equals total food revenue (including reception covers) divided by total food covers (not including reception covers).

tions. In 1978, there was a slight improvement in revenue increase versus cover increase, which is also reflected in the higher average check. Is that the beginning of a trend? Was a new banquet salesperson hired, or did the economy improve at this locality? These are examples of the many questions which a simple chart can bring out into the open. One thing is obvious: the average check did not improve sufficiently to cover the increased cost of doing business and to render an acceptable margin of profit at the same time.

To find a solution to this situation, the menu prices would have to be first reviewed and then evaluated to see whether compensation is being received for unusual services provided. Is the operation getting money for the "extras" (such as oystermen shucking oysters in the banquet room, sommeliers for special wine service, carvers in the room, extra napkins, special linen, ice carvings, labor-intensive food preparations, electrician charges, etc.), or are these bonuses being thrown in for free by the banquet sales staff? What is to be provided free of charge to the guest is a management decision. The need to stay competitive of course must be recognized, but it is essential that the charge policy be reviewed from time to time. In these inflationary times, many items given free for years cannot be provided free today.

Menu, dinner at the Arizona
Biltmore Hotel, December 1967.
The coordination of typefaces,
the use of space and the
arrangement of words on the
page make this an inviting
menu.

ARIZONA BILTMORE HOTEL

December 7, 1967

LA RECEPTION

HANS KORNELL BRUT
SPARKLING MOSELLE MADRIGAL
LANCER'S VIN ROSE

Les Huitres Fraiches en Belle Vue

Les Moineaux des Campagnes Friquet

Les Oeufs Durs des Cailles

LE DINER

La Boula Boula Gratinee

Paillettes D'Or

&

SCHLOSS VOLLRADS KABINETTE
SCHLOSSABZUG FASS III

Filet de Sole a la Belle Normande

&

CORTON CHARLEMAGNE 1964
LOUIS JADOT

L'Oison a la Mecklenbourgeoise, Sous Cloche

&

La Mandarine Givree de Noel

&

CORTON POUGETS 1964
LOUIS JADOT

Le Tournedos de Boeuf Grille Rochelaise

Les Fenouils aux Fines Herbes

Les Pommes de Terre Gaufrettes

&

La Laitue du Kentucky Cressonniere

a L'Huile de Noix et Citron

Le Brie Francais de Meaux

&

DOM RUINART BRUT
BLANC DE BLANCS 1959

La Poire Maxime

Les Mignardises

&

BISQUIT NAPOLEON COGNAC
FINE CHAMPAGNE

Le Cafe Turc

Henry Warren	Franz Nikodemi
Le Maitre Culinaire	*Le Maitre de Cuisine*

Albert Mastboom
Le Maitre du Banquet

Figure 1.5   Seasonal minimum guarantee and menu price minimum.

Wintergarden Ballroom		Minimum	Lunch	Dinner
JANUARY	Weekdays	500	$	$ . . . .
	Weekends	600		
FEBRUARY	Any Day	500	$	$ . . . .
MARCH				
1st 2 weeks	Any Day	550	$	$ . . . .
3rd & 4th weeks	Any Day	600	$	$ . . . .
APRIL	Weekdays	600	$	$ . . . .
	Weekends	700	$	$ . . . .
MAY	Any Day	700	$	$ . . . .
JUNE	Weekdays	600	$ . . .	$ . . . .
	Weekends	700	$	$ . . . .
JULY	Any Day	500	$	$ . . . .
AUGUST	Any Day	500	$	$ . . . .
SEPTEMBER				
1st week		500	$	$ . . . .
2nd week		550	$	$ . . . .
last weeks		600	$	$ . . . .
OCTOBER	Any Day	700	$	$ . . . .
NOVEMBER		700	$	$ . . . .
Thanksgiving week		500	$	$ . . . .
DECEMBER		700	$	$ . . . .
Christmas week		500	$	$ . . . .

SETTING GUIDELINES

Management should provide the banquet sales staff in large banquet operations with a minimum menu price list for each season. When a number of function rooms are available, a list of seasonal minimum guarantees for the different rooms should also be made available (see Figure 1.5). Clear guidelines for room rental charges, arranged according to room and time of day, will also be of inestimable value to your sales staff when they take bookings (see Figure 1.6). It must be stressed here that guidelines are goals set by management. Market conditions dictated by the economy or market competition may make adjustments necessary from time to time, but in every case, guidelines should always have management approval.

That menu prices vary according to the season is logical. The cost of doing business will not vary much in most locations during the year, but banquet space is more desirable at certain times of the year, and this should be reflected in the menu price. After all, when selling banquets, you sell not only food, drink, and a good time, but also space.

A realistic deposit policy must be established for each function room and each type of banquet. Certain groups and most weddings

Profitability

Figure 1.6.   Rental rates chart.

Meeting Room Rental Rates	8:30 AM—11:30 AM	2:30 PM—5:00 PM	6:00 PM to Midnight
Blue Room All Day $	$	$	$ . . . . .
Riverview All Day $	$	$	$ . . . . .
Sutton Suite All Day $	$	$	$ . . . . .
Salon Agnes All Day $	$	$	$ . . . . .
Johnson Suite All Day $	$	$	$ . . . . .
Wintergarden Ballroom All Day $	$	$	$ . . . . .

Rental Rates for Cocktail Receptions

It is our policy, if possible, to charge a room rental fee for receptions. Following is a guide to desired rental:

Wintergarden Ballroom	5:00 PM to 7:00 PM
October to June	$ . . . .
July to September	$ . . . .
Blue Room	$ . . . .
Riverview	$ . . . .
Sutton Suite	$ . . . .
Salon Agnes	$ . . . .
Johnson Suite	$ . . . .
Christopher's Ballroom	$ . . . .
Stephanie Suite	$ . . . .

require complete prepayment of all charges before the function (see Figure 1.7). When prepayment is not required, maximum payment schedules should be available to the party giver and the salesperson.

15

Figure 1.7.   Advance deposit information.

Deposits

Advance deposits are required for all "definite" reservations. The amount should be indicated in the letter of confirmation, as well as in the standard terms and conditions.

Minimum Deposit for each function room

Wintergarden Ballroom	$ . . . .
Christopher's Ballroom	$ . . . .
All smaller suites	$ . . . .

Advance Deposit Requests

In all letters of confirmation a deposit must be requested, based on the established schedule. The paragraph in the letter should read as follows:

> To serve as your confirmation, please sign and return enclosed copy of this letter, within two weeks, with a deposit check in the amount of $ . . . . If you should cancel above function and we are able to re-book this space, the deposit, less a handling charge of $50.00, will be returned to you. If we are unable to re-book this space, the entire amount of the deposit will be retained by us as liquidated damages.

Finally, additional income in the form of commissions can be derived from florists, photographers, orchestras, and decorators. Banquet sales staff members must be aware of which companies to recommend and what their basic charges are (see Figure 1.8).

Figure 1.8.   Specialty services—official recommendations.

Photographer

We recommend the use of the services of . . . . Company because the company is familiar with our establishment. Price list is available upon request.

Audio-Visual Equipment

We use the services of . . . . Company for rental of all audio-visual equipment. Price list is available upon request.

Music and Entertainment

The Hans Lauterbach Orchestra is the official orchestra of our operation and all inquiries should be directed to him. Following is the suggested minimum requirement for each room which coincides with the union minimum.

Wintergarden Ballroom	12 Musicians
Christopher's Ballroom	8 Musicians
All Smaller Suites	4 to 6 Musicians

Menu cover, bicentennial dinner held by the Wine and Food Society, Inc., June 1976. The pen-and-ink eagle evokes the bicentennial spirit.

Flag Day

Getting the Business

It is no easy task to fill banquet space with profitable business day after day. In many cases, banquet space could theoretically be utilized four times a day. Nobody achieves that kind of maximum utilization of space, but it is disturbing to note that many hotels utilize the available space to capacity only 25 to 30 percent of the time.

KNOW YOUR OPERATION'S CAPACITY

To calculate the utilization of banquet space in your facility during a given year, divide the number of covers served in one year by 365 (the number of days in a year). The resulting figure is the average number of covers served per day. Then divide this figure by the number of seats available per day and multiply the answer by 100. This gives you your daily utilization rate: the utilization of your banquet seats per day as a percentage of maximum (100 percent) utilization potential your facility holds (see Figure 2.1).

If the facility is available twice or three times a day (for breakfast, lunch, and/or dinner service) divide by two or three depending on availability. The resulting number is the average utilization by meal period. This figure will shock most people, but remember: it is a bit misleading. To achieve 100 percent utilization, you must sell the facility to capacity every day of the year for every meal function, and, of course, this is impossible.

However, once you have computed these figures you can easily see that banquet space must be sold aggressively regardless of the size or type of establishment. Be creative with your facilities. A small restaurant may have a backroom available for parties. A luncheon club may have rooms that stand empty in the afternoon or evenings. A cafeteria-type restaurant in an office building could make its space available for meetings in the early evening hours. A dinner restaurant could increase its earnings by renting space not needed during lunch. All of these places have one thing in common: the space is there to be sold. Do not sit back and wait until somebody walks in and books a party. For your operation to be profitable, you must market its facilities.

PROFITABILITY: TODAY'S KEY TO SUCCESS

Years ago, volume was the yardstick by which a banquet salesperson's work was judged. Profit-making was left to the people operating the facility. Hotelkeepers used to say, "Volume buries a multitude of sins." This is not true any longer. Today the profitability of the business booked is of major concern, and all business must be scrutinized in terms of profitability. Unprofitable and marginally profitable businesses must be identified in time to correct the situation. In many cases

Figure 2.1.   Computing your facility's utilization.

Step 1. $\dfrac{\text{Number of covers served in one year}}{365}$ = Average number of covers served per day

Step 2. $\dfrac{\text{Average number of covers served per day}}{\text{Number of covers available per day}} \times 100$ = Daily utilization rate

it is better to do a smaller volume of profitable business than a large volume of marginally profitable business.

The Sales Force

Large hotels divide the sales force between the catering or banquet department and the sales department. The sales department is responsible for selling rooms and meeting space. In many cases, especially when the rooms are sold in connection with conventions or with tour groups, food activities are also needed. In some hotels, the sales department books these food functions. This arrangement seems beneficial to the client because the client then needs to deal with only one person, or at least with only one department, to take care of all his or her needs. The disadvantage is that the salesperson in the sales department often does not have the necessary background and time to sell the most profitable food arrangement. Consequently, convention food is often dull and convention banquets fewer. If the salesperson does not convince the convention to book food activities at the headquarter hotel, the attendees will be left to eat wherever they please. This, in turn, benefits restaurants nearby, not the large convention hotel. It is easy to see how a hotel can lose potential revenue when the selling of food is left to a staff untrained in selling food.

Catering or banquet sales personnel deal with food every day; they should qualify as experts in their field. In most fields salespeople must possess a solid knowledge of the product they are selling. In banquet selling, this knowledge should also be required. Salespeople should know food, its seasonal availability, menu making, and beverages; they should also have a good background in service, be versed in social etiquette, and have good taste. They must be able to sell and must not be timid about getting a fair price for the menus they develop.

In many cases, especially when dealing with social business, many people are not sure of what they want and what they think they need. The salesperson must advise and counsel them: most people do not mind spending more than originally planned if the party is a huge success. The banquet salesperson must evaluate each situation. If (s)he does not feel that, within the framework of the proposed budget, a fine job can be done, it is up to him or her to strongly suggest a better format. This not only protects the client but also protects the reputation of the establishment.

While it is excellent to please the person or the committee ordering the menu, if that results in 998 unhappy people, the establishment, not the host or committee, will be blamed for the fiasco. One such fiasco was planned as a very chic pheasant supper. The hostess specified 11:30 p.m. as the service time, although the invitations read 8:30 p.m. A very elaborate program started at 9:00 p.m. and for 2½ hours nobody had a chance to get a drink or a bite to eat. The elegant guests were extremely unhappy, and although the hotel could not be blamed in any way, the dinner still reflected badly on the operation as for years people recalled the party held at place XYZ during which everybody starved. In retrospect, it became clear that the banquet salesperson should have put his foot down and refused to go along with the timetable. If the party turns out to be a failure, the hotel gets blamed and the client will never come back, nor will the many other potential customers who attended the function but were disappointed.

Smaller places, of course, do not employ a catering sales force. Instead, the headwaiter, the owner, or a single salesperson handles all sales. Whoever does it, the same ground rules for selling banquets apply.

Set Sales Goals

It is important to set sales goals. These goals should be realistic and optimistic. In established operations the goals are based on past history. In smaller places that do not keep track of banquet sales, it would be worthwhile to calculate how much additional revenue could be achieved if, for example, the banquet room could be sold at least twice a week, and then set this figure as a goal.

Banquets can generate tremendous volume. In most cases, the seating capacity in banquet facilities is much larger than the capacity of the restaurant. Think how many covers would be sold at one seating in a banquet room and compare that figure with how long it would take to get the same number of covers in a restaurant!

To ensure that banquet covers are profitable, many large operations require the use of a Banquet Sales Report and Monthly Progress Report like the ones reproduced in Figures 2.2 and 2.3. These reports show how much business is booked by each salesperson, how this business is divided between repeat business and new business, how the salesperson ranks in dollar sales and in number of covers, what average check and food cost are achieved, and what the business prospects for each month are.

Figure 2.2.   Banquet salesperson's progress report.

Names	New Bookings Value $	No. of Funct.	Covers	Repeat Bookings Value $	No. of Funct.	Covers	Total Value $	Rank Total #	%	Rank New #	%	Rank Repeat #	%	Food Cost	Aver. Check $
Johns	54,312	12	4,312	30,290	8	2,543	84,602	1	24.48	2	26.03	2	22.11	24.3	12.34
Alton	21,941	8	957	40,187	12	3,514	62,128	4	17.98	5	10.51	1	29.32	21.9	13,89
Mayers	43,878	14	3,618	21,212	16	1,964	65,090	3	18.83	3	21.03	4	15.48	22.7	11.66
O'Tang	62,316	19	5,354	18,936	9	674	18,252	2	23.51	1	29.87	5	13.82	23.1	13.48
Gold	26,212	12	2,396	26,413	7	1,876	52,625	5	15.23	4	12.56	3	19.27	20.9	12.30
													Averages %	22.58	$ 12.73
TOTAL	$208,659	65	16,637	$137,038	52	10,591	$345,697		100%		100%		100%	22.58	12.73

To compute the average check, the total revenue, including reception revenue, is divided by the total covers, excluding reception covers. This method increases the average check, but as long as the same method is used for comparison purposes it is acceptable. To include reception covers would give a distorted picture because the reception food check could be very small and the number of covers could be very large.

The food cost is obtained by costing out each and every menu sold. This is not such a formidable project as it seems because, in many cases, banquet menus are fairly similar. It is important, of course, to keep the figures used for computing the food cost up-to-date. Special menus must be costed out with the help of the chef.

WHAT THE SALESPERSON NEEDS TO KNOW

Before going out to sell banquets, start a promotion campaign, or set up a banquet market plan, it is essential that the salesperson know your own operation and know as much as possible about the competitors. He or she must be able to justify your prices, especially in cases when they are higher. However, antitrust laws must be observed and

Figure 2.3.   Monthly progress report—definite bookings.

Banquet Representative: _____ Month of: _____

Definite Bookings Name of Organization	File No.	New	Rep	Date	Type of Function	Price PP & Attendance	Estimated Value Food Only
Totals							

Original and two copies to be completed and submitted to banquet administrator on the first day of each month.   **Approved by:**

_____ Director of catering

legal counsel is often needed to find out what is legal or illegal; e.g., it is illegal to compare prices.

Sales representatives can learn much by attending banquet functions in other places. Find out as much as possible about the other places, their layout, the staff they employ, the kind of food they serve. Large conventions often like to schedule small, exclusive food functions away from the convention hotel. This provides an opportunity for the smaller restaurants to capture profitable banquets.

The salesperson should have floor plans of all available banquet facilities, with precise measurements of the available space. A short description of the rooms and good color photographs showing the different types of set-ups possible are also very helpful. The banquet sales office can be decorated with photographs of buffets, table set-ups, ice carvings, and wedding cakes. Framed menus from former functions are also very helpful in selling, especially if the function was attended by a prominent personality and his or her name is on the menu.

When preparing to sell banquets, the salesperson must know what the operation has to offer in the areas of both food and service. Does the operation have a good chef? Does the operation still bake on the premises, cut all meat needed, and use fresh vegetables, real

Figure 2.4. Banquet inquiry form.

DATE _____ ESTIMATED ATTENDANCE ___ ROOM _____

TYPE OF FUNCTION _____ TIME ___

ORGANIZATION _____

PERSON IN CHARGE _____

ADDRESS _____

_____

TELEPHONE _____

TENTATIVE _____ DEFINITE _____ DEPOSIT REQ'D ___

MENU & ARRANGEMENTS:

Estimate of Costs
Per Person

Reception _____

Smorgasbord _____

Menu _____

Cake _____

Beverage _____

Check Room _____

Misc. Expenses _____

Gratuities _____

Taxes
Total Estimated Exp.
Per Person _____

FLOWERS _____

MUSIC _____

PHOTOGRAPHY _____

Salesman _____

Date of Inquiry_____

whipped cream, fresh fish, or homemade soups? Frequent visits to the chef are very important for banquet salespersons. I would like to emphasize the word frequent, because conditions in kitchens change rather suddenly and it does no good to promise the guest freshly baked pies if the baker left two months ago. Other facts the banquet salesperson should check out are: Does the operation have better silver than its competitors? Is the silver shiny at all times? Does it have better glassware, perhaps a nicer champagne glass, or better china? Are its facilities better kept, newer, or more elegant? Does the operation have access to better banquet waiters or better uniforms? Is its headwaiter exceptionally knowledgeable? Is the operation more experienced in weddings? Does the band sound better because the acoustics are good? The operation might not be better than its competitor in all respects, but it is sure to have something that the competitor lacks. Every salesperson should know what the strong points of the operation are.

Does the salesperson get the chef involved when planning special menus? The possible extent of the chef's involvement is discussed in chapter 11. The salesperson should remember that many clients are flattered if a special menu is planned personally by the chef.

Does the salesperson know enough about the arrangements that are possible for theme parties? The salesperson should be well versed in what props are available free of charge, what the house carpenters could build (don't forget to charge for that!), what kind of costumes can be rented in town, and how much such rental will cost. Does the salesperson know what your florist is capable of doing? Don't forget, the house might collect a commission on florist sales. What orchestra should the salesperson recommend? How many musicians are needed in the ballroom? Always tell your sales representatives whether your location is better, your facilities newer, your operation's name more prestigious, your parking lot lighting better. These are all important sales points. In a nutshell: to sell successfully, find out as much as possible about your operation, then make sure your sales staff knows.

HANDLING INQUIRIES

Inquiries often come in by telephone. It is very important that inquiries are handled properly. All phones should be staffed as long as possible. In smaller places an answering device should be installed. All calls should be transferred to a pleasant, knowledgeable person. It is most important that the function book always be readily accessible so that an immediate answer can be given as to what space is available on the date in question. In large operations a telephone is installed next

Figure 2.5.   Banquet inquiry form—alternative style.

NAME _____

GROUP OR ASSOCIATION _____

TELEPHONE NUMBER _____

ADDRESS _____

TYPE OF EVENT _____

DATE _____

NUMBER OF PEOPLE _____

QUOTATIONS _____

REMARKS _____

_____

_____

_____

_____

_____

to the function book to make it possible to let the prospective client know right away what dates are available to choose from.

It is advisable to use a preprinted Banquet Inquiry Form (see Figures 2.4 and 2.5). This should be filled out while the caller is still on the phone. However, it is only rarely that a major piece of business is booked over the telephone; in all cases an attempt should be made to make an appointment either at the banquet office or at a place convenient for the caller.

The banquet inquiry forms must be evaluated every night by the person in charge of the catering office. In large places this is the director of catering, in smaller places, the salespeople, the owner, or whoever is in charge of booking parties. At this point, the credit of the prospective client can also be evaluated. If no appointment has been made, an inquiry requires follow-up in the form of a telephone call, a letter, or a visit. If no satisfactory dates are available, the inquiry should be filed or dropped. This decision must be made by the person in charge.

Inquiries are also often made by people who walk in ready to be sold. Obviously, the best salesperson is not always available to take care of the situation. In large hotels, often a junior member of the sales staff is sent to take care of the person who is a walk-in. This is not very wise: the walk-in represents an opportunity to grab business and make a sale. No matter how disruptive a walk-in may be to a set schedule, an experienced salesperson should handle the inquiry and evaluate the situation. If it is impossible to assign a salesperson, the Banquet Inquiry Form should be filled out by the receptionist, and the inquiry then followed up as soon as possible. A person who comes in to inquire is often ready to be sold, so do not miss the opportunity.

MARKETING YOUR FACILITY

It is not possible to depend solely on telephone and walk-in inquiries. Advertising, personal contacts, and repeat business create a certain volume, but banquet business must be actively solicited. In order to do this successfully market areas should be identified. Based on the selected market area a banquet market plan can be formulated. The following list offers potential markets for banquets:

Financial institutions

New office buildings

Airlines

Embassies, consulates (for their national day)

Foreign trade missions

High schools (proms)

Colleges (class reunions)

Fraternities

Social clubs (annual events)

Churches, synagogues, religious organizations

Charities

Hospitals (fund raising)

Weddings

Menu interior, bicentennial dinner. The American culinary spirit is present, even to such details as the walnut oil dressing.

Menu

Four Regional Buffets
Various American Champagnes

Canapé of Spring Quail & Quail Eggs
Mondavi Fumé Blanc 1971

Consommé with Old Madeira

Lobster Wenberg
Freemark Abbey Pinot Chardonnay 1972

Braised Ham & Baby Turkey
Sauce Schramsberg
Bercut-Vandervoort Sonoma Pinot Noir
bottled in 1965
Whole Hominy & Green Bean Purée

Limestone & Bibb Salad
Walnut Oil Dressing

Illinois, Vermont & Wisconsin Cheeses
Mondavi Cabernet Sauvignon 1969

Nesselrode Ice Cream Bombe
Henri Marchant White Labrusca
An Array of Great American Cakes
Coffee ··· Hennessy Cognac Bicentenaire

We wish to express our appreciation to Jas. Hennessy & Co and to the
Peel Street Wine Merchants for their generosity and to
Alan Lewis, Director and to André René, Chef de Cuisine

Bar mitzvahs

Ethnic clubs

Newspapers

Trade groups

Political parties

Bus tours

Seasonal parties

Unions

Department stores

Chambers of commerce (especially in smaller cities)

Corporations with growth potential

Convention and visitor's bureaus

Obviously, not every market is a potential source of business for every operation. Select a number of market areas that seem to offer the most potential for your operation.

There are a number of methods to use in establishing contact when starting to solicit business. For example, marketing can be achieved even as a function is held. All available banquet personnel should wear name tags and mingle with guests during functions. Guests can be asked what other functions they attend; sometimes it is possible to obtain a name to contact this way.

The social pages of the newspapers must be read carefully for announcements of weddings and other social affairs. In larger cities, the bulletin boards of competitors should be checked every day. This will establish what groups are in town, and some of that business could be secured the next time around.

When large conventions are coming to a town, the pertinent industry or professional organizations should be solicited. Often, a lot of entertaining goes on while a convention is in town. Some of that entertaining will not take place in the convention hotel. Effective marketing can draw that business to your organization.

Catering personnel should belong to organizations like Rotary, the Chamber of Commerce, and other civic organizations. If the place of business pays the membership fees, the value of belonging to the organizations should be reviewed every year. Be alert to small committee meetings as well, as they too can bring in big business.

The sales staff should also remember to treat secretaries with friendliness and respect. Secretaries bring valuable skills to the catering organization and can be an important resource in getting busi-

Menu, dinner in honor of the King of Sweden, April 1976. This meal was served to over 500 guests.

MENU

Striped Bass in Aspic
Sauce Verte
Chenin Blanc   Pritchard Hill

Roast Saddle of Veal
Buttered Snow Peas
New Potatoes rolled in Dill
Cabernet Sauvignon   Sterling Vinyard

Salad of the Season
Hot Cheese Tart

Crown of Praliné Ice Cream
California Strawberries
Carlshamn's Flagg Punch

Crisp Petits Fours

Demi Tasse

ness. If your secretary has large social circles outside of her job, she should be able to steer a lot of social business to the banquet office. Even after her social contacts are exhausted, her knowledge of the organization and her experience in handling customers should continue to promote business and profits.

The social market is primarily a referral market. A successful charity ball has a direct influence on the wedding market. Weddings go to places of prestigious happenings. In smaller towns, glamorous charity balls will bring wedding inquiries. A number of successful weddings bring more weddings because the facilities are seen during the reception by many prospective brides. After the wedding is over, do not forget the bride. A tasteful anniversary card sent by the catering director will keep the name of the establishment in her mind, and, if she liked the place, she will refer business to it.

Political dinners, in turn, have little or no influence on the social market, but they do expose the facilities to a large portion of the business community. If the sales staff is around and visible, many important contacts can be established.

MAINTAINING THE BANQUET FILE

When the contact is called to solicit business, either by phone or by going out and ringing doorbells, a Banquet Call Report Form (see Figure 2.6) is made out. The Banquet Call Report Form goes in the banquet file and is the basis for future evaluation.

Large hotel chains usually have a computerized banquet file and trace system at their headquarters. Possible dates mentioned on the Call Report Form are sent to the hotel in question well ahead of time to allow for solicitation. Banquet files contain historical data on local businesses that have active and continuous food functions. Solicitation and follow-up of these functions is the responsibility of the Catering Department. Banquet files must contain sufficient information concerning the prospect, previous functions, with records of correspondence and suggestions for solicitation of future business.

New banquet files can be obtained from several sources; they include:

All Banquet functions held in the establishment on a regular or repeat basis

All other banquet functions held in the city on a regular or repeat basis

Newspaper leads on new functions planned or considered

Figure 2.6.   Call report form.

Date:_____

Group:_____   File No._____

Contact:_____   Title:_____

Address:_____   City:_____

Telephone:_____   Best time to call:_____

New prospect?   ( ) Yes   ( ) No   What Month and Year?_____

Number of persons:_____ Type of function:_____

Comments:_____

Date of decision:_____   By whom?_____

Report made by:_____   Trace Date:_____

Inquiries coming into the operation regarding possible future bookings

Personal contacts established

All files must be reviewed monthly at least eight months prior to the potential event to allow sufficient time for solicitation (see Figure 2.7). Every time a solicitation is made, a Call Report Form must be filled out and added to the file. If the solicitation effort was not successful, a Lost Business Report is made out (see Figure 2.8). The Lost Business Report must be reviewed with the person in charge to determine why the business was lost.

Smaller operations cannot afford all the paperwork large banquet hotels require, but some of the same techniques can be used by the small entrepreneur. It is always necessary to solicit business, and it is essential to know why business was lost. Studying Lost Business Reports can establish trends or patterns that then can be righted. Are the prices too high? The rooms too small? The equipment not up to date? The food not good enough? The service bad? If you know why business was lost, you can zero in and find a solution.

Figure 2.7. Banquet solicitation record.

HOTEL   **DATE**

Monthly Booking Report
Banquet Solicitation Program

Definite bookings

Name of Organization	File No.	New Business	Repeat Business	Date	Type	Size	Estimate Value
TOTALS							

Number of outside calls:_____ I.B.M. completed for this month: Yes _____ No _____

Number of "C" files this month:_____ Number of newspaper leads followed this month:_____

Number of "C" files killed this month:_____

Salesperson_____

Approved by _____
Director of Catering

BANQUET STAFF MEETINGS

Since a large marketing effort costs money the results obtained must be evaluated. Earlier in this chapter we described the monthly Salesperson's Progress Report. The same report can be prepared for a shorter or for a longer period of time. A longer period will show a trend which can be evaluated. The weekly report can be used at the weekly banquet staff meetings. In most larger operations, the banquet or catering department meets once a week. At these meetings every salesperson should report on his or her bookings and on how much the business volume done the prior week differs from the goals set or the forecast that was made.

Figure 2.8. Report of lost business.

_____

Hotel_____ Date _____

City _____

_____ Gen. Mgr.—Hotel Reporting

_____ Gen. Sales Office

_____ Div. Sales Office

_____ File

Name of Group:_____ File No._____

Secretary or Contact:_____ Title _____

Date of Function or Convention:_____

Type of Business: _____

Size: (Estimated no. of guest rooms, attendance of banquet food functions, receptions, etc.)_____

_____

Hotel Selected: _____

Source of Lead and Date Received: _____

_____

Report of Solicitation: (Briefly and specifically outline steps in solicitation, date of first contact, and

follow-up action taken.)_____

_____

Reasons for Losing Business: _____

_____

_____

Sales Manager or Catering Manager

Problems with operations should also be discussed. It is not necessary for the chef and the headwaiter to attend every banquet meeting, however, at least once a month they should also attend. This provides an opportunity for them to discuss menu problems, service problems, and to exchange ideas with the banquet sales staff.

There are three levels of space bookings: confirmed, tentative, and prospective. Confirmed bookings have been ensured by written agreement and perhaps by monetary deposit. Tentative bookings have been entered in the diary but the necessary letters of confirmation (mailed to the clients by the banquet operation) have not been returned. Prospective bookings are those for which space is being held but for which confirmation has not yet been requested. There are also two kinds of bookings: those for banquets and those for meetings. At the banquet meeting, all these aspects of the booking process should be discussed. Cancellation of tentatives and prospectives should be reported so that space can be released for further business. Space blocked by the sales department for meetings should be discussed. In order to book a large convention securely, the sales department often blocks more space than ultimately needed. Once final requirements are known, space not required for meetings should be returned to the banquet department.

To project the best possible image, correspondence from the catering and sales offices should be on attractive stationery. Letters should be accurately typed and they should be polite and well-written. Form letters of course can be used, but only as models from which the personalized letter is composed. The sales staff should remember that in correspondence the direct and personal approach will best influence the customer to book business with you. For sample form letters, please see appendix A.

Menu, dinner for Georges
Pompidou, March 1970. A
simple yet elegant French menu.

MENU

Consommé Lagrandière

❖

Meursault 1966
Sichel & Fils Frères

Bar rayé au champagne
Pommes nouvelles persillées

❖

Beaune
Clos des Fèves 1962
Chanson Père & Fils
en Magnum

Contrefilet aux cèpes
Céleri braisé au jus
Haricots verts sautés

❖

Krug Brut
Private Cuvée
en Magnum

Glace Casanova en couronne
avec garniture de pêches Chantilly

Petits fours

❖

Café des Antilles

Menu interior, dinner for a
Japanese gala, May 1973. An
unusual example of the special
event banquet menu.

million dollar

Japanese Gala

Program

INTRODUCTION OF DIGNITARIES   Mr. Charles T. Carey
                                        Chairman, Washington Committee

H.E. The Ambassador of Japan   H.E. The Ambassador, Consul General of
    and Mrs. Ushiba   Japan and Mrs. Sawaki
        Prince and Princess Paolo Borghese
              International Chairmen
Mrs. H. Donald Sills,   Dr. Norman Molomut
    General Chairman   Scientific Director
        H.E. The Ambassador of Japan to the U.N.
                and Mrs. Nakagawa
H.E. The Ambassador of Turkey   H.E. The Ambassador of Ireland
    and Mrs. Esenbel   and Mrs. Warnock
H.E. The Ambassador of Italy   H.E. the Ambassador of New Zealand
    and Mrs. Ortona   and Mrs. White
H.E. the Ambassador of Tunisia   H.E. the Ambassador of Singapore
    and Mrs. El Goulli   and Mrs. Monteiro

NATIONAL ANTHEMS   Kimigayo and The Star Spangled Banner

"SALUTE TO JAPAN" CEREMONIES   Mrs. H. Donald Sills

ENTERTAINMENT INTERLUDE   Miyoko Watanabe Dance Company

DRAWING OF TOP TEN PRIZES
    DE LUXE PRIZES   Mr. Herbert S. Cannon
                            Mrs. Jane C. Murchison, Vice-Chairman

    TREASURY OF PRIZES   Mr. James J. Duffy, Journal Chairman
                                    Mrs. Rafael Ramos Cobian
                                     Chairman for Puerto Rico
        Balance of Prizes Will Be Drawn and Posted in the East Foyer

CONTINUOUS DANCING, GAMES OF CHANCE, BROWSING ALONG THE GINZA

                Processional Attendants:
            *Miss Margit Berge, Junior Committee
        Miss Ayako Ikebe, Mitsubishi Int'l Corp.
        Miss Emiko Sawaki, Consulate General
          Miss Nami Tayooka, Mitsui & Co.
        Miss Eiko Uematsu, Japan Air Lines
        Koto Music By: Fusako Yoshida & Reiko Kamata
                The Joe Carroll Orchestra

*Pearls – Richter Jewels

"For the Dignity of Man"

million dollar

Japanese Gala

MONDAY, MAY 7, 1973
THE WALDORF ASTORIA

COCKTAILS
Hot and Cold Hors D'Oeuvres   Hibachi Tid-Bits
        Nippon   Benihana

DINNER MENU
Smoked Brook Trout en Gelee
        Sauce Wasabi

Bean Curd Soup Misoshiru

Chicken, Beef, Shrimp Matsutake
        on Bamboo Skewers
with Water Chestnuts and Shoyu Sauce

Gekkeikan
Sake

Four Seasons of Gomokuni
Bean Sprouts, Onions, Zucchini
    and Bamboo Shoots

Satsuki Green Salad
Spinach, Lettuce, Watercress
    and Sesame Seeds

Gekkeikan
Plum Wine

Cherries Flambe on Mt. Fuji Snow
    Japanese Petit Fours

Tea   Coffee

Menu cover, Les Dames
d'Escoffier, New York, February
1978. An elegant band of ribbon
is the cover's only decoration.

Collecting Information

Selling a banquet is different from selling shoes or automobiles. When you sell a banquet, you sell a memorable event and often a unique one, such as a wedding, an anniversary, a Bar Mitzvah, a jubilee, a debutante ball. Even small business luncheons can be memorable, celebrating the signing of a contract, featuring a prominent guest speaker, or entertaining a senior officer of the corporation as guest of honor.

ADVISING THE CLIENT

No party is routine. A good banquet salesperson, therefore, must have an inquiring mind and a good measure of curiosity. She or he must start a process of communication which will turn up as much information as possible about the prospective group, asking the right questions about the group and, in turn, giving honest answers to questions asked. The salesperson must try to think about the party as the prospective guests will. A banquet salesperson sells not only the event but also hope: hope that the upcoming event will be unique and successful.

In many cases, the prospective client is not familiar with all aspects of social etiquette or the catering business. A good salesperson will counsel and, if necessary, strongly advise against something he or she feels is not proper for the occasion. After the day and date are established and a proper room is selected, the salesperson must keep in mind the season and time of year. Food eaten at Christmas is different from food eaten during July. Perhaps there is a holiday theme that will fit the occasion.

To make sure that banquet plans are appropriate, the salesperson also needs to know the following: What is the make-up of the group? Are the guests mostly young or elderly? What is the economic background of the group? The fact that the party giver is willing to spend money does not mean that his guests are going to enjoy caviar. People have strong likes and dislikes in food, and what is elegant to some is inedible to others. I have seen elegant food served that came back hardly touched. The menu chosen in such cases just was not the right type of food for the guests being served.

Is the group all male, all female, or mixed? A group of women may well like a different menu than one for a group of men. Is the occasion going to be festive, formal, or business-like? Food should reflect the mood of the event. For evening events, it is also important to have food chosen that can be eaten gracefully without danger of ruining a carefully selected evening gown or tux. Also remember that people like to show off their evening clothes; a function room with a wide staircase may add to the elegance of such an occasion.

Menu interior, Les Dames d'Escoffier, New York. The dinner, entitled A Showcase of Women Chefs, celebrates the culinary achievement of outstanding women chefs.

RECEPTION

Gardner's Bouquet
Hot and Cold Piquant Sauces

Veuve Cliquot La Grande Dame 1969
Joseph Garneau Company

Marquis de Goulaine Muscadet de Sèvre-et-Maine 1976
Robert, 11th Marquis de Goulaine
Schieffelin & Co.

DINNER

Consommé Les Dames d'Escoffier

🐝

Mousse of Massachussetts Bay Scallops
White Wine Sauce

Meursault 1972, Réserve Sainte-Anne
Patriarche Père & Fils
Peartree Imports Inc.

🐝

Breast of Long Island Duckling Leslie
Poached Bosc Pear
Winter Parsnips
Brussel Sprouts

Chassagne-Montrachet 1969
From the cellar of a member of Les Dames d'Escoffier

🐝

Salad Sorbet Helene

🐝

Pastry Extravaganza

Tokaji Aszu - 5 Puttonos 1973
Heublein Wines International

🐝

Demi-tasse
Confections
Conversations with the Chefs

Delamain Cognac, Pale and Dry
Bénédictine D.O.M
Julius Wile Sons & Co., Inc.

A business luncheon or dinner, on the other hand, can be less elaborate than a social event, yet still be elegant. The food should be delicious but have fewer frills. In most cases, the length of the luncheon must also be limited because most business people do not want to spend too much time over lunch. To make a business luncheon a special event, the salesperson should be sure to ask about the guest of honor. What are the preferences of the guest of honor? Does (s)he have a favorite dish? Should the guest of honor's home state be reflected in the menu? Unexpected little touches such as those make the occasion memorable.

For a wedding luncheon, successful planning depends on similar facts. Does the bride or the immediate family have a favorite dish? In some families a certain type of food brings back memories of happy family times. Perhaps one of these dishes can be included in the menu. What is the color scheme planned for the bridal party? The colors can be reproduced on the wedding cake decoration.

It may be important to know the religious background of the guests. Jewish groups usually have kosher affairs, supervised by a Rabbi. However, sometimes only a small percentage of the invited guests are Jewish. If that is the case, will they require a special meal? Perhaps only the guest speaker or guest of honor is Jewish. Would (s)he appreciate being served a sealed, airline-type kosher meal, or would (s)he be embarrassed if served different food than the rest of the group? Finding this out in advance will assure that the affair runs smoothly.

Talking About Costs

At this point the salesperson has not yet talked about the budget. Of course, most people shop around and have a fair idea of the price structure in your establishment. Obviously customers must be able to afford your place, otherwise they would not be considering it. Price is something that should be discussed only after the client has become convinced that your place can make his or her event successful and memorable and after the salesperson has shown genuine interest in the affair.

Because of anti-trust laws you cannot ask a prospective client how much a competitor has quoted. However, if the prospective client has shopped around, (s)he will probably mention the price quoted by a competitor. A price mentioned by a prospective client has to be scrutinized. What does it include and what does it exclude?

Menu interior, dinner of La Confrérie de la Chaîne des Rôtisseurs, March 1968. A many-course menu: note the use of capital letters and the unusual motif that separates course descriptions.

Réception

Avant l'Oeuvre
Le Caviar Beluga sur Socle
Les Escargots d'Alsace

Taittinger Champagne Blanc de Blancs Brut 1959
Byrrh
Chablis Cassis

Le Dîner

L'Essence de Céleri aux Quenelles
Les Paillettes d'or

Le Bar Noir Plaza

Montrachet, Baron Thenard 1960

La Noix de Ris de Veau en Vol-au-vent
Le Granité au Calvados

Marcobrunner Riesling Spätlese, von Simmern, 1964

L'Aiguillette de Faisan au Genièvre
La Purée de Marrons
Les Endives Braisées

La Laitue du Kentucky Cushman a l'Huile de Noix et Citron

Chateau Mouton Rothschild 1962

Les Grands Fromages Français

Pommard Épenots Louis Latour, 1962

La Pêche de la Grande Dame Dorothy
Les Petits Fours

Piper Heidsieck Extra Dry (en Magnum)

Café

Les Liqueurs
Cordial Medoc
Grand Marnier
Hennessy VSOP Cognac
Crème de Menthe

Le Chef de Cuisine
Harry M. Rose

Le Maître d'Hôtel
Ron C. Varga

LES INTRONISÉS

CHEVALIERS AND DAME

Mr. Adolph J. Macina	Mrs. Gustave Sirot
Mr. Norman Holmes Pearson	Mr. Johannes B. Van Der Horst
Mr. Harry M. Rose	Mr. Edwin P. Weber

CADETS

Mr. Andre B. Bonniere	Mr. Ronald A. MacDaniel
Mr. Steven F. Havrilla	Mr. Dennis Lee Powell
Mr. James L. Hennessy	Mr. Elliott R. Sharron
Mr. Richard S. Herman	Mr. Dennis W. Tyler
Mr. Ronald A. Lacroix	Mr. John C. Wiser

MEMBERS AND GUESTS

Mr. Joseph Amendola	Mr. Robert F. Meyer
Mr. Robert E. Bengtson	Mrs. Norman Holmes Pearson
Mr. Edward H. Benenson	Mrs. Natalie A. Robbins
Mr. John H. Bogrette, Jr.	Mr. and Mrs. Carl Roessler
Mr. I. M. Bomba	Miss Sara Rosenberg
Mr. Leonard P. Drabkin	Mr. and Mrs. Jacob Rosenthal
Mr. LeRoi A. Folsom	Mrs. Nils G. Sahlin
Mr. Reuben A. Holden	Mr. Arno Schmidt
Mr. Sidney Levy	Mr. Frederick A. Snyder
Mr. Alphonse S. Marcello	Mr. Paul A. Spitler
	Mr. and Mrs. Matthew Walsh
Mr. and Mrs. Robert A. Meyer	

PARTY CHECKLIST

Since every party is different, additional information must be collected. The following checklist outlines the subjects that the salesperson and client should discuss.

Time. When does the reception start? When does the dinner commence? When will the meal be over?

Control. Who will control the collection of tickets? Who will pay the collector? Are security guards needed? Can party crashers be expected?

Signs. Are any signs necessary or desired? What kind of signs can be put up? Who will pay if special signs are requested?

Checkroom. Will the client pay for the checkroom? I.e. is the checkroom charge included in the arrangements, or is individual tipping appropriate?

Beverages. What kinds of beverages will be served? What style of service will be used? (See chapter 8 for a complete discussion of beverage sales and service.)

Decorations. What is the client's choice of color in linen, flowers, special tapered candles, and candle sticks? Will there be elaborate decorations put up by professional decorators? How long will it take to put up the decorations? Will the room be out of commission for an excessive amount of time? Should rental be charged?

Gifts, door prizes. Will gifts be received? Will prizes be given? Who will receive, control, and distribute them?

Music. Will the house orchestra be used? How much rehearsal time is needed? Will there be dancing between courses?

Amplification. How much amplification is needed for the orchestra? How much is needed for the guest speaker? Are microphones needed on the floor?

Photographer. Will the house photographer be used? Will members of the press attend? Are press photographers to be allowed on the floor?

Room set-up. Should the room be prepared reception, buffet, or butler style? Should there be bars in the room or will liquor be passed on trays? A number of different sizes and shapes of tables are available (see Figure 3.1). Are tables for eight or for ten persons desired? Is a dais, a

Figure 3.1. Banquet table chart.

List of Standard Banquet Folding Tables

The height of all tables is 30 inches. Space requirements for calculating banquet capacity is normally ten square feet per person for a sitdown meal.

Round Tables	2½ ft.	Cocktails	54 by 54 in. tablecloth
"	3 ft.	"	64 by 64 in. "
"	4½ ft.	"	64 by 64 in. "
"	5 ft.	10 persons	84 by 84 in. "
"	5½ ft.	10 persons	90 by 90 in. "
"	6 ft.	12 persons	90 by 90 in. "

Rectangular Tables	6	by 1½ ft.	used for buffets with skirts
" "	6	by 2 ft.	" "
" "	6	by 2½ ft.	seats 3 persons on one side for head tables and dais
" "	6	by 3 ft.	used for buffets with skirts
" "	5	by 2½ ft.	" "
" "	4	by 2½ ft.	" "
Square Table	2½ by 2½ ft.		" "
Half-Round	5	ft. by 30 in.	" "
Quarter-Round	30 in. by 30 in.		" "
Crescent	6	ft. by 36 in.	" "

Large Oval Table, for 16 guests: Two Half-Rounds 5 ft. by 36 in. Four Rectangular 6 by 2½ ft.

Hollow Buffet Table: Combination of four Crescent tables and a sufficient number of 6 by 3 ft. or 5 by 3 ft. tables.

Clover Leaf: Four Half Round Tables 5 ft. by 36 in.
Sixteen Rectangular Tables 6 by 2½ ft.
One Square Table 2½ by 2½ ft.
90 by 90 in. tablecloths are normally used for draping under lace.

Room Set-Ups

Theater Style: Rows of chairs facing the speaker's table or lectern

Schoolroom Style: Rows of 6 ft. by 1½ ft. or 6 by 2 ft. rectangular tables with chairs placed behind them facing the speaker

Vanderbilt Style: Round cocktail tables scattered informally around the room

headtable, a family table, or a table of honor needed? Is a children's table a good idea? Where will the people to be seated at the head table line up?

Flags. Any flags needed? Who will pay for rental if the flag is not available free?

Programs. Who will print the programs? When is the deadline for the menu? Who will proofread the menu copy? Who will deliver the menus and to whom? Who will pay for menu printing? Do you have a policy about ads solicited from the establishment for souvenir programs? Does the establishment provide a prize for a raffle in connection with a charity ball?

Sales tax. Is the group exempt from local sales taxes?

Seating list. If seating is to be formal, who will supply a seating list? The salesperson should inform the client that the catering department will supply a diagram to the client and that it will also supply number stands.

Master of ceremonies/announcer. Is there to be a master of ceremonies? Will one be needed? Is there a program or a speech? When will it take place: during the dinner, before the main course, or after the dinner? Fund-raising speeches are often held before the dinner to keep the guests in the room. How long will these speeches be?

Mechanical. Is a spotlight operator needed? Must lighting in the room be dimmed at some point during the function? If a production is given on the stage, who will supply the lighting instructions to the hotel staff? Is extra power needed? Are carpenters needed to hang banners or do other work? Is an upholsterer needed to drape a runway or to drape tables?

National anthem. Will it be played? Will it be on tape? Will our flag be spotlighted?

Permits. Are any special permits needed to comply with local laws? Is special insurance needed for displays?

Arrival. What entrance should be used?

As this list indicates, there is much more to discuss than food and service. A price will mean very little unless all information is available. The cost of the complete package must be considered in setting the price to be quoted.

Figure 3.2.   House policy form.

BANQUET POLICY

All reservations and agreements are made upon, and are subject to the rules and regulations of the hotel and the following conditions:

1. The quotation herein is subject to a proportionate increase to meet increased costs of foods, beverages, and other costs of operation existing at the time of performance of our undertaking by reason of increases in present commodity prices, labor costs, taxes, or currency values. Patron expressly grants the right to the Hotel to raise the prices herein quoted or to make reasonable substitutions on the menu, and agrees to pay such increased prices and to accept such substitutions.

2. In arranging for private functions, the attendance must be definitely specified at least 48 hours in advance. This number will be considered a guarantee, not subject to reduction, and charges will be made accordingly.

3. All federal, state, and municipal taxes which may be imposed or be applicable to this agreement and to the services rendered by the Hotel are in addition to the prices herein agreed upon, and the Patron agrees to pay them separately.

4. No beverages will be permitted to be brought into the Hotel by the Patron or any of the Patron's guests, or invitees from the outside.

5. Performance of this agreement is contingent upon the ability of the Hotel management to complete the same, and is subject to labor troubles, disputes or strikes; accidents; government (federal, state, or municipal) requisitions, restrictions upon travel, transportation, foods, beverages or supplies; and other causes whether enumerated herein or not, beyond control of management, preventing or interfering with performance. In no event shall the (Hotel) _____ be liable for loss of profit or for other similar or dissimilar collateral or consequential damages whether based on breach of contract, warranty or otherwise.

6. PATRON AGREES TO BE RESPONSIBLE FOR ANY DAMAGE DONE TO THE PREMISES DURING THE PERIOD OF TIME THEY ARE UNDER PATRON'S CONTROL OR THE CONTROL OF ANY INDEPENDENT CONTRACTOR HIRED BY PATRON.

7. THE (HOTEL) _____ WILL NOT ASSUME ANY RESPONSIBILITY FOR THE DAMAGE OR LOSS OF ANY MERCHANDISE OR ARTICLES LEFT IN THE HOTEL PRIOR TO OR FOLLOWING PATRON'S PARTY.

8. Payment shall be made in advance of function unless credit has been established in advance with the Hotel.

Menu interior, the Culinary Olympic Dinner, December 1977. Novelle cuisine combines with Kosher laws to produce a rich banquet menu.

. . . In the Spirit of Nouvelle Cuisine,
we observe Ancient Dietary Laws. . .

Dinner

The Reception

Table No. 1

Minsk Beef Borscht
Negev Chicken with Almond Velouté
Barcelona Fish Caldo
Frankfurt Purée of Cabbage

Table No. 2

Salmon en Croûte • *Watercress Purée*
Calf's Feet à la Mode de Caën
Anchovy Coulibiac

Table No. 3

Fruits of Many Lands
picked from the tree and prepared by our Chefs

Also

Mojavi Dates with Lamb
Zucchini with Eggplant
Cucumber Boats with Smoked Salmon

Ackerman Sparkling Vouvray

Bouquet Imperial Valley
Poached Atlantic Striped Bass Ambassador

✻

Canard Duchene Cote de Champenois

Granité of Cranberry and Apple
à la Sidney

Veal and Sweetbreads Leventhal
Braised Fennel

✻

Bichot 1973 St. Emilion

Breast of Roast Squab Victor
Appropriate Fruits

✻

Domaine Gerin 1971 Cote Roti

Refreshment of Fresh Pineapple
with Crunchy Caramel
Pistachio Genoise Stanley
Sammy's Sabayon

✻

Fontanaprodda Asti Spumante

Demi-Tasse

✻

Domecque Don Pedro Brandy

At this point questions must be asked about the credit rating of the prospective client. The house policy regarding deposit, prepayment, and extension of credit must be explained fully and perhaps provided to the client in writing (see Figure 3.2.). The banquet salesperson also has a right to ask how the client expects to pay the bill. Smaller operations providing simple banquets often use a preprinted form to aid the banquet salesperson in asking the necessary questions. This form varies from place to place but one can be made up very easily by culling the pertinent questions from the previous pages and combining them on a simple form. A Banquet Order Form facilitates banquet booking tremendously, especially in establishments where the booking is done only occasionally by personnel normally engaged in other tasks.

Having a banquet is like having guests in one's own house: one can never know too much about prospective guests if the group and the host are to part as friends when the party is over.

Planning

4

The catering industry is characterized by widely varying demand. Days of peak business are followed by days of very low activity. This wide fluctuation of business has a variety of causes. The economic situation, tradition, the prevailing political condition, trends in social life, changing social customs, the manner in which the competition operates, even the weather, all these can contribute to catering demand. It is, therefore, very difficult to forecast banquet business precisely. Sometimes even the best forecast can be way off target because a traditionally large annual function does not live up to expectations. On the other hand, a small, relatively unknown account can schedule an event that grows by leaps and bounds at the last minute.

Such fluctuations often require last minute changes in assignment of rooms, room set-up, and sometimes even in the menu selection. Good planning is, therefore, essential in the banquet business, but that planning must always be flexible enough to allow reasonable changes when requested. The banquet business is part of the hospitality industry, and success lies in being hospitable to the guests. That requires consideration of the client's every wish or whim. Every plan can be changed if the change helps and is profitable.

THE FUNCTION BOOK

Function space is controlled through the use of a diary or function book. This book has one double page for every day of the year, listing the day, date, and all available function space. The space is normally divided into columns for morning, lunch, afternoon, reception, and dinner.

In hotels, the function book is used primarily by the sales department, since that department is responsible for selling hotel sleeping rooms in connection with events which often also require function space for meetings and activities where food is served. It is also used by the catering department, which is responsible for selling food functions. There is often a conflict about function space between a hotel's sales department and its catering department. Since hotels are vitally interested in filling sleeping accommodations, the sales department should have preference in booking the available function space (convention bookings are often dependent on having meeting space available). It is imperative for the sales department to get such meeting schedules as quickly as possible in order to make unneeded function space available to the catering department. In large operations it is not unusual to book a ballroom for an all-day meeting and also to sell the room in the later afternoon for a reception and dinner. Being able to re-set a room quickly can add considerable revenue. Every hotel com-

PAC CHRISTMAS PARTY

Waldorf-Astoria / Friday, December 17, 1971

Program

Reception and cocktails at seven p.m. in the
East Foyer and Astor Gallery.
Dinner at eight, and dancing till one a.m.
in the Grand Ballroom.
Music by: Joe Carroll and his orchestra.

Dinner

Jellied Madrilene

Bouquet of Pascal Celery & Olives
Choice Nutmeats

Roast Yuletide Hen
Old English Bread Stuffing
Cognac Sauce
Brussell Sprouts with Chestnuts
Candied Sweet Potatoes

Emerald Dry

Southern Cross Salad
Romaine Lettuce, Hearts of Palm
and Pimiento, Lemon Dressing

Queen Madge's Plum Pudding
Flaming Rum Sauce

Sugar Plums & Marzipan

Coffee

pany has rules established concerning how quickly the space must be released.

In order to maintain proper control of function space assignments and to assure that the space available for sale is clearly apparent, the diary or function book must be maintained in a neat and orderly fashion. In an operation doing a large banquet business, only one person, the function clerk, is authorized to make entries in the function book or diary. In smaller operations, all salespeople may make entries in the diary, but all entries must be initialed to make identification possible.

There are two types of entries: definite and tentative. A tentative booking is made when a prospect has expressed definite interest, but a letter of confirmation has not been received. This entry should be made in the diary or function book in pencil. A definite booking is made when proper written confirmation has been received from the customer accepting the proposal of the house. A definite booking should be entered in the diary or function book in ink.

FORECASTING REVENUE

Forecasting is looking ahead and estimating as precisely as possible how much business will be done in the future. Every businessperson should know how much revenue can be expected during the coming month. That is the only way to allocate expenses properly. Large corporations make a five-year forecast, a yearly forecast, and a monthly forecast.

Forecasting for the banquet business is based on the diary or function book. As noted earlier, large fluctuations in business are common in the banquet industry. The figures entered in the diary or function book are only estimated attendance figures given by the client. When the date of the function draws nearer, these figures can change considerably. This is when experience and records of past history of the account's acitivities demonstrate their importance. It is easy to see that forecasting cannot safely be based on copying the business listed in the function book. Instead, it must be a realistic estimate of how business will materialize. A considerable amount of walk-in business may also exist for certain operations. Walk-in business can be estimated by knowing what is going on in town, how the competition is doing, and having faith in the abilities of the sales staff. An example of the revenue forecast of a large hotel is shown in Figure 4.1.

Menu, PAC Christmas dinner. From nutmeats to sugar plums, this banquet menu is filled with traditional holiday delights.

Figure 4.1.   Sample revenue forecast for a large hotel.

Date	Name of Function	Forecasted Covers Type	Number	Food Revenue	Beverage Revenue
7/1	Teachers Reunion	Hospitality*	0	$0	$1,000
	Fiesta Hispana	Dance*	0	0	5,000
	Pick-up			300	100
	Total to Date			$300	$6,100
7/2	Mutual Life	Reception and Dinner	35	$1,288	$400
	Teachers Reunion	Dinner	800	12,000	4,000
	Pick-up			300	100
	Total Today		835	13,588	4,500
	Total to Date		835	$13,888	$10,600
7/3	Masterson	Lunch	25	$300	$100
	Airport News	Reception	125	1,875	1,500
	Pick-up			300	100
	Total Today		150	2,475	1,700
	Total to Date		985	$16,363	$12,300
7/31	State Conference	Lunch	300	$3,600	$1,800
	Werner Wedding	Dinner	275	5,300	3,600
	Pick-up			600	100
	Total Today		575	9,500	5,500
	Total to Date		6,750	$102,300	$40,090

*Hospitality and dance functions do not count as covers in these cases because no food is served.

Banquet Department Revenue Forecast Summary July 1979

		FOOD	BEVERAGE	TOTAL
Forecasted	July 1978	$85,000	$36,000	$121,000
Actual	July 1978	96,000	31,500	137,500
Forecasted	July 1979			
Actual		$79,000	$36,300	$115,000
Pick—up		23,300	3,790	27,090
Total		102,300	40,090	142,390

	July 1978 Actual	July 1979 Forecasted
Covers	8,787	6,750
Average check	$10.90	$15.14

BANQUET MEETINGS

It takes a team to run successful banquets. All members of the team should always be aware of how things are going. In large banquet operations, it is very important to call formal banquet meetings between management, the banquet sales staff, the head waiter, the chef, and the head houseman to discuss pertinent problems. In smaller places, the banquet meeting can be a friendly get-together over a cup of coffee to evaluate past functions and discuss problems encountered.

Subjects to be included on an agenda for banquet meetings, as suggested by the Hilton Hotels Corporation, are listed below. It is recommended that no more than five items be discussed at one meeting.

Weekly review of files covered by each banquet salesperson

Review of high food-cost menus

Lost business reports

Referrals

Call reports

Year's sales goals for each banquet salesperson

Review of progress report of business booked for each month

Evaluation of quality of food and service

Evaluation of effectiveness of guidelines

Review of high labor costs

Review of Banquet Profit and Loss Reports

Late distribution of menus

Guarantees

Condition of banquet space

Engineering charges

Condition of "big four"—china, silver, glasses, and linen

Progress report of the banquet market plan

EQUIPMENT MAINTENANCE

The condition of banquet space and the condition of the "big four" are among the most important points on the banquet manager's agenda. The condition of the banquet space can make or kill a sale. Keeping the chairs in good repair, maintaining walls and carpets in good order, and having a room arranged in a neat and orderly manner when not in use are important factors in the impression made on a prospective client when the room is being shown. The staff working in the room is often most aware when damage occurs and what repairs are needed.

Menu, autumn dinner. This
formal French menu is so
descriptive that it reads like text.

Le Diner d'Automne

IN THE TERRACE ROOM

Avant de passer à table

Vermouth-Cassis
Dubonnet, Sherry, Byrrh

LE CAVIAR FRAIS SUR GLACE
LE PATE DE FOIE GRAS DE STRASBOURG
accompagnés
d'Amuse Bouche Chauds

———

IN THE GRAND BALLROOM

Pouilly Fumé 1954
Château du Nozet

Le Festival commencera par
LE CONSOMME DOUBLE A L'ORLEANAISE

On servira ensuite

LE ZEPHIR DE TURBOTIN A L'AURORE
garni de NYMPHES VIERGES

Suivra

Bordeaux —
Château Lafite 1952

LE CUISSEAU DE VEAU PIQUE GASTRONOME
accompagné, de Rizotto aux Cêpes Provençale
et le Céleri Braisé Colbert

On continuera avec

Chambertin, Clos de Beze
Domaine Jules Regnier 1949

LE PERDREAU ROTI ARROSE DE SON JUS
sur son gratin à la Fine Champagne
avec une bonne Salade d'Automne

Enfin on savourera

LE FROMAGE DE BRIE A POINT

———

Intermède pour permettre à la critique de
s'exprimer en attendant

Heidsieck Dry Monopole 1947

LES CERISES JUBILEES "ESCOFFIER"
Servies avec des Petits Palmiers

LA CORBEILLE DE FRUITS D'AUTOMNE

Et pour aider la digestion
on dégustera

Martel — Cordon Bleu

Un bon MOKA bien chaud

Le Chef de Cuisine: HUMBERT GATTI

The headwaiter, the captains, the waiters, and bartenders should be encouraged to report immediately any damage or accident hazards noted.

The management, however, must decide when to schedule routine maintenance and complete rehabilitation of banquet space. Rooms used frequently for industry shows receive more wear and tear than rooms used for social functions. As a rule, the carpets must be shampooed at least every three months, the curtains and drapes dry cleaned once a year, and the room scheduled for a major redecorating job every five to seven years. Banquet chairs must be inspected frequently. Sometimes the welded seams start to crack because of heavy use and frequent stacking, and nasty accidents can occur when a chair collapses under a guest.

The "big four" is an expression used in the industry to describe china, silver, glasses, and linen. These items are needed in large quantities and have a limited usable life. Since the replacement cost is considerable, it behooves good management to stress care and prudence in the use of the "big four."

Careless handling of table linen and napkins can result in stains that only excessive amounts of bleach will remove, which will ruin the original color. Occasionally, napkins find their way into the kitchen where they are used as kitchen towels, ruining them for public use. Cigarette burns damage tablecloths, but can at least partly be prevented by supplying sufficient clean ashtrays on time. Chipped glasses can be avoided by proper bussing methods and by racking the glasses the moment they come from the diningroom. China must also be handled carefully. Much silver is lost in garbage by careless employees. Very large operations rake all garbage and easily recover their labor cost through the silver they find. Skidproof kitchen floors prevent slipping accidents, cutting down on injury, human misery, and equipment breakage.

Sufficient space for storage of dirty utensils coming from the dining room is very important. I have seen major ballrooms built without space adequate to quickly unload dishes coming from the dining room. I realize that space is precious, but I often wonder if savings in breakage might not be worth a little more space in back of the house.

Since banquet business fluctuates widely, it is prudent to keep as much equipment as possible under lock and key when not needed. The additional labor involved in storing these items is probably much less than the value saved by preventing breakage and pilferage. Increasing pilferage by guests and employees alike is a problem that plagues operators. The only effective and legal solution is to be vigilant and to have as few pilferable items as possible lying around.

Figure 4.2.   Sample Captain's report.

Captain's Report

Name of Function:_____ Date: _____

Name of Host:_____ Price: _____

Guarantee:_____ Number of guests attended:_____

Reception scheduled when:_____ Reception started when:_____

Food function scheduled   Food function started
    when:_____   when:_____

Beverage included in price: yes_____ no _____

Sale of beverage a la carte: $ _____

Heavy wine sales: yes_____ no_____

Heavy drink sales: yes_____ no_____

Heavy bottles sales: yes_____ no_____

Party closed on time:_____

Overtime required:_____

Observations:_____

Excessive consumption of "big four" items has put some banquet houses out of business. Another book would be needed to describe all the ideas that have been tried and proved successful in controlling the "big four." I think awareness of the problem by management and staff is the key to success.

There are smaller items used daily in banquets which also add up to a major expense item, such as candles, paper goods (primarily doilies), and Sterno. All three items are often left unprotected, free for all to take. Candles are dropped and break, or too many candles are taken to a function room and those not needed are not returned. Paper doilies often stick together, and most waiters take two or three because they do not bother to take the doilies apart. Sterno is often used in excessive amounts. Here again, management and staff awareness of the expense improper usage incurs can lead to major savings for the banquet business.

CONTROLS

There are different methods of controlling the number of main courses taken by the waiters to the function room. In smaller operations, probably no controls are needed since the function room is close to the kitchen and the waiters are few. In large places, however, some waiters take away many more dinners than needed because the distance to the kitchen is considerable, and they want to be sure to have sufficient food at their tables without having to walk back. This practice leaves the kitchen short of food, which in turn encourages waiters to take a little more the next time so as not be short.

This vicious cycle can be broken by issuing "roast slips" to the waiters. These slips can be made out by the captain in charge or by a control person in the kitchen. Every waiter reports his table number and the number of guests seated. A preprinted slip is quickly filled out with this information. The waiter then hands the slip to the chef or steward in exchange for food.

Beverages must be controlled the same way to avoid abuses (see chapter 8 for further details). Because the control of energy has become a major concern, in some operations the closing captain fills out a short checklist covering the turning off of lights, air conditioning, fans, etc. The closing captain also fills out a Captain's Report (see Figure 4.2).

Every function should be attended by the person who sold the party. The salesperson should be dressed appropriately for the occasion, greeting the host or person in charge, and remaining available throughout the function to ensure that all instructions agreed on with the client are carried out. However, the salesperson should not play headwaiter or chef. The salesperson is a liaison between the host and the professional staff. "Too many cooks spoil the broth" is a saying which also applies to banquet service. After the function the banquet salesperson should fill out a Banquet Follow-Up Form which will go in the file for future reference (see Figure 4.3). This provides yet another means of banquet cost control.

SAFETY PROCEDURES AND LEGAL LIABILITIES

Important to any function arrangement are the plans made for emergencies. Legal counsel is needed in setting up these procedures; in some cases the house is open for liability suits if an employee recommends a doctor. If a fire breaks out, are the employees trained in the proper procedures? All employees should know that their responsibility is first to call the Fire Department, then to help vacate the premises of all persons present, and then try to fight the fire.

A constant safety problem is storage of chairs and tables. Function rooms need differing numbers of chairs and tables, and storage space

Figure 4.3. Banquet follow-up form.

Banquet Follow-Up Form

Name of banquet: _____

Date of banquet: _____

Name of banquet salesperson
who booked the banquet: _____

Time when banquet concluded: _____

Time when banquet salesperson
said goodbye to customer: _____

Name and position of person to
whom banquet salesperson
said goodbye: _____

Were any comments made at
that time? Please summarize: Good _____
                                      Acceptable _____
                                      Poor _____

Date when follow-up letter
sent out by banquet salesperson: _____

Was acknowledgment received? _____

Please summarize comments made: Good _____
                                      Acceptable _____
                                      Poor _____

This form is to become part of the permanent banquet file.

Figure 4.4.   Dance contract.

Dance Contract

All confirmations for Non-package-plan dances must contain the following stipulations:

1. Rental.

2. Special dance gratuity of 10 percent of the above rental for supervisory personnel.

3. Salesperson will be responsible for the minimum dollar beverage consumption of_____. Should Guest fail to purchase this minimum, the difference will be charged to the master account.

4. No corkage will be permitted of any beverage in the Hotel. This fact should be clearly specified on the dance admission tickets.

5. Client hereby indemnifies and hold harmless_____ and each of them against and from any and all claims, liabilities, damages or costs of whatsoever nature, including reasonable attorney fees, and whether by reason of death or of injury to any person, loss of or damage to any property, or otherwise, arising out of or in any way connected with the agreement, the event taking place in the Hotel or any related act by the Client, its agents, contractors, servants, employees, licensees or invitees, and whether or not occasioned or contributed to by the negligence of_____ and/or _____ or any agent or employee of_____ and/or _____ .

6. The Hotel requires the attendance of uniformed security guards. Please contact_____ to make specific arrangements.

7. A public dance permit is required and must be presented prior to the event. The permit can be obtained from _____ .

8. All public advertising must be reviewed by the Publicity Department, of_____ before publication.

9. For tables set but not occupied or occupied by less than six guests, a charge of $10.00 per table will prevail.

10. Full payment of all anticipated expenses is required by cash or certified check no later than 72 hours prior to the dance.

Figure 4.5.   Sample list of taxable items and exemptions.

NEW YORK STATE SALES AND COMPENSATING USE TAX
BANQUET CHARGES

Taxable

Amplification
Banquet Waiter Overtime
Bar and Bartender
Book Matches
Candles
Carver's Labor
Caterers (Food)
Chair Rental
Chef's Labor
Corkage
Door Signs
Dry Ice
Flags and Decorations
Flowers
Gold Service
Hostess
Menus
Oysterman
Photographer
Piano Tuning
Place Cards
Playing Cards
Portable Dance Floor
Projection
Quill Toothpicks
Rabbinical Service
Skull Caps
Special Napkins
Special Tablecloths
Spotlights and Operator
Telephone Installation
Typewriter Rental

Non-Taxable

Announcer
Cashiers
Engineer Service and
    Labor (Electrical and
    Carpenter)
Flower Girl
Music
Protection
Screen Rental
Special Cleaning
Ushers

is seldom available in sufficient size. Special attention must be paid to be sure that legal exits are never blocked with furniture. The temptation is great to block a fire exit "just for a little while," but must be avoided.

With blackouts becoming more frequent, instructions must be issued to the staff regarding blackouts, especially about the location of emergency lighting, and what to secure first. If there is no danger to guests and staff, the first thing to secure would be the cash register, and next the bars.

In many localities, dances require a dance permit. It is prudent to get a dance contract drawn up by legal counsel to spell out the necessary permits and limits of liability. The liquor license can be in jeopardy if liquor is brought in during a dance by outsiders and then dispensed to minors. A sample dance contract is shown in Figure 4.4.

Exhibitions require filing of documents with the board of underwriters in certain cities. Legal advice is needed to limit the liability exposure of the establishment as much as possible.

In states and cities which have a sales tax, certain groups are tax exempt. All tax-exempt organizations must provide the operation with a tax-exempt certificate. The certificate must be in possession of the operation prior to the function. The operation cannot carry the tax liability while waiting for the approval of the exemption. In case the certificate is not furnished in time, the operation should ask for an amount sufficient to cover the liability, and keep the money in escrow until the certificate is available. The way in which the sales tax is charged can also be confusing. The law varies from state to state, and proper information about sales tax charges must be available to the banquet salesperson if he or she is to charge the tax properly. A limited sample list of New York State taxable items and exemptions appears in Figure 4.5.

Insurance claims have become of major concern to operators. It is prudent to consult a competent insurance expert and secure "Hold Harmless" forms. These forms should be signed by anybody who does any kind of work in the building and is not employed by the house. A man can put up a display in his booth during a show. If he uses a ladder from the house and falls down, he can sue the house.

MENU COORDINATION

Throughout this book the necessity of coordination between the chef and the salespeople is discussed. Menu coordination is essential to making the work in the kitchen as efficient as possible. Sales personnel certainly should be encouraged to sell, but they also should be

Menu interior, dinner in honor
of Robert Audelan, June 1964.
Another beautifully written
French menu.

Les Aperitifs

PERNOD, VERMOUTH, DUBONNET

CASSIS, BYRRH

CANADIAN CLUB and G & B

 Le Menu

L'ÉLIXIR DU CHAROLAIS

PAILLETTES DORÉES

On boira:
CHÂTEAU DE SELLE
Grande Réserve
Domaine ' Ott

QUENELLES DE BROCHET BOURGUIGNONNE

NOUILLES FINES AU BEURRE

On boira:
BEAUJOLAIS SUPERIEUR
Latour 1962 (Beaune)

ROGNONNADE DE VEAU À MA FAÇON

ENDIVES BRAISÉES À LA MOËLLE

PETITES CAROTTES BELGE

POMMES DAUPHINE

LAITUE DU KENTUCKY

PARFUMÉ AU CITRON ET À L'HUILE D'OLIVES

LES FROMAGES DE FRANCE

LES BAGUETTES FRANÇAISES

On boira:
LE CHAMPAGNE MERCIER

LE MONT BLANC

LE MOCCA DES ÎLES

◇

GRANDE FINE CALVADOS

Exécutif Chef des Cuisines
ANDRÉ RENÉ

given guidelines as to the type of food that can be best produced and served. The importance of this kind of cooperation cannot be over-emphasized.

This process starts with the production of attractively printed banquet menus to be used in sales presentations. These menus should not be printed like a telephone book, with all dishes listed according to price. Banquet menus, if possible, should not have prices at all. They should rather have a selection of attractive dishes for different occasions.

It may create difficulties if proper accompaniments are not listed with the main courses. If a choice of potatoes in several forms, vegetables, and other starch dishes are listed, the client at times selects items which just do not taste well together. If the proper vegetables and starches are listed next to the item, many guests will still want to change them. Probably the best solution is to give the banquet staff a list of soups, potatoes, and vegetables for each day of the week. This list can be a two-week cycle and can be updated according to season. The banquet salesperson, in turn, will select from this list the side dishes she or he thinks proper and will then try to sell the selection. Most people will buy the choices offered if they are sold properly. This method will limit the dishes the kitchen has to prepare and at the same time give a seasonal selection of vegetables to the guests. It might even be possible to have fresh vegetables for large banquets.

Custom menus for certain groups will always be necessary. This is part of the banquet business and cannot be avoided. Management must set policies, though, regarding custom selections the sales staff can sell. It is possible to get a Cadillac automobile in many different colors and with many accessories, but it would be pretty hard to get a Cadillac with a Lincoln motor. The same situation holds true in kitchens. Many different dishes can be made from the same basic ingredients, but if ingredients are introduced that are not readily available, the back of the house falls in disarray.

I know of one hotel which gave its sales staff permission t sell any menu as long as they got the proper price for it. Whatever was promised by the sales staff had to be prepared by the kitchen. The result was constant chaos; no kitchen today is able to prepare everything at all times and in all quantities. The management of this hotel had a complete disregard for today's labor situation. Management must set realistic guidelines for all to follow.

Simple common sense is the main criteria for banquet menu planning. It would be foolish to sell a convention of truck drivers dainty tea sandwiches for their opening reception. Substantial food like rounds

Menu interior, dinner for La Confrérie des Chevaliers du Tastevin, November 1970. An example of how art can be used on the menu page.

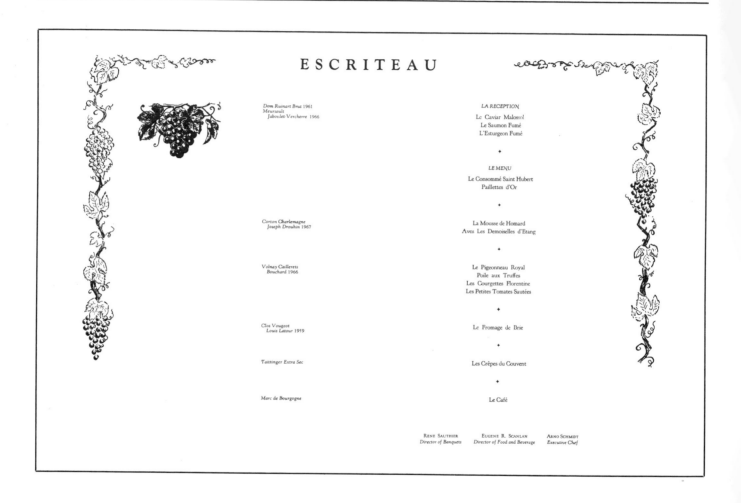

ESCRITEAU

Dom Ruinart Brut 1961
Meursault
Jaboulet·Vercherre 1966

LA RECEPTION

Le Caviar Malossol
Le Saumon Fumé
L'Esturgeon Fumé

✦

LE MENU

Le Consommé Saint Hubert
Paillettes d'Or

✦

Corton Charlemagne
Joseph Drouhin 1967

La Mousse de Homard
Avec Les Demoiselles d'Etang

✦

Volnay Caillerets
Bouchard 1966

Le Pigeonneau Royal
Poile aux Truffes
Les Courgettes Florentine
Les Petites Tomates Sautées

✦

Clos Vougeot
Louis Latour 1959

Le Fromage de Brie

✦

Taittinger Extra Sec

Les Crêpes du Couvent

✦

Marc de Bourgogne

Le Café

RENE SAUTHIER
Director of Banquets

EUGENE R. SCANLAN
Director of Food and Beverage

ARNO SCHMIDT
Executive Chef

of beef, blocks of cheese, and chafing dishes full of hearty items would be much more appreciated. Similarly, to sell an oysterbar with one oysterman to serve 800 persons is also foolish. An experienced oysterman can open no more than three bushels of oysters an hour. There are about 220 pieces of Blue Point oysters to the bushel. Little Neck clams are smaller, about 400 pieces to the bushel, and he can open no more than 1½ bushels every hour without rest. Cherrystone clams are larger, about 275 to 300 pieces to the bushel, and an oysterman can open about 3 bushels every hour in the diningroom while people are waiting. These figures must be kept in mind when a menu is being planned; they are examples of the importance of good planning. More details will be presented in chapter 7.

STYLES OF SERVICE

Another important planning decision concerns the type of service offered. The kind of service chosen for a function not only influences the price, but also dramatically affects the atmosphere of the function itself. Let us review service terminology briefly.

In **French service**, food is served from silver platters or other large dishes. Sufficient food for one table (normally a table of ten guests) is on each platter. One waiter serves the meat and sauce, the other waiter the potatoes and vegetables. The service is fast, and the platters can be garnished attractively in the kitchen. The service staff must be skilled. In true French service as practiced in private homes and embassies, guests help themselves. This practice is not very practical for banquet service. Extensive information on French service can be found in my book Notes from the Chef's Desk (Boston: CBI Publishing Company, Inc., 1978.)

"A la Russe" is an expression used in New York when food is served on individual plates. In true Russian service the food is served from platters by the waiters, a practice now called French service.

Plate service is the most widely used form of banquet service in the industry. Food is plated in the kitchen. Cold food can be plated ahead of time if sufficient cold storage is available. Large roll-in refrigerators are very helpful. The cold plates are covered or separated by stacking rings, and placed on stainless steel shelves in large carts or trucks. A five-tier truck or cart is called a Queen Mary. These trucks can be kept refrigerated and can be rolled to the banquet room at the moment of service.

Hot food must be plated at the moment of service. A large kitchen staff is needed during the short service period. For larger parties a number of stations are set up in the kitchen, and each station handles a share of the work load. Certain types of food or, when no sufficient staff is available, all hot food can also be pre-plated and kept in portable or stationary heaters. However, the quality of most hot food suffers when pre-plated. Plate service requires less skill on the part of the service personnel and less investment in equipment. (In French service, the investment in silver can be considerable.)

With **family-style** service, enough food for each table is put on platters and in bowls. These are then taken to each table. There is no service; each guest passes the food, or one guest serves the food for everybody. This service is informal and is often used in resort hotels, children's camps, or family-style restaurants. It is not suitable for fine banquet service.

Buffet service is suitable for all types of meals, from breakfasts to receptions to dinners. Hot and cold food is attractively displayed and decorated. Guests walk up to the buffet and help themselves. Proper equipment is of prime importance because of the visual impression it makes on the guests. Before they can see the individual food presentations, the guests first look at the buffet from a distance. Gleaming silver or copper chafing dishes, large ice carvings, beautiful platters, attractive flowers, lace- or satin-skirted tables, proper lighting, and a uniformed crew behind the buffet set the mood for a pleasurable experience. Most people love buffets because they offer them the freedom to choose among many dishes, and it is imperative that a reasonable selection continues to be available for the last guests. On elegant occasions, foods for the reception are often presented as a buffet to allow the guests to mingle, and then the dinner is a sit-down affair. At other functions, the first course is served by the waiters, the main course is on the buffet, and then the dessert is served at the table.

Pre-set service is employed when faster service is needed. On occasions when the schedule is tight, the client can request that the first course be set on the table before the guests sit down. The first course in such a case could be a cold soup, melon and Prosciutto, or perhaps another cold appetizer. For business luncheons sometimes the dessert is also placed on the table before the guests sit down. However, the client should be aware that food is normally not at its best when pre-set.

Butler style is most often used during receptions when food in tidbit size is put on platters. Waiters then circulate among the guests with the platters. Only fingerfood should be passed butler style. I have seen Oysters Rockefeller served butler style with one waiter passing the oysters and another waiter trailing behind with tiny bread and butter plates, oyster forks, and napkins. How the hapless guests managed to eat the food and hold a glass at the same time I do not know.

The type of service offered depends very much on physical exigencies such as the equipment, the staff available, the layout of the rooms, the layout of the kitchen, and the distance from the kitchen to the dining rooms. Of course, it should also reflect the wishes of the guests. The banquet industry must operate as efficiently as possible in order to earn an acceptable profit and, consequently, attract the capital necessary for expansion and replacement of existing facilities. Nobody would think of taking an abandoned truck factory and starting to manufacture dresses without major modifications. In the banquet industry, however, facilities are often built before a decision is reached as to where to put the banquet facilities and what kind of service to offer. In many cases, additional costly construction is required after the building is opened to make the food facilities function.

THE IMPORTANCE OF TRAINING

The best building, however, cannot by itself make a food facility function. It takes pleasant, well-trained employees to make the difference between an empty shell and a viable business. In some cases, interested amateurs know more about food, wine, and service than many "professionals" who serve them. The lack of a knowledgeable staff can cost the operation valuable business. Part of planning is a genuine concern for employee training.

The banquet business is probably the only major industry that does not train in an organized fashion. There are notable exceptions, of course. For an excellent example, see the Banquet Waiter Rules from the Waldorf-Astoria Hotel in appendix B. But, in many cases, training is still left to the fellow across the street. Good training costs money. Many training aids are available to the operator, and, with goodwill, some money, and an open mind, a good training program can be established.

Logistics

5

This chapter will outline how to write menus that can be produced efficiently. As discussed earlier, promising a customer something that the kitchen is unable to deliver will not keep your operation in business very long. The salesperson must never forget that all the dishes on a banquet menu stencil must be turned into reality in the kitchen. All too often, banquet sales personnel concentrate on forecast, profits, goals, and the sale, and do not remember the production problems in the back of the house. Today nobody can ignore production problems. Of course, the salesperson should want to sell the best possible menu at the best possible price, but it is the responsibility of the banquet salesperson to write menus that can be produced as promised.

KNOW THE EQUIPMENT

To understand the relationship of the written menu and the produced meal, a good banquet salesperson will spend time in the kitchen and get acquainted with the equipment available. In most kitchens there is never enough equipment; how efficiently that equipment will be used, therefore, depends very much on the chef—and the chef's goodwill. Cooks are normally ingenious, but the chef may become even more resourceful when the banquet salesperson comes to see him (or her— many fine chefs these days are women) and discuss possible problems.

Still, there are limits; a good salesperson should know them and keep them in mind. I remember a fine, new hotel with a large ballroom seating about 1000 people. There was no broiler in the banquet kitchen and only two broilers in the main kitchen to take care of the restaurant, the coffeeshop, and room service. You guessed right: the first dinner booked for the ballroom called for filet mignon! As a result, the chef did not stay very long, and the party booked its dinner in another hotel the next year. Clearly an awareness of equipment limitations on the salesperson's part could have benefited the kitchen, the client, and the hotel.

Additional equipment can always be rented, and lack of equipment should never be a deterrent to selling a banquet. Still, smart selling can avoid extra costs and keep customers happy. Linen should always be kept in mind. Most places have a list of linen types and colors available, but the sales staff should remember: when linen is used, it must be sent to the laundry and normally will not return until the next day. Banquets should not be sold promising linen of a certain color scheme if that linen is scheduled to be used the day before. Similarly, if the salesperson knows how many round platters the operation can provide, or how many chafing dishes are available, the client can be

Menu cover, 218th anniversary banquet of the Saint Andrews Society of New York, December 1974. The society's seal is embossed in gold.

guided to stay within these limits. Not only is the life of the steward made easier, but the salesperson avoids making promises that cannot be kept.

BROILER CAPACITY

A standard broiler has a broiler rack with a finishing oven on top, though models omit the finishing oven, instead providing a double rack. The capacity for broiling steaks is about the same on both models. A large model broiler will hold a standard sheet pan measuring 18 by 24 in. Thirty-five filet mignons in the weight range of 6 to 8 oz. can be placed on one such sheet pan. An experienced cook will place one tray on the rack under the flames and the other tray in the finishing oven. In a few minutes, the first tray can be put in the finishing oven, and the second moved under the flames. In this way 70 filet mignons can be cooked in about ten minutes. It is, therefore, easy to calculate how long it will take to cook 500 filet mignons with existing equipment. Larger quantities take a little longer because of heat lost while cooking more food. In addition, the human factor should be considered; after 25 minutes work in front of two or three hot broilers, the banquet cook will probably be less productive than at the beginning of the shift.

If the same banquet requires sirloin steaks, the time factor is different. Sirloin steaks cannot be broiled very well on a sheet pan; instead they should be cooked directly on the broiling rack. About 20 to 25 sirloin steaks can be placed on the rack at one time. These steaks must be turned, and, in order to turn them, the cook must pull out the rack. While the rack is pulled out, it does not receive any heat. Consequently, the first batch of steaks will cook in about ten minutes, but the second batch will take considerably longer because the broiler has spent its heat. Before the third batch can be cooked, the broiler must be allowed to heat up again, losing still more production time.

Because of this slow-down, some chefs brown steaks under the broiler, then put them on sheet pans to be finished in the banquet kitchen's oven. This system works quite well, but the steaks will not be very good because the fat often does not cook enough. In addition to timing problems, there is always the danger of fire when a large quantity of sirloin steaks are broiled. The salesperson should be aware of these difficulties. Once familiar with them, the salesperson understand the advantage of selling filet mignons instead of sirloin steaks for large banquets.

ROASTED ITEMS

A standard roasting pan measures about 25 by 22 or 24 in. If a rib of beef is roasted with the bones, it will weigh between 20 to 24 lbs. and will provide about 20 portions for a banquet. These sizes will vary from house to house, but represent the average.

Normally, two ribs in the 20 to 24 lb. range are cooked in a roasting pan; on busy banquet days, three ribs can be crowded into one pan. A rib takes about 3½ hours to roast. That means, under the best circumstances, each oven can produce 60 slices every 4 hours. Time must also be allowed for the meat to rest before it is sliced and for the staff to load and unload the oven. Roast rib of beef can be roasted many hours before actual serving time if all sanitary precautions are taken. However, the salesperson should know the kitchen's capacity: if a place has limited oven capacity, it is foolish to book a large lunch and a large dinner each requiring roast ribs of beef on the same day. No small kitchen could handle such demand well.

The same roasting pan can accommodate four shell strips of beef, each weighing about 10 to 12 lbs. trimmed or eight beef tenderloins weighing 3½ to 4 lbs. trimmed. Each shell strip will provide between 16 to 20 portions for a banquet. The roasting time is about 50 minutes, with another ten minutes must be allowed for loading the oven. Therefore, the same oven that produces 60 portions every hour from rib of beef roasts can produce 64 to 80 portions every hour from shell strips of beef. Each beef tenderloin provides eight portions. The roasting time is 25 minutes. Each pan yields 64 portions in one-half hour.

Another possibility for roast meals is poultry. Here too the salesperson would be wise to understand cooking details. The standard roasting pan will take a maximum of eight whole ducklings in the weight range between 4 and 5½ lb. Normally one-half duckling is a portion. It takes about 2½ hours to roast a duckling which results in a capacity of 16 portions every 2½ hours.

On a normal 18 by 24 in. sheet pan 20 double breasts of chicken in the weight range of 20 to 22 oz. can be cooked at one time. Normally, 30 minutes must be allowed for a pan of chicken breasts. Since the chicken breasts are not very high and many ovens have a rack, it is possible to roast two sheet pans at a time. (In that case, however, the roasting time must be increased because the hot air cannot circulate as efficiently.) It is possible, then, for each oven to produce 80 portions in a little more than a half hour. From these figures the salesperson can see that selling a roast breast of chicken is not only attractive in terms of food cost angle, but also in terms of utilizing the equipment to the utmost.

Menu, the Saint Andrew's Society of New York banquet. A gala presentation of traditional Scottish fare.

Bill o' Fare

Cock-a-Leekie

———

HAGGIS FRAE CALEDONIA
Bashed Neeps   Oatcakes

———

Nairn Mutton
Perth Tatties   Glesga Sprouts

———

Fraserburgh Greens

———

St. Kilda Ice

———

Ither Orra Things   A Tassie O'Coffee

———

Music by
Patrick Walsh and his orchestra

SOUP PRODUCTION

Soups are normally very low in food cost and can be prepared efficiently if sufficient steam kettles are available. It takes only minutes to bring 30 or 50 gallons of liquid to a boil in a steam kettle provided with 40 lb. steam pressure, while it will take agonizing hours to do the same thing on a rangetop. If you want to sell homemade soups in any quantity, you must have steam kettles. Otherwise you tie up valuable range space that could be put to better use.

If soups are served from tureens filled in the kitchen, service is fast and simple, even when the individual cups are filled in the kitchen. However, there is always the danger of accidental spills in the dining room. If conditions will be very crowded at the function, the salesperson might be wiser not to advise serving a soup, encouraging the client instead to start the meal with a pre-set appetizer. If it proves necessary to serve a soup under crowded conditions, the salesperson should remember that it is better to serve a clear soup rather than a cream one: burns are less painful and spots normally easier to handle.

Sometimes very large banquets can strain the capacity of the kitchen. In such cases little things can make a lot of difference. When the banquet is to be very large, it is worthwhile for the salesperson to remember that vegetables should be easy for both the kitchen crew and the service personnel to serve. Asparagus cannot be handled easily, for instance, nor can whole stalks of broccoli. The salesperson should discourage the inclusion of such vegetables on the menu of an especially large function. The best vegetables to serve come in walnut-size shapes: zucchini chunks, tiny whole carrots, bottoms of mushrooms and similar items that can be scooped up very quickly. The salesperson should make every effort to sell this type of vegetable when a large banquet is being planned.

AVOID TOO MANY MENU CHOICES

Offering more than three vegetables at a large banquet will slow up service. The salesperson should understand this and make the fact clear to the client. Even where the customers are expected to help themselves at the table, more than three vegetables slow up service, and the platter looks very messy after the fourth person has been served.

The salesperson should understand that the number of items served is also a consideration for cheese trays. Four varieties are sufficient: a soft cheese like a Camembert or Brie; a semi-soft cheese like Port Salut, a blue cheese from the many available, and a harder cheese like Cheddar or Monterey Jack. If an exotic goat cheese is needed, one of the other cheeses should be eliminated.

Menu, dinner at the Four Seasons in Florida, December 1967. Compare the layout of this menu to others in this book: the design here is clear, but noticeably less creative.

8

LE DÔME OF THE FOUR SEASONS, FORT LAUDERDALE, FLORIDA, December 10, 1967

L'Escriteau

AVANT PROPOS

Pommery & Greno 1961 *Magnums*	Les Bagatelles Apéritives
	Le Caviar Beluga et Ses Blinis

I ère ASSIETTE

Tio Pepe Jerez	La Soupe de Tortue
	et Ses Paillettes D'or

II ième ASSIETTE

Puligny Montrachet 1964 Clos du Cailleret	Le Soufflé de Langouste
	au Parfum Des Caraïbes

III ième ASSIETTE

Chambertin 1961 Clos de Béze	La Selle de Mouton en Chevreuil
	Sauce Poivrade
	Barquette de Marrons
	Laitue Braisée

IV ième ASSIETTE

Musigny 1959 Cuvée Vieille Vignes .. Domaine Comte de Vogué	Le Perdreau Rôti Sur Canapé
	Pommes Dauphine
	Carottes Glacées
	La Salade Tropicale à
	L'Huile Vierge et Citron

Vième ASSIETTE

Château Haut Brion 1957 Ier Grand Crú Classé	Le Plateau de Fromages
Château la Tour Blanche 1959 Ier Cru Classé	Bombe Glacée Aux Violettes
Cordial Médoc Hennessy XO Crème de Cacao "Chouao" Marie Brizard	Le Moka
	Mignardises

LES MAÎTRES DU BANQUET   LES MAÎTRES CULINAIRES

Georg Haringer — Robert Rogers   Robert Morency, Chef des Cuisines
Maurice Blanchar — Hans Regnery   Antoine Agnoli — Roger Boule
                                          Denis Rety — Maurice Bonfils

Music by HERB and ELENA AYERS

Sometimes the client desires fruit to be served with the cheese. This can become a very awkward situation, and the salesperson should know why. The kinds of fruit that go well with cheese are largely limited to grapes, pears, apples, and perhaps figs or kiwi fruit. It is easy to separate a bunch of grapes into little clusters convenient to serve and to eat. The other fruits are different. To serve a whole apple or pear to a customer at an elegant banquet creates a difficult problem. The fruit can only be eaten gracefully when cut into little pieces, yet cutting it would be a messy process for the banquet. The alternative is to cut the fruit in wedges in the kitchen. However this is not much easier. It must be done at the very last moment, since apples and pears oxidize rapidly. Figs and kiwi fruit must also be cut in half. The fruit can be put in lemon water, or Delicious Apples can be used because they do not oxidize as rapidly as other apple varieties, but the fact remains that the fruit must be cut into wedges just before service by expensive kitchen labor.

Often a salad is served with cheese. The salad can be very elaborate if necessary but, if possible, the salesperson should convince the client to limit the dressing choice to one good dressing. It is very time-consuming to pass around a tray containing three or more varieties of dressing, and many times the banqueter does not even want to be bothered with making a choice at that point in the dinner. When selling a dinner, the salesperson should offer a dressing that has proven popular and suggest that the same dressing be served to everybody. Incidentally, the salesperson should remember to be very careful with garlic at social gatherings—and never to schedule garlic at a business meeting! It is also inadvisable to recommend strong smelling cheeses for a large banquet. Five hundred people eating strong goat cheese in one room will not be very pleasant for anybody attending.

HOLDING PRE-PLATED ITEMS

We have outlined the pitfalls of serving soup to very large groups, but the question of other individually pre-plated items must also be considered. The thing to remember is that anything pre-plated must be stored until service time. In most cases they will be held under refrigeration. Properly fitting lids are imperative if these items are to be stacked and stored properly. This may sound too basic to mention, but in one large banquet operation I saw over a thousand plates littering every available corner in the kitchen because no covers were provided for stacking.

Items like fruit, melon, and marinated vegetables can be prepared in units of ten, and service personnel can put the food on the plate

Menu interior, dinner for La Confrérie des Chevaliers du Tastevin, January 1977. A page of English culinary notes accompanied this menu.

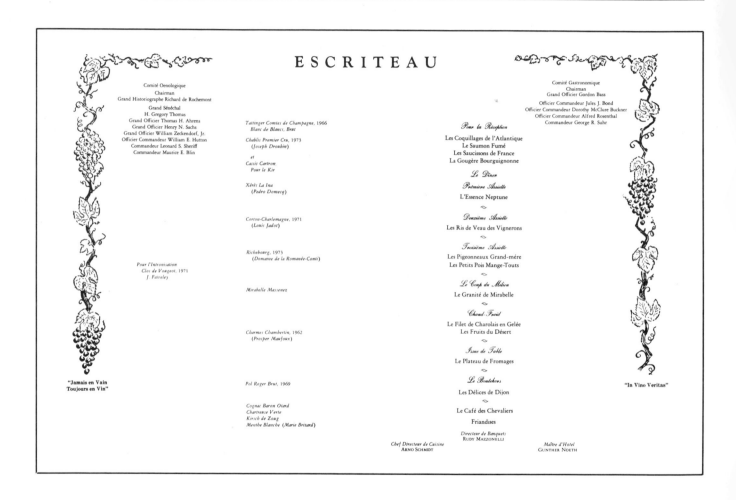

ESCRITEAU

Comité Oenologique
Chairman
Grand Historiographe Richard de Rochemont
Grand Sénéchal
H. Gregory Thomas
Grand Officier Thomas H. Ahrens
Grand Officier Henry N. Sachs
Grand Officier William Zeckendorf, Jr.
Officier Commandeur William E. Hutton
Commandeur Leonard S. Sheriff
Commandeur Maurice E. Blin

Comité Gastronomique
Chairman
Grand Officier Gordon Bass
Officier Commandeur Jules J. Bond
Officier Commandeur Dorothy McClure Buckner
Officier Commandeur Alfred Rosenthal
Commandeur George R. Suhr

Tattinger Comtes de Champagne, 1966
Blanc de Blancs, Brut

Chablis Premier Cru, 1973
(Joseph Drouhin)
et
Cassis Cartron,
Pour le Kir

Xérès La Ina
(Pedro Domecq)

Corton-Charlemagne, 1971
(Louis Jadot)

Richebourg, 1973
(Domaine de la Romanée-Conti)

Pour l'Intronisation
Clos de Vougeot, 1971
J. Faiveley

Charmes Chambertin, 1962
(Prosper Maufoux)

Pol Roger Brut, 1969

Cognac Baron Otard
Chartreuse Verte
Kirsch de Zoug
Menthe Blanche (Marie Brizard)

Pour la Réception
Les Coquillages de l'Atlantique
Le Saumon Fumé
Les Saucissons de France
La Gougère Bourguignonne

Le Dîner
Première Assiette
L'Essence Neptune

Deuxième Assiette
Les Ris de Veau des Vignerons

Troisième Assiette
Les Pigeonneaux Grand-mére
Les Petits Pois Mange-Touts

Le Coup du Milieu
Le Granité de Mirabelle

Chaud-Froid
Le Filet de Charolais en Gelée
Les Fruits du Désert

Issue de Table
Le Plateau de Fromages

Les Boulehers
Les Délices de Dijon

Le Café des Chevaliers
Friandises

Directeur de Banquets
RUDY MAZZONELLI

Chef Directeur de Cuisine
ARNO SCHMIDT

Maître d'Hotel
GUNTHER NOETH

"Jamais en Vain
Toujours en Vin"

"In Vino Veritas"

shortly before the customers arrive. Individual salad bowls often stack well with sheet pans placed between them. Some banquet operations use wooden blocks to separate sheet pans filled with dishes. Today there are also roll-around racks with plenty of shelf space for sheet pans. If there are no stairs between the banquet room and the kitchen, these racks can be rolled into the banquet room before the customers arrive.

Large banquet hotels may have several different banquet kitchens not all equally equipped. The distance from a banquet kitchen to a banquet room can also vary tremendously. The salesperson should consider all this when making up a menu. Proper consideration of the effect of logistics can keep both chef and client happy.

Food warmers play an important part in banquet success. I remember a banquet salesperson who habitually sold large banquets a menu of hot soup, hot appetizer, hot main course with two or three hot vegetables, cheese with hot french bread, and a hot dessert. As might be expected, the existing heater space was never sufficient for his parties, and food spilled out over makeshift warmers heated with Sterno. One day I pointed out the problem to him; he told me that, frankly, he had never thought about it. He changed his menus somewhat, and I am sure his clients received better service, even if they did not know why.

TIMING THE SERVICE

I would like to stress how important it is for the kitchen to know when a dinner will be served. At any banquet, we expect the food to be hot and delicious, and we also expect the chef to run his crew in the most efficient manner. This combination is possible only if the serving time is defined. I have seen banquet stencils with menus listing the meal function from 11 A.M. on. How can a chef schedule his crew and plan the food efficiently with such an indefinite schedule? To ensure the best service, the salesperson should determine the exact starting time for the meal as definitely as possible, and should note this information on the front page of the banquet form.

Breakfast

It should be obvious to every salesperson that when the function's timing is vague, the program is not well defined, or many guests are expected to arrive late, it is better to choose a dish that can stand a little longer without too much damage. Therefore, the salesperson should understand the holding characteristics of various foods. Let's start with breakfast. Scrambled eggs keep well if kept in heavy china crocks. Thick china has low heat conductivity and prevents the eggs

Menu interior, spring dinner of
La Commanderie de Bordeaux,
April 1966. A simpler French
banquet menu.

LES VINS

Champagne Krug Brut Reserve
Private Cuvée

Château Carbonnieux 1962
(Graves)

*

Château Haut Brion Blanc 1962
(Graves)

*

Château Lascombes 1959
(Margaux)

Château Ducru-Beaucaillou 1955
(St. Julien)

*

Château Ducru-Beaucaillou 1949
(St. Julien)

Château Lascombes 1926
(Margaux)

*

Château d'Yquem 1959
(Sauternes)

*

Hennessy Grande Fine Champagne
V. S. O. P. Reserve

Chartreuse V. E. P.

AVANT PROPOS

Petits Cromesquis   Saumon Fumé d'Ecosse
Cuisses de Grenouilles en Aspic   Little Necks and Cherrystones

* * *

LA MATIERE

Consommé de Caneton aux Quenelles

*

Alose Sauté aux Câpres

*

Baron d'Agneau de Lait Rôti
Petits Haricots Verts au Beurre — Pommes Anna

*

Fromages de Saison

*

Charlotte Russe aux Fraises

*

Café des Commandeurs

Director des Banquets
Jerome Horvath

Chef de Cuisine
Arno Schmidt

Bordeaux, Toujours Bordeaux!

from cooking further and getting too dry. Metal, however, conducts heat quickly and will ruin egg dishes. Poached eggs can stand a while in a heater if they are covered with a lid to prevent their drying out. Cooked eggs will tarnish silver. French toast keeps well for some time; as a matter of fact, it can be made beforehand and reheated, a good point to remember if you are planning a series of large breakfasts for an in-house convention. Corned beef hash is another breakfast item that keeps well; the top can be browned in a pan or under the broiler. Waffles, however, should be avoided. They take too long to make and for that reason are not practical for banquet service. Griddlecakes are inexpensive but must be eaten fresh: warmed griddlecakes look and taste like shoe leather.

The Main Course

Fried food must be served while still crisp. Obviously that is possible only when enough fryer capacity and enough personnel are available to do the job properly. This is also true for fried fish or chicken, which means a fried fish platter or a breaded and fried chicken dinner is usually not a good idea for banquets. If such a meal must be sold, the kitchen staff should cover the fried food lightly with an unstarched napkin before serving, never with a heavy lid that traps all the steam.

Poached fish keeps well when covered with a moist cloth. Fish covered with a rich fish sauce and browned under the broiler in a process called "glazing" also keeps well providing the heater that holds it is not very hot. Excessive heat will curdle the rich sauce.

Roasted poultry keeps well when covered, as does pot roast, roast veal, veal scallopini, and similar items. Lamb is a little more tricky. It should be cooked to medium when served to most people, and that means it has to be sliced at the last moment. Roast beef can wait quite a while because it is such a bulky piece of meat. Roast beef tenderloin, by comparison, will cook through and become too well done.

When a banquet features roasts that must be sliced at service time, it is normally up to the headwaiter in charge of the banquet to let the kitchen know when to start slicing. Roast rib of beef usually is sliced on slicing machines; with two machines, 500 slices can be sliced in 20 minutes. Roast shell strip (sirloin) is often sliced two slices per person, and it will take about 35 minutes to slice 500 portions. Roast filet of beef (tenderloin) is sliced by hand. A portion is two slices, with eight portions in a trimmed tenderloin. How quickly roast filet of beef can be sliced depends on the skill of the culinarian, but it will necessarily be slower than machine-slicing of meat. All this should be taken into account when scheduling the start of the main course.

Vegetables

Green vegetables do not stay green very long in a heater. If the client expects many dishes to be plated or wants the vegetables put in silver Escoffier dishes, it might be worthwhile for the salesperson to suggest an alternate to green vegetables. Grilled tomatoes, zucchini saute, glazed carrots, puree of white turnips, braised celery hearts, fennel hearts: all of these hold their color well. If green vegetables must be included on the banquet menu, the salesperson still can urge preferable choices. Green beans will stay green for a while; so will creamed spinach if it is kept in a china casserole. Snow peas (pea pods) will not stay green very long and should be avoided if the vegetable must be kept in the warmer a while.

Desserts

Ice cream cakes should never be covered with whipped cream because the cream will freeze solid. The salesperson should recommend that the cake be covered with meringue and the whipped cream be served on the side. Any cake covered with fondant icing must be stored in a dry room, never in the refrigerator, because the icing will attract the moisture of the refrigerator and will melt. I note this because somebody once wanted to have a large wedding cake filled with pastry cream (perishable) and glazed with fondant—a recipe the salesperson should know is headed for disaster!

MEETING MENU NEEDS

A good banquet salesperson anticipates the needs of a particular group. If the majority of guests are expected to prefer meat cooked medium to well-done, this fact is marked on the banquet menu, and the chef can prepare to provide it. If the chef is not prepared, there will be chaos in the kitchen when an unexpectedly 50 percent of the clients request well-done meat.

The salesperson must also remember that purchasing today is no easy task. In most localities there are no commercial deliveries of fish, meat, or produce on Saturdays, Sundays, and certain holidays. That means that a menu for a lunch on Monday should be in the kitchen no later than Thursday noon. The reason is simple: food must be ordered Thursday for Friday delivery so it will be available for Monday morning preparation. Many of our national holidays fall on Mondays; when a function is planned for the Tuesday after such a Monday, the menu must be in the kitchen on Thursday before noon.

The time of the year should also be taken into consideration. All growing things have seasons and are more readily available in better quality during that time. A banquet salesperson who sells strawberries in December, melons in January, or grapefruit in July just does not know what he or she is doing.

Nothing irritates a chef more than to have major banquet functions treated in a casual fashion. The salesperson who drops the banquet menu off in the kitchen a few hours before service is neither reasonable nor realistic. Even a small typing error can cause great problems in the kitchen. I think some banquet salespersons do not visualize the large quantities of food which must be ordered, received, stored, transported to the preparation area, cleaned, trimmed, cooked, and finally dished up to feed 1000 guests. A banquet menu is a work order for a production department. It must be handled with care and made out with precision.

Menu cover, 192nd meeting of
the Wine and Food Society,
October 1970. The cover shows
the Cartier building where the
dinner was held.

Kitchen Layout and Equipment

When Mr. Statler built his famous hotels in the early part of this century, he designed the back of the house very carefully. Whenever possible, the food storeroom, the receiving dock, and all production kitchens were arranged on the same floor, in a manner that would achieve the most direct work flow.

The chef's office was close to the storeroom so the chef could keep an eye on the incoming merchandise. Butchershops and bakeshops were close to the storeroom to keep the movement of raw materials to a minimum. The soup kitchen, the pantry, the garde manger, and the hot cooking line were arranged so they were all easily accessible to the dining rooms. When it was necessary to have ballrooms on different floors from the main kitchen, sizable elevators connected them with the kitchens and made the transportation of food, china, glass, dining room supplies, and garbage as speedy as possible. Warewashing was located close to the source of dirty dishes so that transportation and resultant breakage at this stage could be kept to a minimum.

IMPORTANCE OF KITCHEN DESIGN

Hotel companies today try to follow Statler's example, and some have produced very well-designed new kitchens. However, I have also seen some very unworkable new kitchens, kitchens so poorly designed that any banquet professional could tell the kitchen could not work. An endless procession of chefs (who were either fired or left on their own), costly turnover of kitchen help, constant complaints from customers, and negligible food profit result from such ill-designed kitchens.

These kitchens were not designed poorly deliberately. In many cases, a building is designed by a developer who invites hotel companies to manage the property only after the building is under construction. The hotel company then has to fit restaurants and function rooms within an established design. The leftover space becomes the kitchen. Occasionally insufficient funds are left to equip the kitchen properly, and often the investor lacks understanding of what a functioning kitchen requires.

I have seen kitchens with all freight elevators located in the middle of the space, creating continuous traffic through the kitchen. There are ballrooms with hundreds or thousands of seats and no place to put dirty china. Planners seem to have no conception of how many glasses are required for a banquet of 800 guests, or how much soiled china can accumulate when a major function room is cleared. And though labor cost and energy cost could often be saved by holding soiled dishes from smaller functions to be washed together, planners often omit space to store shelved carts near or in the main dishwashing area.

Menu, the Wine and Food Society dinner. An elaborate formal buffet menu, written in elegant French.

LA RECEPTION

Les Endives en Surprise
Les Rondelles de Brioche au Foie Gras
Les Tartelettes de Venaison
Les Canapés de Saumon Fumé

LE SOUPER
LA PREMIERE ASSIETTE
Le Borschok à la Russe et
Le Pirogui Chaud

LE BUFFET
LE PREMIER APPROCHE
La Mousse d'Ecrevisses à l'Aneth
Les Truites au Bleu en Gelée
La Galantine d'Anguille au Riesling
Les Fruits de Mer Niçoise
Le ''Grave Lax'' Suédois
Les Concombres à la Hongroise

LE RETOUR
La Selle de Chevreuil Baden Baden
Le Jambon Fumé Harrington aux Figues
Le Gigot d'Agneau en Croûte
Les Cailles Farcies à la Vendangeuse
Le Paon Marie Antoinette
Le Filet de Boeuf Strasbourgeoise
Julienne de Celerie Rave
La Salade d'Orange aux Marrons

LA DORURE
Les Fromages de la Belle France

L'APOTHEOSE
Le Croquembouche
Les Oeufs à la Neige
Les Raisins Smitaine
La Charlotte au Mocca
La Mousse Violette
Les Macarons Waldorf

*

Le Café de Colombie

Being able to roll items around is also very important: banquet food is food prepared in bulk, and the best way of moving bulk loads is on wheels. Yet some kitchens are still designed on different levels, banquet rooms built with steps going up or down, and hotels created so that food received in the basement must be prepared in kitchens on the second floor.There are even places where garbage must be hand-carried over long distances because planners left no facilities for putting the garbage cans on dollies.

Get Professional Advice

Kitchen design and construction should be closely supervised by an experienced person who knows how kitchens operate. Without such guidance, even well-financed projects can turn out imperfectly. I remember a new hotel where walk-in refrigerators were installed. The laying of the kitchen's tile floor was not coordinated with the installation of the refrigerators. The brick layers laid the floor too low; no space was allocated for insulation under the refrigerators. As a result the floor inside the walk-in box had to be raised two inches above the kitchen floor. This necessitated the construction of a ramp, which in turn caused countless spills and slipping accidents. I have also seen walk-in refrigerators with a tile floor slightly lower than the kitchen. Every time the kitchen floor is cleaned, water runs into the refrigerator. Poor conditions such as these could have been avoided by better planning.

Lack of sufficient floor drains is another mark of inexperienced planners or poorly-financed construction. The necessary number of kitchen floor drains should be provided and kitchen floors should be properly graded away from walls, toward the various drains. The kitchen floor should also be made as slip-proof as possible. A number of excellent kitchen tiles for this purpose are now on the market. The floor in a busy kitchen will always be slippery even in spite of frequent cleaning during the day and the thorough cleaning every night; cooks used to learn from their elders how to walk in a kitchen before they were even allowed to come close to the stove.

MANY USES FOR STEAM

Steam is a versatile tool, extremely useful in the professional kitchen. The most efficient way to keep kitchen floors clean and kitchens roach-free is by steam cleaning. In large operations, such as city hotels and large resort hotels, steam is normally available. Many smaller places, however, do not have steam, which makes their operation as banquet kitchens more difficult. Cooking is the more important use for steam. Kettles, steamers, and large steam tables are indispensable for large production cooking. Steam generators are available in different sizes, capable of producing 40 pounds of pressure, the pressure needed for kettles. Though such generators require a high initial investment, they soon pay back through more efficient operation.

The compartment steamer is another useful cooking tool. The basic model of the compartment steamer has not changed in many years. The basic compartment steamer can be used for many types of food preparation—boiling potatoes and eggs, poaching fish, and steaming assorted root vegetables. For poaching hot mousse, compartment steamers are indispensable. Compartment steamers are not very satisfactory for cooking green vegetables since vegetables vary so much in required cooking time. If the space, the steam, and the money is available for compartment steamers, they should be installed. However, I would not want to give up a steam kettle or a tilting frying pan for a compartment steamer.

Steam Kettles

Perhaps the most useful piece of equipment for volume banquet operations is the steam kettle. Steam kettles come in different sizes and in two basic designs: tilting kettles and kettles with drains. Each type of kettle has its own advantages. (There are also tilting kettles with drains available, combining the advantages of both.) When there is only room and need for one kettle, I would choose the tilting kettle with drain. If more space is available I recommend an equal number of kettles with drains and tilting kettles.

Kettles with drains come equipped with a strainer basket and a drain spout at the lowest point of the kettle. These kettles are used for making stock. Fat floats to the top of any liquid, so when a stock or broth is drained from a kettle, it is fat free. Any kind of stock or broth can be made in these kettles with the greatest ease.

The tilting kettle has no drain spout and no strainer basket. It has a smooth, stainless steel liner ideal for making any kind of stew, soup, heavy sauce, roux, seafood newburgh, pastry cream, and similar items. The crucial difference between one type of kettle and the other is the strainer basket and drain. When sauteeing food, the strainer basket is in the way, while when making roux in a kettle with a spout, the fat will first collect in the drain spout, the flour will fall through the strainer cap and those ingredients are completely lost. This will not happen in a tilting kettle, because it is smooth all around and has no drain. The kettle can be emptied by simply tilting it.

Steam kettles connected to an outside source providing sufficient steam are amazingly fast. Even large kettles holding 50 or 80 gallons come to a boil within minutes, whereas a 10-gallon pot put on a range top takes much longer. When installing steam equipment, the amount of steam pressure is all important. The standard industry pressure is 25 pounds per inch. This pressure is not sufficient to operate large kettles in the most practical manner. Forty pounds per inch pressure is preferable. Compartment steamers work with reduction valves and operate on much lower pressure. Some kettles on the market generate steam right in the unit. A gas or electric heater turns water into steam, which, in turn, heats the kettle and its contents. In my experience these kettles have been very slow though better models may be available now.

Kettles with drains are most practical for cooking green vegetables. Green vegetables, especially once frozen, should be cooked rapidly for the shortest possible period of time. It is therefore very important to have a strong heat source when cooking vegetables. Steam kettles markedly shorten the time between the addition of vegetables to boiling water and when the water boils again.

Steam Kettle Installation

Proper kettle installation is important. Kitchen designers frequently put kettles in small, shallow stainless steel pans or depressions in the floor. In most cases, the pans are only two inches deep. When kettles are installed in recessed pans, pots must balance precariously on the edge of the draining pans. When the kettle is emptied, most of the water misses the pans altogether because they are too small. The remaining water hitting the pans splashes out because the pans are too shallow. As a result, the floor around the kettles is covered with water every time a kettle is washed, an unsanitary and dangerous condition.

Kettles should be installed above a deep, wide trough covered by level floor grating of sturdy metal. The floor should be pitched toward the trough. This arrangement not only makes cleaning the kettles faster and safer, but also makes the transfer of hot liquids from the kettle into pots safer, because the pots can be placed level under the kettle.

Hot and cold water should be available from a swing arm over the kettle for easy filling of kettles. More sophisticated installations have water meters that fill the kettle with the desired amount of water automatically. Heat-and-chill kettles are also available, in which circulating water chills the kettle as desired. Very large operations have electric stirring devices installed in their kettles; others have wire basket inserts to remove food rapidly, and in some installations the baskets can be lowered and lifted by an overhead hoist. These last installations are more for canning factories and institutions providing food in very large quantities. There are not many hotels or banquet operations large enough to warrant an investment in such devices. Strong stainless steel paddles, long-handled whisks, and hand-held wire baskets are usually sufficient. Perhaps a shovel can be kept close to the kettles to remove bones after the stock has been drained off. Better installations have wall-mounted steam kettles to facilitate cleaning. Other models are floor-mounted with only two or three legs.

In a smaller operation with no need for a floor steam kettle, a small electric kettle mounted on a table can be very helpful. A low candy stove is also helpful since a stockpot can be left to simmer on it in an out-of-the-way location, eliminating the need to lift the pot on and off the range.

TILTING FRYING PANS

One of the most versatile pieces of equipment now available in this country is the tilting frying pan. In Europe, tilting frying pans have been in use for generations. Tilting fying pans are square or rectangular stainless steel pans with a pouring spout. They are available in several sizes with a standard depth of about seven inches. The heat source can be gas or electric. I have found electric frying pans more reliable than gas-heated pans. The electric unit that lights the pilot on a gas-heated pan can get wet and be shortcircuited; through careless cleaning, the pilot light can also be extinguished and is time-consuming to light again. For these reasons, an electric frying pan may well prove more convenient in the professional kitchen. When buying tilting frying pans, note that the more expensive models have a thick bottom that permits heat distribution and prevents hot spots and cold corners. A floor trough with grate and a water faucet makes cleaning an easy task.

What can be prepared in these pans? Practically everything. The tilting frying pan can be used as a frying pan to saute chicken or stew meat, a pot to braise rice, a saucepan to make sauces, a poacher to poach large fish; cooks are always inventing new uses for these pans.

STEAM FOR FOOD HOLDING—THE BAIN MARIE

The bain marie is a copper or stainless steel pan or basin, large enough to hold pots of food, that can keep food either hot or cold. The most practical way to heat a bain marie is with steam. Most establishments have steam coils on the bottom of the pan; the coils are covered by a sturdy grate to prevent the coils from getting crushed when heavy pots are placed on top of them. These grates must be easily removable to make cleaning between the coils possible. Some years ago I decided to pipe live steam directly into a bain marie. This, of course, heated the water very rapidly. This system turned out to be much better than steam coils which clog occasionally, but it is a little noisy.

A bain marie must have a good drain, operated by a valve, not a plunger, and the pan must be pitched properly so that the water drains off rapidly. The steam valves must be easily accessible. Here again proper supervision during construction is important. Plumbers have been known to put steam valves for kettles and the bain marie at the back of the equipment. When such kettles boil over or the bain marie splashes over, it is virtually impossible to turn off the steam without risking a severe burn. It costs a lot of money to rectify such a situation.

Bain maries to be used in banquet service differ from steam tables. In a-la-carte kitchens, steam tables are about waist high. Banquet bain maries should be about 20 in. high and about 12 in. deep: this makes lifting heavy pots into the bain marie as convenient as possible. Bain maries should also be equipped with a hot and cold water valve and have an overflow built through the wall. A cold water valve turns the bain marie into a chill tank, very useful when soup or stock must be chilled and kept overnight.

HOLDING CABINETS AND FOOD CARTS

Holding cabinets heated with steam can be used to heat and keep china hot, as well as to hold hot prepared food. The temperatures of these cabinets cannot be controlled with thermostats. Controlling the heat by adjusting the steam valves is also difficult. However, steamheated cabinets are rugged, and their interiors can be steam cleaned, two factors in their favor. In cabinets used primarily for holding food, moist heat prevents the drying out of certain dishes. Moist heat can be provided easily by running a separate steam line with tiny holes drilled in it through the cabinet. The line must have its own shut-off valve to cut off the live steam when not necessary. Moist heat is desirable, for example, when keeping turkey hot, but it would ruin sliced roast beef or patty shells.

Cabinets heated by electricity are also widely used. They have the advantage of being thermostatically controlled. This somewhat reduces the operating cost since the cabinets are turned on only when needed. On the other hand, steam cabinets are often left on for the whole banquet season, regardless of their design. Electric units can burn out and often have a musty smell after prolonged use.

Holding cabinets on wheels can be heated by either electricity or canned solid fuel. In many banquet operations, plates with food on them are placed in movable heaters and rolled to the function rooms just before time for service. If the carts are heated electrically, suffi-

Menu, dinner in honor of Chef
Joseph Castaybert, June 1967.
This menu features the special
contributions of distinguished
chefs.

Menu

Dédie au Musée Auguste Escoffier, Villeneuve-Loubet, France

* * *

LES BAGATELLES APERITIVES
pour les Toques-Blanches

*

UNE PETITE MARMITE
d'après l'Illustre Antonin Carême

*

Puligny-Montrachet
Jos. Drouhin
1962

LE TURBOT FARCI ET BRAISE
à la Façon du Grand Vatel

*

Château Trotanoy
Premier Grand Cru, Pomerol
1961

LA SELLE DE VEAU
comme l'Aimait le Maître Auguste Escoffier

*

LES ASPERGES EN BRANCHE
traitées selon un Principe du Maître Cuisinier Prospere Montagne

*

Beaune
Clos des Fèves
1959

LES FROMAGES CHOISIS AVEC RAISON
sur un Plateau à l'Unisson

*

Bollinger, Brut
Special Cuvée

UNE GOURMANDISE GLACEE DU RAINBOW
un Chef d'Oeuvre du Chef Pâtissier

*

Delamain
Grand Fine
Champagne

LE CAFE SPECIAL
du Gros Bonnet

Directeur Général	Chef Directeur	Chef de Cuisine
Brian Daly	Max Putier	Max Thomas

cient outlets in strategic locations must be planned so it is easy to position the carts in convenient locations. Canned solid fuel, of course, eliminates this need. Canned solid fuel used in food holding carts is available under several trade names. It provides strong heat, but the burning fuel leaves a slight odor. Canned fuel should be kept on hand as it is very useful in giving a heater just a little extra boost before the food is served. Canned fuel is also used extensively in the dining room to heat chafing dishes.

Food carts should have large, sturdy wheels. Small wheels get clogged and cause the cart to ride very unevenly over tiled kitchen floors. One pair of wheels should swivel, the other pair should be stationary. When both pairs swivel, the wheels tends to go in all directions when pushed, making the cart difficult to maneuver. Ideally, food carts should be pulled rather than pushed, but this is not always possible.

Many different types of food carts are on the market, and a visit to a hotel and restaurant show is the best way to find the proper models for the intended use. Carts must be able to withstand abuse and should be sturdy. Strong crossbraces, angle irons rather than tubular steel, normally indicate well-built carts. Cabinets on wheels, also classified as carts, come in handy for transporting and storing standard size sheet pans of food. Low flatbed trucks are useful for transporting food from the storeroom and for taking heavy pots of soup and stew to a banquet kitchen. Carts of table height can easily be repositioned wherever they are needed and are handy all day long.

BROILERS

Two basic types of broilers are on the market: broilers with a finishing oven on top and broilers without a finishing oven but with a second broiler unit instead. All other differences between broilers pertain to the source of heat, the heat output, the distribution of heat, and so on. Here we need only consider the advantages and disadvantages of the two basic types.

A broiler with a finishing oven on top can be used like a combination oven-broiler. Meat, fish, or poultry can be browned under the broiler and then cooked through in the oven on top. This is very practical, especially when preparing banquet food. However, when preparing a lot of steaks, a broiler without a finishing oven is faster because twice as many steaks can be browned at the same time. Which of the two models to choose is a difficult question. If the amount of equipment is limited, it is probably better to have broilers with finishing ovens unless the operation specializes in steaks at banquets.

When buying broilers for the banquet kitchen it is very important to get the proper size. I once bought some high quality broilers for a banquet kitchen and discovered too late that a standard size sheet pan, measuring 18 by 24 in., barely fitted under the broiler. The heating elements were recessed 4 in. from the front and 4 in. from the back of the broiling unit. As a result, any food placed close to the edge of the pan did not get heat. Broilers are available that take sheet pans easily with all the product on the pan exposed to even heat.

Gas broilers are made either with or without an electric fan. The electric fan creates a stront air current that spreads the flames evenly over the heating elements. Often the elements are constructed to create infrared rays. The models without a fan may have gas jets spread over ceramic plates that, in some cases, also create infrared rays. Electric broilers also work well, providing the heat element is large enough to cover the whole surface of the boiler. However, most commercial broilers are gas fired. I have worked with both types of broilers, and have found both excellent, as long as the sheet pans fitted well. For banquet use, try to buy equipment that is as rugged and simple as possible. For this reason I often choose broilers without electric fans, since fans constitute one more item that might break, burn out, or be tampered with. Also, in many places banquet kitchens are used intermittently, and extra personnel are often employed. Extra cooks, unfamiliar with the equipment, can turn the broilers off after use, but forget to turn off the fan motor. There is a safety light that should indicate the motor is on, but that light can burn out. On one occasion I know, an extra night cleaner turned a water hose on the broiler where the fan motor was still running. It was a miracle he was not killed; the short circuit he created was truly spectacular.

Whatever type of heat is used there is always danger of fire when working with broilers. It is imperative to keep broilers properly cleaned, a difficult task, and even a clean broiler can be the source of a fire when fat gets spilled or a pan of food starts to burn. You might consider a precaution introduced in my kitchen. Our kitchen mechanic installed simple metal baffles over the ducts in the back of the broilers. These do not interfere with air ventilation, but prevent flames from jumping from a broiler into the filters.

Some banquet operations specializing in steaks employ char-broilers very successfully. These gas-fired broilers are made of strong iron grills over beds of treated stones, heated red hot by gas. These broilers come in different sizes and can be installed side by side. In most such broilers, the steaks are seared on both sides, placed on sheet pans, then heated in an oven at the moment of service.

OVENS

In banquet cooking, ovens are probably the most important equipment. There can never be too many ovens in a kitchen producing banquet food. Some foodservice designers design kitchens for looks rather than practicality, and will install cook stoves without ovens underneath. These flat top or open burner stoves on four thin legs look attractive, and cleaning underneath is easy. However, in my opinion they waste space and represent relatively little savings, as a stove with an oven would not cost much more.

In banquet food preparation, many items require the use of an oven although the menu might not indicate it. For roasting foods in a banquet kitchen the least desirable ovens are the so-called deck ovens. These are ovens on four legs, one placed above the other, the deck top about chest high. This is a very convenient height for light items such as buns or potatoes, but it is dangerous for heavier food such as ribs of beef or even chicken. For roasting heavy pieces of meat in smaller quantities, the range-type ovens are most practical. The oven is close to the ground, making it easy to turn the roast as necessary. When the roast is finished, it can be lifted up to a cart or table with relative safety.

For many years, large banquet operations have used rotating ovens. These ovens come in several sizes and models. A hot air flow like that of a convection oven bakes and roasts very evenly. Rotating trays operate in ferris-wheel style, bringing food to the level of the oven door at the flip of a finger. Rolling steel tables made exactly the height of the oven door makes loading and unloading the oven even easier. However, when using rotating ovens, remember to use pans of proper size. Pans too large for an oven will jam during the first turn.

True convection ovens have a fan with a motor installed that forces hot air around the food. The motor will burn out eventually, but, overall, convection ovens are well suited to banquet kitchens.

Some new ovens on the market are very suitable for large banquet production. Some allow the food to be roasted after being placed on carts. Some have timers that can be set so that carts are turned around after a period of time to expose the food to even heat. Some also have a reverse air flow switch that blows cool air into the oven to chill the food after the programmed cooking process is over. These ovens are excellent when operated by conscientious, well-trained employees.

Microwave ovens are seldom used in banquet kitchens. I have visited food processing companies where a hundred meals are assembled on conveyor belts every minute, and I am chagrinned how far behind this performance certain segments of the banquet industry are today. In some hotel kitchens producing a banquet of a few hundred covers is an effort accompanied by anxiety, screaming, confusion, and frustration. Having the proper equipment, frame of mind, and know-how is essential when serving banquets. Only concern for productivity and proper investment will make this possible.

OTHER KITCHEN EQUIPMENT

When there are enough steam kettles, tilting frying pans, ovens, and broilers, **stoves** are of less importance in banquet food preparation. However, when none of the above equipment is available, banquet food must be prepared on conventional stoves. This is most often true for smaller restaurants where only occasional small parties are booked. Such establishments do not need equipment for heavy food production. In these operations, however, a good **heater** is indispensable. I have seen small places that had to stop all service to restaurant guests while a banquet was being served. The restaurant guests did not like the delay, and neither banquet nor restaurant guests were completely happy. A heater enables the staff to prepare at least the vegetables ahead of time.

Deep fat fryers are essential when the banquet menu calls for fried items. When there is no space for fryers in the banquet kitchen, menus without fried food must be planned. Because it gets soggy when held, fried food is tricky to handle for banquet service. Sufficient fryer capacity is a must if fried foods are to be featured.

Table space is at a premium in the banquet kitchen. Regardless of whether the service is from plates or from silver platters, there must be enough table space to slice the meat and hold dishes in which garnishes or accompaniments are placed. Tables should be stainless steel. The space underneath can be used as heater space. **Electric heat lamps** over the service table are also desirable. Many places install hanging lamps, which heat only a small circle on the table. I was not satisfied with this and persuaded our electricians to install electric space heaters, which look like fluorescent lamps but have a heat rod in place of the tubes. These heat the whole table during the service period.

In most operations, roast rib of beef and similar items are sliced by a gravity-fed **slicing machine**. Electric outlets must be provided where the meat is to be sliced so the machine can be plugged in. The slicing machines should be portable and should be locked up when not in use to prevent vandalism and theft.

Vertical cutter/mixers are available in a range of sizes. They are useful for making mousse, stuffings, farces, spreads, as well as fillings for the garde manger and the pastryshop. Stale rolls can be made into breadcrumbs in a vertical cutter/mixer with little effort. Even the saucecook can use the machines once in a while. **Meat grinders** and **buffalo choppers** can also be useful.

No banquet kitchen is complete without a **menu board.** All banquet menus must be displayed in a neat and orderly fashion. This display is crucial if all banquet food is to be ready on time and in the right quantity.

It is especially important to have the right number of **coffee urns** of the proper capacity. A gallon of coffee provides 20 cups. It should not be difficult to calculate the coffee-urn capacity required from the number of available seats. If large banquets occur only rarely, it would be foolish to install a coffee urn of maximum capacity. Instead, for the occasional large banquets, invest in thermos containers: coffee to fill them can be made in the smaller machines and stored in the thermos containers until time for service. This will not provide the freshest coffee, but it will be acceptable if done with care.

Dishwashing machines are an important aspect of banquet service. The size of the parties to be served will dictate capacity of equipment needed. For banquet kitchens designed for sizable production a three-tank conveyor machine is probably the best for china and silver; for glasses a three-tank rack machine is most practical. When installing the dish machine, a sufficiently large **scrapping table** with openings for garbage cans must be provided. If possible, a person should be able to work in a space in the middle of the table, sorting and feeding dishes to the people who are feeding dishes to the machine. When all the dishes come rolling in at the same time at the end of the banquet, the dish table must be ready to receive them.

There are many more facilities for the banquet kitchen than those I have described: a room for polishing silver; a place to store china and glasses; a linen room; a uniform room; a storeroom for paper goods, candles, and other miscellaneous items; storage space for tables, chairs, carpets, portable dance floors, platforms, and spotlights; a service bar to serve liquor; a liquor storage room. Food must be received and stored properly. Garbage must be disposed of. To perform all of these functions, much planning is needed. The choices made should be determined by the type of banquet food to be prepared and the quantity to be sold. If a machine shreds 1000 pounds of vegetables in an hour, while the ballroom seats only 500 persons, the machine is obviously too large. If pureed soups and creamed spinach are never sold for banquets, it is not necessary to have a straining device for the mixing machine. But if these items are sold often, this device is indispensable. Sound professional advice in planning can avoid costly mistakes and achieve maximum productivity.

1971

Basic Rules of Menu Construction

There are definite rules to follow in menu-making. Well-made menus should contain a harmony of flavors. Dishes should balance each other. The dishes on menus change over the years because our taste changes, but the basic rules concerning menu-making remain the same.

RAW INGREDIENTS

First look for contrast in raw ingredients. A menu featuring creamed chicken a la king should not start with a cream soup and finish with a rich ice cream. Obviously, that would be too much cream. A menu planned around roast beef should not start with beef consomme. A menu which includes applesauce with the main course should not conclude with apple strudel. A menu that starts with onion soup served with grated cheese should not list cheesecake for dessert. Mushroom soup should not be followed by mushroom sauce. The menu maker must avoid repetition of ingredients on the menu.

Figure 7.1.

Contrast in texture, color, and flavor create harmony in the meal.

Cold Appetizer	Melon Balls in Port Wine
	*******
Hot Soup	Old-Fashioned Vegetable Soup
	*******
Main Course	Roast Shoulder of Veal
	Mushroom Sherry Sauce
Vegetables	Creamed Spinach sprinkled with Croutons
	Saffron Pilaff Rice
	*******
Salad	Lettuce, Avocado, and Arrugola Salad
	*******
Dessert	Coconut Sherbet with
	Fresh Raspberries in Cointreau
	*******
Coffee	Coffee
Petits Fours	Petits Fours

Menu cover, 44th annual dinner of the American Association of the Master Knights of the Sovereign Military Order of Malta, January 1971.

Figure 7.2.   Formal menu featuring excellent visual contrast.

Hot or Cold Soup	Beef Consommé with Fine Noodles and Chives
	*******
Hot Appetizer	Poached Salmon in Sorrell Sauce Golden Fleurons
	*******
Main Course	Roast Rack of Lamb Persillé
Vegetables	Baby Lima Beans with Tomatoes
	*******
Salad	Endive, Watercress, and Romaine Salad Mustard Dressing
	*******
Dessert	Pistachio Coffee Ice Cream Bombe Flaming Cherries
	*******
Coffee	Coffee

COLORS

There should also be a pleasant contrast of color from dish to dish as well as on each of the plates. This can be done, but it requires planning. Avoid bad sequences such as these: tomato soup, lobster, Golden Rich cheese, raspberry sherbet; brown oxtail soup, brown stew, dark cake; chestnut soup, sauerbraten, apple crumb cake. Such sequences offer almost no visual contrast. Harmonize the colors on the plate. Visualize how the food items will look together when served. Platings with poor color combinations or little color contrast do not appeal to the eye. A white fish mousse and a white wine sauce; sauerbraten with red cabbage and carrots; creamed chicken with white rice; strawberry ice cream bombe with hot cherry sauce; all of these would be poor menu choices because of the colors they combine. I have even seen canapé selections that consisted of smoked salmon, cherry tomatoes filled with ham mousse, and salami. It is easy to imagine how dull the platter looked!

TEXTURES

There should also be a contrast in texture. Bland and soft foods should alternate with crisp foods; food items that are round should be followed by foods shaped in long sticks. Texture contrast can be subtle,

Figure 7.3. Texture and flavor contrast lighten a rich meal.

Hot Soup	Game Consommé flavored with Dry Sack
	*******
Hot Appetizer	Mousse of Sole, Sauce Cardinal Golden Fleurons
	*******
Sorbet	Sorbet of Apple Jack
	*******
Main Course	Roast Filet of Beef Sauce Bordelaise
Vegetables	Tomato filled with Purée of Peas Endive Meunière
	*******
Cheese and Salad	Pont l'Eveque and Port de Salut Romaine Lettuce with Watercress French Bread
	*******
Dessert	Mocha Mousse decorated with Violets Lady Fingers Crème Chantilly
	*******
Coffee	Coffee

yet it adds tremendously to menu harmony. A good example of contrast within a single dish is Zuger Kirsch-torte, a cake consisting of a soft, liquor-drenched center layer between crisp top and bottom layers. Other possibilities are crunchy water chestnuts blended into string beans, creamed spinach served with a crisp corn fritter, toasted brioche accompanied by pate de foie gras, or crunchy lettuce with creamy cheese. Praline or croquant sprinkled over ice cream is a traditional use of contrast. So is crisp puff paste with a creamy filling and crisp bacon bits on spinch salad. The examples go on and on.

Contrast cooking methods as well. To serve a broiled fish before a broiled steak is not very imaginative. Nor is it good menu practice to serve a clear soup before a boiled dinner; a potato croquette, fried main course, and apple fritters as dessert; a smoked fish appetizer followed

Menu, Knights of Malta dinner.
The menu describes an elegant
meal, using a combination of
French and English terms.

Menu

Dry Sack	CONSOMMÉ DE TORTUE PARISIENNE
	✛
	LOBSTER NEWBURG
	✛
Chateau *Pontet Canet* *1964*	TOURNEDOS OF BEEF ROSSINI CROWN OF SPINACH GLAZED BELGIAN CARROTS PERSILLÉES
	✛
	SORBET AU DUBONNET
	✛
Pommard Clos *de la Commaraine* *1964*	CROWN OF HAM MOUSSE AU MADERE ESCAROL AND CHICKORY SALAD
	✛
Veuve Cliquot *Ponsardin* *1964*	SOUFFLÉ GLACÉ AU CHOCOLAT STUFFED MARZIPAN DATES
	✛
Liqueurs	LE CAFÉ NOIR

Dinner Committee
JAMES T. TYNION, *Chairman*
PAUL B. MURRAY   HARRY C. HAGERTY

by a smoked ham dinner; or a patty shell filled with creamed mushrooms and creamed peas to accompany it.

When reading about these rules, it is easy to think that such unsound combinations would not happen. I have seen them all, though, and have even committed some of them myself. Thoughtful planning is the key to menu design.

MISTAKES TO AVOID

The following menu was created by an overly ambitious banquet salesperson. The customers were a group of men who got together once a year in a major hotel. The event was a jovial, informal one, the dinner framed by drinking. This is the menu that was suggested:

DINNER MENU

Vol au Vent of Mushrooms

***

Grilled Filet Mignon
Sauce Bearnaise
Three Purees
White Turnip, Carrot, Green pea

***

Salad of Bibb Lettuce
Watercress & Endive
Oil and Lemon Dressing
with Dijon Mustard

***

Charlotte Russe au Chocolate
Fresh Lady Fingers on the outside
Top decorated with fresh whipped cream

***

Petits Fours

***

Coffee

Menu, dinner from the
Distinguished Chef Series of the
Statler Inn's School of Hotel
Administration, October 1975. A
banquet presentation of classical
German cuisine.

Menu

Flor Fino Sherry   *Apertif*
Almaden   *Aperitif*

Toulouser Pastete
The Queens patty shell filled with a delicate ragout

Wildkraftbruehe "St Hubertus"
Game Consomme with Quenelles

Niersteiner Oelberg   *Forelle Blau mit Sahnemeerrettich*
Riesling Kabinett   *Fresh Poached Brook Trout with whipped horseradish*
1972

Champagner Sorbet
Champagne Sherbet

Kalbsruecken "Orloff"
Kartoffelcroquetten
und
Rosenkohl
Saddle of Veal
Croquette Potatoes
Brussels Sprouts

Salad Komposition
Mixed Salad

Croquant Halbgefrorenes
Demi Frozen

Kaffee
Coffee

As you can see, the menu was loaded with cream, starting with the creamed mushrooms, followed by three pureed vegetables, the dollop of Bearnaise Sauce that accompanied the meat, and a creamy dessert served with whipped cream. This menu lacks texture contrast appropriate to any banquet. Moreover, it is certainly not a menu to recommend to a group getting together to drink.

Here is another menu, once served to a group of church women in April:

LUNCHEON MENU

Mushroom and Barley Soup

***

Half Broiled Chicken, Giblet Gravy
Continental Brown Rice
Candied Yams
New Garden Peas

***

Hot Apple Charlotte, Vanilla Rum Sauce

***

Coffee, Tea, Milk

The first noticeable thing is that the menu is rather heavy, especially for this group at this time of year. There is no feeling of spring in this menu. A heavy, starchy, thick soup is followed by two starches. The dessert is served hot and is relatively heavy. It can also be argued that a barley soup should not be followed by rice because of the repetition created by two whole grains on the same menu.

In the first chapter I stressed the need to communicate with the client in order to learn the party's requirements. The salesperson must work with the clients to determine what kind of food will serve their needs best. When that is done, more appropriate menus are sure to result.

Variety is the key to a good menu, but harmony must tie it all together. It takes good taste to make a good menu; the designer must think of flavors, textures, colors, and cooking methods, and, at the

Figure 7.4. Rich meal for a winter banquet.

___

Hot Soup	Cream of Wild Mushroom Soup
	*******
Main Course	Roast Rib of Beef au Jus
Vegetables	Potato Croquette
	Braised Celery
	*******
Salad	Spinach Salad sprinkled with Beets
	House Dressing
	*******
Dessert	Warm Apple Tart
	Sauce Sabayon
	*******
Coffee	Café

same time, keep in mind the group to which the menu will be served. The right balance between dishes must be found. When it is, the result will be an excellent menu: filling yet light, satisfying, interesting, and delicious.

FOLLOW MENU TRENDS

New trends in menu-making must be considered. Clients like to appear up-to-date and often want their catered parties to reflect the new trends in entertaining. For example, in years past most menus started with oysters, and many menus served sweetbreads as an entree. Today, these dishes have lost their popularity for large banquets, but other foods such as pureed and raw vegetables are "in." Imagination and boldness are needed in banquet menu-making. Menus are not meant to be copied like a dress, but rather to be used as a model or pattern. Each new menu should be custom-made for the occasion.

Desserts

When making menus, pay special attention to desserts. As the last course served, it will be the longest remembered. As the old German saying goes: "If the end is well, all is well." Desserts should be spectacular yet, light and refreshing, especially if the courses preceding them are many and filling.

Seasons

The season during which the menu will be served should also be taken into consideration. This can be hard when the menu is planned months ahead of time, yet it is very important. The season will affect not only availability of food but also the guests' response. Chestnuts and oranges contribute to the Christmas spirit; green asparagus, herbs, rhubarb, along with pastel colors and blossoms indicate spring. Berries, fruits, chilled soups, and iced or light food convey a summer feeling; game, gamebirds, turkey, squash, root vegetables, and grapes reflect fall. In our suggested menu selections I sometimes mention the time of year when a particular menu can be served.

Lunch and Dinner

There should also be a difference between luncheon dishes and dinner dishes. Actually, the difference is often contradictory and is frequently based on tradition. Luncheon menus can be simpler. For instance, they can list stews, swiss steak, chopped steaks, sliced turkey on broccoli, and similar items. Fish served for lunch is often of a less expensive variety than that served for dinner: Boston scrod, mackerel, flounder, or finnan haddie are all acceptable for lunch menus. Luncheon dishes should also be light because most people must go back to work after lunch. This is especially important when arranging business luncheons: nobody wants to hold a meeting with overfed, drowsy attendees.

Dinners can be more festive and, in some instances, can have many courses. Again, all details should be considered. If the dinner is to be very late, it should offer lighter food than an earlier dinner. If a long program is planned, dinner food should also be light. A dinner dance, on the other hand, can feature more substantial dishes—in good taste, of course—because people get up and dance and get hungry again. Foods that are very heavy, filling, and difficult to digest should be avoided, and very fatty foods are not appreciated.

There is a strong trend toward lighter food selections today. The intake of starch especially is monitored carefully by many guests. For that reason starch in the form of potatoes, rice, noodles, or dumplings should appear on a menu—lunch or dinner—no more often than once, and in many cases not at all. I also believe that an item baked in a crust like a beef Wellington or a turnover of meat should not be served with an additional starch accompaniment or garnish.

Menu, dinner from the
Distinguished Chef Series of the
Statler Inn's School of Hotel
Administration, November
1975. A superb selection of
classical Northern Italian
cuisine.

Menu

Soave Classico Superiore	*Antipasti Grissini*
	Assorted Hors D' Oeuvres
	Italian Bread Sticks
	Mille Fanti
	A Florentine Soup
	Crostaced Peoceta Veneto
	Shellfish with Brandy Sauce Venetian
	Risi-Bisi
	Rice and Pea Dish Venetian
Valpolicella Classico	*Insalata Giardinetto*
Superiore	*Fresh Garden Salad with Sweet Basil Dressing*
	Manzo Stufato al Barolo
	Braised Beef in Barolo Wine Sauce
	Zucchini Genovese
	Gorgonzola-Bel Paese
	Tasty Italian Cheeses
	Pane Italiano Caldo
	Hot Italian Bread
	Gelato con Zabaglione Amaretti
	Italian Ice Cream and Marsala Egg
	Custard Macaroons
Cafe Sambuca Liqueur	*Caffé Té*

Figure 7.5.   Three simpler menus that offer contrast.

Menu One
    Cold Appetizer   Iced Tomato Juice

****

    Cold Main Course   Avocado stuffed with Tunafish

****

    Hot Dessert   Hot Apple Strudel
                               Whipped Cream

Menu Two
    Hot Soup   Seafood Bouillon with
                               Saffron and Fennel

****

    Cold Main Course   Smoked Chicken
                               Wax Bean Salad
                               Watercress
                               Pommery Mustard

****

    Cold Dessert   Floating Island with
                               a scent of Cointreau

Menu Three
    Hot Appetizer   Baked Meat Canneloni Bolognaise

****

    Cold Main Course   Chicken Salad with Pineapple Chunks
                               Curry Dressing

****

    Dessert   Lime Sherbet
                               Walnut Sauce

MENU-MAKING TECHNIQUES

There is a technique which can make menu-making easier. Take a piece of paper, divide it horizontally in as many sections as there are courses. Now take a pencil, and start planning the menu with the main course. It is foolish to spend time discussing a proper soup or a suitable

Two dinner menus from the Greenbriar, November 1973 and September 1977. Information about events of the evening here are blended into the menu as a whole.

La Réception

Le Caviar Beluga Malossol
et les Gourmandises Épicure

Les Apéritifs

"Le Festin"

L'Essence de Tomates Fraiches Nicoise
et les Paillettes Dorées au Gruyere

Le Roi des Crustaces "Monseigneur"
Le Riz Pilaff

Dezaley l'Arbalete, 1970, Suisse
Mise en Bouteilles par J. Testuz

Le Supreme de Faisan "St. Hubert"
avec les Fonds d'Artichauts Farcis a la Puree de Marrons
Medoc Cruse 1969, Bordeaux
"La Dame Rouge"

Intermede de Musique

Pour se Rafraichir
Le Granite d'Orange "Caesar Ritz"

Le Zephir du Jambon de Virginie "Southern Belle"
a la Gelee au Porto Accompagne d'une Salade de Celeri Normande
Chateauneuf du Pape 1970
Vallee du Rhone, Barton et Guestier

La Tourte Glacee "Sarah Bernhardt"
Enrobee de Sucre Voile et la Sauce Melba
Mumm's Cordon Rouge Brut 1966, Magnum

Le Cafe des Maitres

La Parade des Pompadours Parisienne
avec ses Douceurs

———

On Terminera la Soiree a "Kate's Mountain Lodge"
Parmi les Culinariens du Spa

Le Greenbrier
Dans la Salle de Cristal   *Le Vendredi, 16 Novembre, 1973*

Diner

Donne En L'Honneur de
Monsieur Hermann G. Rusch
a l'Occasion de son
Septantieme Anniversaire
Par la Direction du Greenbrier

La Reception

Les Gourmandises a l'Aristocrate Accompagnees des Aperitifs

. . . Le Festin . . .

La Tortue Claire Christophe
Les Paillettes Dorees au Gruyere
Williams and Humbert Dry Sack Sherry

En Suite
Le Roi des Crustaces et les Crabes du Maryland
a l'Americaine
Le Riz Pilaff
Dezaley l'Arbalete, Premier Cru 1975: Suisse

Le Medaillon de la Plume de Veau "La Violette"
Artichaut Gregoire et les Pommes "Cheri"
Chateau Kirwan, Bordeaux Grand Cru 1973

"Intermede Musical" par les Populaires

Pour se Rafraichir
Le Citron Givre "Vatel"

Comme Entree Froide
Les Aiguillettes de Canetons "Southern Belle"
a la Gelee au Porto Garnies des Delices de Floride et la Sauce Cumberland
Gevrey Chambertin, Bourgogne, 1970

Puis
Le Fromage de Stilton et de Brie avec les Galettes a l'Anis

Pour Terminer
La Tourte Glacee "Escoffier" Enrobee de Sucre Voile
et le Jus de Framboises
Champagne, Blanc de Blanc Almaden 1973

La Parade des Creations du Patissier avec Leures Douceurs
Le Cafe des Maitres
Les Liqueurs

"Le Gateau d'Anniversaire"
Musique par L'Ensemble Knud Moller

Dans la Salle de Cristal
Le Greenbrier   Le Lundi, 26 Septembre, 1977

Figure 7.6.   Well-coordinated banquet menu.

Cold Appetizer	Red Pimientos, Anchovies, Olives and Fennel Sticks
	*******
Hot Soup	Cream of Watercress Soup with Toasted Croutons
	*******
Hot Appetizer	Striped Bass saute with Almonds and Grapes
	Red Bliss Potatoes
	*******
Main Course	Broiled Filet Mignon
	Sauce Bordelaise
Vegetables	Chestnuts and Brussels Sprouts
	*******
Salad and Cheese	Brie Cheese with Winter Greens
	Crisp French Bread
	*******
Dessert	Pears poached in Red Wine
	Macaroons
	*******
Coffee	Columbian Coffee

dessert only to choose afterwards an incompatible main course. The main course is the pivot around which the whole menu turns.

When the main course is established with the client (and the reason for using a pencil is the main course selection will probably be changed many times), start thinking about suitable garnishes or accompaniments for the main course. Point out to your client, though, that these do not have to be finally decided. These items can easily be added later. Discuss the rest of the courses one at a time—fish course, dessert, salad, soup, fruit, or whatever they may be. When each course is in place and safely anchored to the main course, the rest of the dinner will "fall in place." Minor adjustments can come later, perhaps a different vegetable than first thought of or a different sauce with the dessert.

Now the bread, the butter service, and, of course, the proper wines should be discussed. (Wine service will be discussed in chapter 8.) Normally, the food is sold first, then the wine. An exception might be made for members of a gourmet society, planning to taste a particular wine on the evening of the dinner. Such clients would, consequently, want a menu that would complement the wine. However, such situations are rare.

In the menu sequences that appear throughout this chapter, you will note that the salad is sometimes listed before the main course, except where the salad is to be served on a fish plate as a separate course. This listing formality is followed even if the salad is to be served before the main course itself. There is also some confusion regarding the service of the cheese course. Cheese is normally served with red wine; for formal dinners this would be a very fine, heavy burgundy wine. Such wine cannot be truly savored after ice cream or other sweet. Therefore at a formal meal, the cheese is always served before the dessert, and this should be reflected in the menu.

The Champagne Gala

The Wine
and Food
Society, inc.
NEW YORK

Beverage Sale and Service

This chapter covers the subject of selling beverages, tells how to list them properly on the menu, and how to serve them at a banquet or function.

In a well-run hotel, departmental beverage profit can be as high as 60 percent of sales. In other words, of every dollar taken in for beverage sales, about 60 cents is departmental profit. Of every dollar taken in for food sales, only about 10 to 15 cents remains as profit. This fact underlines the tremendous importance of selling beverages for banquets.

Many banquet salespersons put all their selling skill into selling food. A high banquet food check is important because it brings in dollars to cover the overhead. A high banquet beverage check added to the food check brings in the additional profit we all need to stay in business. Given the importance of beverage sales to the profit picture, it stands to reason that every banquet salesperson should have a basic knowledge of beverage sale and service. It is not necessary to be a sophisticated connoisseur of wines, but it is essential to know the different groups of wine and spirits in order to advise the clients properly.

PRE-BANQUET BEVERAGES

Most gatherings of people start with a reception. Because it is most unlikely that all of the individuals attending a function will arrive at precisely the same time, a reception allows something to be served while the guests gather. This makes everybody feel comfortable, breaks the ice, and makes waiting easier. Also, the reception period is often the only time when guests can move around and talk to each other. Beverage service is an important part of this time.

Some party givers, often corporate clients, do not want an open bar during the reception. If it is a question of budget (i.e. lack of money) the banquet salesperson should at least try to sell champagne or white wine passed butler style by waiters or waitresses during the reception. This makes the occasion a little festive without adding too much to the expense. The wine should be sold to the client by the glass, and a budget should be established to provide so many dollars, or glasses, per person.

For the host who wants a bar available, but who does not want to pay for any drinks, the banquet salesperson should suggest an open bar equipped to sell drinks. When a bar is used, it is customary to charge the host a labor charge for the bartender(s) and for the cashier(s). Some clients will argue about the fairness of this charge, but it should be pointed out that the hotel must engage the necessary help without any guarantee of sales. This justifies charging the client for

Menu cover, champagne gala held by the Wine and Food Society, Inc., December 1970.

115

Menu interior, champagne gala.
A light supper compliments the
tasting of French champagnes.

Menu

Hot Salmon Mousse
Dill and Oyster Sauce
Fleurons

Cold Fricandeau of Veal Florentine en Gelée
Tonnato Sauce
Salade Suprême

Croquembouche

Café

Champagnes

Bollinger · Brut · 1964   Kobrand Corporation
Charles Heidsieck · Brut · 1964   Austin Nichols & Co. Inc.
Dom Ruinart · Brut · 1964   Schieffelin & Co.
Krug & Co · Brut · 1962   Dreyfus, Ashby & Co.
Lanson · Red Label · 1964   Peartree Imports Inc.
Laurent Perrier · Brut · 1964   Munson Shaw Co.
Mercier · Brut · 1962   Dennis & Huppert Co.
Moet & Chandon · Brut Imperial · 1964   Schieffelin & Co.
G. H. Mumm Cordon Rouge · Brut · 1964   Browne Vintners Co.
Piper-Heidsieck · Brut · 1964   Renfield Importers, Ltd.
Pol Roger & Co · Brut · 1964   Frederick Wildman & Sons, Ltd.
Taittinger · Brut Reserve · 1964   Kobrand Corporation
Veuve Clicquot Ponsardin · Brut · 1964   The Jos. Garneau Co.

the bartenders and cashiers. This charge is an industry practice, and the banquet salesperson should not omit it from the client's bill.

It is advisable to have the cashiers sell drink tickets that cover the cost of the drink including gratuities and tax. It is best to have only one kind of ticket for all drinks, unless, at the request of the host, some very expensive and rare wines and liquors are to be available. This is very unlikely, however.

The cashiers should be located away from the bar and should be clearly visible, even before the bars are visible if possible. The guests first buy tickets, then exchange them at the bar for drinks. A good traffic flow is important so that clients can avoid having to fight through crowds. Make it convenient for the guest to get a second drink! Remember the 60 percent departmental profit!

When the client is willing to pay for an open bar, only the labor charge for the bartender(s) will apply; no cashiers will be necessary. One bartender is needed for about 80 to 100 guests if good service is to be maintained. If the host is willing to pay for more, so much the better.

In this situation beverages can be sold by charging for individual drinks, by charging a flat rate for each hour, or by charging by the bottle of liquor used. Selling by the drink is the most profitable arrangement. In most cases, a beverage budget is established setting a certain dollar amount to be spent per guest. A price per drink is established, and the beverage manager issues the proper quantity of liquor to the bars. The beverage budget can be exceeded only with written authorization. If this figure is reached the labor charges can be automatically voided.

At dances without food sales, a room rental charge must be established, plus a beverage guarantee that should be paid in advance by the committee. This paid guarantee applies whether the drinks are sold by the bottle, a la carte, or by the hour. We must remember that a ballroom represents valuable real estate that must be paid for. To schedule a ballroom for a dance, without any guaranteed income, does not make economic sense.

BANQUET BEVERAGES

Beverage sales need not stop with the reception, of course. A banquet salesperson should try to sell wine with the dinner, and perhaps a bottle or two of whisky. Normally, two bottles of red or white wine for each course will be needed for a table of ten. When hard liquor is desired, it is advisable to sell one bottle of scotch and one bottle of bourbon or rye with the customary mixers for each table. Liquor preferences

Menu interior, wine tasting and
reception, Waldorf-Astoria
Distinguished Alumni,
November 1976. An unusual
menu design that emphasizes
the featured wines.

	WINES		MENU		
	WHITE	**RED**			
U.S.A.	CALLAWAY WHITE RIESLING, 1974 Estate Bottled *A white wine that was selected for Her Majesty, Queen Elizabeth II, which comes from the most southern wine region of California.*	FREEMARK ABBEY CABERNET SAUVIGNON, 1969 *Refined, elegant and aged example of a Napa Valley Cabernet Sauvignon, with a generous bouquet.*	SMOKED TURKEY ROAST FILET OF BEEF ON SOUR DOUGH		MONTEREY JACK
FRANCE	CORTON CHARLEMAGNE, 1971 Estate Bottled by Louis Jadot *Big wine with an astonishing combination of richness and dryness. The greatest of white Burgundies.*	CHATEAUNEUF-DU-PAPE, 1967 Domaine de Mont Redon Estate Bottled *Robust, spicy, full-bodied, ruby red wine with a remarkable deep fruity bouquet.*	PATE DE FOIE GRAS IN ASPIC SLICED SADDLE OF VENISON "GRAND VENEUR"		CAROLLE
ITALY	PINOT GRIGIO, SANTA MARGHERITA *A white wine from the northern Alps, with a dry, full aroma and fine bouquet.*	RUFFINO RISERVA DUCALE, CLASSICO, 1967 *Long-aged, premium Classico Chianti with a full bouquet, which had time to develop bottle complexity.*	VEAL "TONNATO" SHRIMPS SAUTEED WITH FENNEL		STRACCHINO
GERMANY	MAXIMIN GRUNHAUSER ABSTBERG, SPATLESE, 1971 *A full bodied, semi-dry Moselle. A great vintage year for German white wine.* SCHLOSS REINHARTSHAUSENER HATTENHEIMER WISSELBRUNN RIESLING, AUSLESE, 1966 *An attribute to German wines. A sweet, long-lasting fine Rhine wine.*		WESTPHALIAN HAM SLICED BRATWURST AND BAUERNWURST ON SAVOY CABBAGE		CARAWAY TILSIT
JAPAN	UMESHU *A good example of fruit wine with a flavor of plum and slight taste of almonds.* SAKE *A dry wine made from steamed rice. Professionals consider it a beer.*		TORI ROAST AGE (ROASTED CHICKEN) SEAFOOD AND VEGETABLE TEMPURA		

vary in different parts of the country. Clients should be allowed to exchange unopened liquor for a different liquor in the same price range or be allowed to pay for any difference in cost between what has been provided and what they want.

If the client does not want to pay for alcoholic beverages to be served during dinner, provisions should be made to allow the waiters and waitresses to sell liquor a la carte, unless the client specifically requests otherwise. To sell a la carte, time is needed and the banquet salesperson should try to provide for this in the program. Sometimes guests would like a drink but cannot because the program is so tight.

If there is any chance that beverages can be sold a la carte during a banquet, the salesperson must make provisions with the service staff and in the back of the house. The service staff should be supplied with an abreviated, compact wine and liquor list, and the service bar and cashier station in the back must be sufficiently staffed. These labor costs are not charged to the client and a certain amount of risk is therefore involved. When parties do not drink as much as expected, the labor cost is partly wasted.

It is hard to say which is more profitable for the establishment: to sell a banquet package with a moderate beverages allowance included in the dinner price, or to sell all beverages a la carte. When beverages are provided by the host, guests are generally reluctant to buy additional drinks. However, the inclusion of beverages in dinner package assures the operation of some beverage income, no matter how little may be consumed. The operation also avoids the expense of staffing a service bar and having checkers on hand.

People do not necessarily buy drinks every time they are given the opportunity. Many people do not order wine when at a banquet because they feel obligated to share the bottles with their table companions. Others do not like to drink hard liquor with their meal. Some may order only a modest bottle of beer. Yet I have seen banquets with fabulous a la carte beverage sales. It is up to the banquet salesperson to assess each situation, check available records of previous functions, and then decide how to sell.

LIQUOR CONTROL

It should be made clear to the client from the beginning that "brown-bagging" of liquor is not permitted. Especially at dances, where tickets are inexpensive, people are tempted to bring in a bottle of liquor, put it under the table, and then order only "set-ups" of glasses, ice, and soda. The banquet headwaiters and service personnel must keep a sharp eye out for such cheaters.

Menu interior, 116th dinner of the Lucullus Circle, May 1973. Note the information provided about each wine.

LA DÉGUSTATION

Pour se Faire la Bouche

CHÂTEAU LA HAUTE GRAVIÈRE 1967
Blanc de Graves
SANCERRE-CHAVIGNOL 1971
Estate Bottled by Delaporte
PINOT-CHARDONNAY 1971
Estate Bottled by Roland Thevenin
PINOT NOIR 1969
Estate Bottled by Roland Thevenin
CHÂTEAU FABRIS 1970
de Montaigne, St.-Emilion
GAMAY 1970
de la Vallée de la Loire
Domaine Pierre Cartier et Fils

Les Amuse-Bouche

LES AMUSE-BOUCHE
LES MOUSSES CLASSIQUES
DE LA GRANDE CUISINE
D'ANTONIN CARÊME

Pour la Maison

CHÂTEAU SAINT CHRISTOLY 1966
en Magnum

L'ESCRITEAU

SERCIAL SOLERA 1900

CHASSAGNE-MONTRACHET 1970
Estate Bottled by Roland Thevenin
POUILLY-FUISSÉ 1970
Domaine de la Chapelle
Estate Bottled by Charles Piat

CHÂTEAU LASCOMBES 1959
Deuxième Crû Classé de Margaux
Château Bottled en Magnum
CHÂTEAU LYNCH-BAGES 1959
Cinquième Crû Classé de Pauillac
Château Bottled

CHÂTEAU LAFITE 1958
Premier Crû Classé de Pauillac
Château Bottled en Magnum
CHÂTEAU COS-D'ESTOURNEL 1958
Deuxième Crû Classé de St.-Estèphe
Château Bottled

CORTON-BRESSANDES 1969
Estate Bottled by
Domaine Laleure-Piot
NUITS ST. GEORGES
CLOS DE CORVÉES-PAGET 1969
Estate Bottled by Charles Viénot

DOM RUINART 1966

HENNESSEY BRAS D'OR
MIRABELLE
from Massenez

1ère Assiette
LE CONSOMMÉ DE TORTUE
DES ÎLES DES CARAÏBES
EN GELÉE
2ème Assiette
LES QUENELLES DE BROCHET
AVEC UNE SAUCE AU CHAMPAGNE
LES BARQUETTES D'ÉPINARDS

3ème Assiette
LA SELLE D'AGNEAU DE LAIT
À LA LUCULLUS
LES FRUITS DU POTAGER

l'Intermède
LE GRANITÉ AU KIRSCH D'ALSACE

4ème Assiette
LES AIGUILLETTES DE CANETON
AU FOIE GRAS DU PERIGORD
LES FEUILLES DE LAITUE

La Dorure
LES FROMAGES DE FRANCE

l'Apothéose
LA CHARLOTTE ROYALE
AUX FRAMBOISES MELBA
LES MIGNARDISES

———

LE MOKA

Employees can also be cheaters. A service person can bring in a concealed bottle of liquor from a store, then, at the opportune moment, serve the liquor and present a check from a different table. Another method of cheating occasionally practiced by employees is to collect liquor left on the tables by guests, combine the left-overs in a bottle, and sell the resulting full bottle to an unsuspecting customer. Needless to say, this practice is unethical and unsanitary as well as illegal.

To minimize such practices some operations put brightly colored stickers on all liquor bottles. The color of the sticker changes from function to function. A banquet captain or headwaiter can look out for bottles without stickers and spot the cheaters.

The basic house rule should be that no liquor can be brought in by anybody, and exceptions to that rule should require managerial approval. Occasionally there are exceptions, such as gourmet dinners serving very unusual wines that have been donated, an affair where unusual liquors not easily available are to be served, or a charity ball where wine has been donated. However, such cases should remain exceptions: liquor profit is very important to the establishment.

When somebody is given permission to bring in wine or liquor, a high corkage charge should be imposed to compensate for the beverage revenue that the operation would otherwise receive. In union hotels, a gratuity of 15 percent of the estimated selling price of the wine is also added as a separate charge. This practice usually makes it financially unattractive for the host to bring in his or her own beverages.

Liquor must be tightly controlled at all times in the back of the house. Many books have been written about food and beverage control, and various control systems are possible. Nothing in the way of a beverage should be issued without a check or a beverage slip present to cover it. Banquets are festive occasions, attended by large groups of people in a happy, generous mood. It is easy for someone to say, "Bring more wine for my friends at table 65," or "Send a bottle of Dewar's to the head table." Such informality, though, results in unauthorized additional purchases and unpleasant disputes when the bill is presented. To avoid such awkwardness, it is essential that the banquet captain have complete control over his personnel and that he personally approve any additional liquor issued.

SELLING SPECIAL WINES

At times, banquets require a special wine to be served. Working this out is complicated: the operation must estimate the amount needed, purchase that amount, and, if it is not all used, possibly absorb the cost of the amount left over. Though liquor laws vary from state to state, in most states the distinction between a restaurant license and a retail license makes it illegal for restaurants or other foodservice operations to sell liquor in bulk to private individuals. Consequently, the leftover liquor cannot be sold to the party giver. In some cases wholesalers will not take back unused liquor; in some states they are forbidden to do so; and in most cases they are reluctant to take broken cases even if they are allowed to take back liquor. To avoid these problems, a banquet operation should have a realistic wine list geared to preferences of the local market and availability, and the banquet personnel should make every effort to sell from this wine list only. It is very hard to sell odd bottles or cases of wine which have accumulated during the year. Liquor that is purchased and not sold represents money lost.

Vintage

When it is impossible to sell from the wine list and special wines must be sold, it is wise to inquire first about availability. It is easy to get two cases of wine of a certain vintage, but it is much harder to get enough for a party of a thousand guests. It can also happen that a wholesaler has sufficient quantities available when the wine is suggested for a banquet, but by the time the client signs the contract the wine has been sold to somebody else. The quality and price of wine can vary greatly from one vintage to another. If one vintage has been promised and another must be substituted, the host must be made aware of the changes. Unless the giver of the banquet is very wine-conscious, I recommend omitting from the printed menu the vintage of the wine that is being served. This will let you substitute another vintage if more wine is needed than has been ordered. Of course, the host should be notified of this possibility. The beverage office must be made aware of any guarantee changes as soon as possible, so they can keep abreast of the situation and the need for any changes in the amounts to be ordered. As is true in selling food, the banquet salesperson can sell only what the house can produce. The salesperson should not make promises that cannot be kept.

Menu Description

When wine is served with a dinner that has a printed menu, the menu should describe the wine as accurately as possible. At an elaborate dinner it is inadequate to describe the wine simply as chablis or red burgundy. Of course it is best to be wary about indicating the vintage, but the shipper, the domain, and the name of the chateau or the vineyard should always be mentioned.

Service

In connection with providing information about the wine being served, I must mention an unfortunate habit of many banquet waiters. They wrap the wine bottle in a napkin as tightly as possible, with only the neck showing, as if the bottle were a baby in a bunting. It is certainly advisable, especially when the wine has been iced, to carry a side towel and wrap it partially around the neck; this prevents the bottle from dripping on the table. But it is a discourtesy to the banquet giver not to show the label to the guests. The guests should be able to see that they are getting what the menu promised. If the menu does not describe the wines, there is even more reason to let the guests know what they are drinking. If the wine is iced, especially if the bottles are cooled in tubs filled with crushed ice, it is prudent to slip rubber bands over the labels to keep them in place during the chilling process. Water will make the labels come off, and it certainly is not impressive to be served wine from a bottle without a label.

Wine Serving Temperatures

Everybody knows that white wines and champagnes should be served chilled, red wines at room temperature. "Room temperature" means only slightly warm: wine that has stood in hot, back-of-the-house kitchen areas and is served in a hot, overcrowded ballroom, will certainly not taste as it should. In fact, for large banquets, red wine should be slightly chilled. By the time a few hundred bottles have been opened and lined up on the service bar, it will be just the right temperature. Further details of wine service are described in chapter 12.

Glassware for Wine

If wine is to be sold, an operation should have proper glasses. For banquet operations it is not necessary, but it is desirable, to have different glasses for different kinds of wine. An all-purpose wine glass will do, of course, providing the glass is large enough. It should hold between 8 and 10 ounces. The glass should never be filled to the rim, of course; the space left at the top of the glass will allow the wine to develop a bouquet inside the glass. For champagne, many houses use a saucer-shaped glass. It is the least desirable glass for champagne since it allows the effervescent bubbles to escape too quickly. A better and much more elegant glass is a tulip-shaped champagne glass. However, this style breaks more easily than the saucer-shaped glass, and is much more expensive.

Cordials after dinner require separate glassware. Normally, two kinds of glasses will do, a brandy snifter and a so-called pony glass. In many cases, the waiters roll a cordial cart around the room, and we can expect and, therefore, safely calculate that every guest will take a drink. A variety of about six kinds of cordials is sufficient: a brandy, a fruit brandy, two or three sweet liquers and perhaps one that is bitter.

If the banquet salesperson is able to sell beverages from the reception, through the main course and conclude the service with cordials, (s)he will have made a substantial addition to the profits for the event. To do this, beverage service must be skillful, the beverages must be properly served, and the appropriate glasses must be used. Controls must also be exercised to safeguard profits earned.

E II R

LUNCHEON FOR

HER MAJESTY QUEEN ELIZABETH II

AND

HIS ROYAL HIGHNESS

THE PRINCE PHILIP, DUKE OF EDINBURGH

NEW YORK · JULY 9 · 1976

The Banquet Stencil

The original banquet menu with the attached instruction sheet becomes a legal document—a contract between the operation and the client—as soon as it is signed. From the original banquet menu and instruction sheet, copies are made for distribution; we refer to these copies as banquet stencils. The banquet stencil is a work order. The banquet salesperson must make sure that all the notes scribbled down during meetings with the guest, all the promises that were made, and all information pertinent to the party are put on paper in language clear enough for all employees to understand. In large banquet operations, hundreds of employees are involved; all of them must be able to carry out the salesperson's written orders. Orders that are unclear provide an easy excuse for poorly executed work, and if the job is not done properly, the client does not receive the service paid for.

Obviously the banquet stencil must be handled with great care. Imagine a few hundred guests coming into a room which is not set up, or a party arriving at a room that has been sold to somebody else, or an assembled luncheon party having to start the meal with the main course because the soup chef mislaid the menu. All these unfortunate things can happen if banquet stencils are not precisely written and distributed to the necessary people under careful supervision. For the purposes of this chapter, I have included a sample banquet stencil (see Figure 9.1). As each feature of the banquet stencil is discussed, you can refer to the appropriate item in Figure 9.1. You may want to look at further samples though when you are finished with this chapter. For this reason, a number of sample banquet stencils—for events ranging from a reception for 100 guests to a banquet for 1200—are included in appendix C.

Figure 9.1. Sample banquet stencil.

Menu cover, formal lunch in honor of British royalty, July 1976.

1 Distribution code: O MK MP GM B1 B2 PQT PAS 1C SR PD

6 Thursday, May 20, 1979

5 Mirror Ballroom Suite

7 Time: see schedule below

4 Reception and Dinner 860 covers

2 State Department/in honor of Prince Jacob

3 Mr. Bradley Allendale, in charge

Figure 9.1. Sample banquet stencil (cont.).

---

8 MENU

Reception Menu

Assorted Tidbits, complimentary

Dinner Menu

Smoked Colorado Trout

Sauce Raifort

Garniture of Knob Celery

****

Consomme with Almonds

****

Roast Tenderloin of Beef

Sauce Perigourdine

Asparagus with Hollandaise Sauce

Rissole Potatoes

Broiled Tomato

****

Salad of Bibb Lettuce, Endive

Vinaigrette Dressing

****

Frozen Orange Excelsior

****

Assorted Cookies

Coffee/Tea/Sanka

9 Charge: $--- per person

EXTRA ITEMS AND ARRANGEMENTS

Time Schedule:	GOH Reception—Stephanie Room	6:30 PM to 7:50 PM
	General Reception—Mirabelle and Agnes Rooms	6:30 PM to 7:50 PM
	Dinner	

Figure 9.1.   Sample banquet stencil (cont.).

Grand Ballroom—Doors open 8:00 PM

Guests Seated by	8:15 PM
National Anthems and Toast	8:20 PM
First course	8:30 PM
Intermission	8:50 PM
Second course	9:05 PM
Intermission	9:30 PM
Main course	9:50 PM
Intermission	10:30 PM
Dessert and coffee	10:45 PM
Master of Ceremony Perf.	11:00 PM
Adjournment	12:00 AM

10 Beverages:

We will provide three (3) bars and bartenders in the Mirabelle Room and the Agnes Salon. One single bar and one double bar. Charge $———— each for total of $————. Serve assorted highballs and cocktails at bottle prices. Provide mixers, white and red wine and Heinekin beer available at bar. Budget: $———— per person.

Bar to close promptly at 7:50 PM.
In the Stephanie Room there will be no bar, only waiter service. This room is only for GOH. Guarantee 150 covers.

Wines. During dinner we will provide two bottles per table of White Chablis Bin # 8644, $———— in buckets on tables. (NO PLASTIC) Two bottles of red wine, Beaujolais Villages, $———— Bin # 8364 to be opened on tables. Two optional bottles white or red by request of guests. Headtable (2 tables of 14) wine is to be served NOT set on tables. Wine charged to Master Account. During dinner a la carte service of drinks.

In Oak Room please provide soft drinks and coffee for 30 entertainers, added to account.

11 Control:

Provide four (4) control tables in JADE Corridor at entrance to East Foyer. Tickets are to be collected by waiters after seating in the Ballroom. Formal seating. No tickets collected at GOH tables.

12 Programs/Menus:

To be placed on tables by waiters.

13 Room Set-Ups:

Stephanie Room. Few cocktail tables and chairs. Remainder to remain empty.

Figure 9.1.   Sample banquet stencil (cont.).

Agnes and Mirabelle. Two double bars and one single bar in each room. Few cocktail tables and chairs Vanderbilt Style.

Trianon Room. (Per Special Diagram) two reserved tables of 14 guests each. T-shaped red carpet (see diagram).

West Foyer. Set early with several tables and chairs for floral arranging. At about 6:00 PM provide six rolling racks and tables and mirrors for the entertainers. Set up as dressing room. Entertainers to enter thru pantry. Hi-rise elevator entrance to stage.

Near ballroom checkroom provide two six-foot tables draped, for gifts to be given after dinner.

14	Decorations:	Linen. White. Candles. With gold shades. Floral. Own arrangements.
	Mechanical Requirements:	Radio Room. One mike in each room, complimentary. Six (6) additional mikes at $——— each. One (1) standing movable mike with long cord. One (1) piano mike, one on piano, one (1) mike for base player, one for GOH table and one spare.
	Music:	Own arrangements.
	Piano:	Provide two (2) pianos on stage of Ballroom. One tuned grand piano and also regular piano.
15	Flags:	One (1) ——— and one (1) American flag in each room.
	Carpenters:	Two (2) carpenters to be on duty to handle curtains and moving charged at $——— per hour.
	Red Carpet:	See diagram.
	Stage:	See diagram.
16	Security:	Outside security from ——— Government and Hotel security.
17	Tax:	———% sales tax, added to the account.

Figure 9.1.   Sample banquet stencil (cont.).

---

18 Gratuities:

_____% of Food and Beverage Sales will be added to your account, of which _____% will be distributed to waiters, waitresses, and, where applicable, bus help and/or bartenders engaged in the function, and _____% to supervisory, sales, and other banquet personnel.

19 Guarantee: Not later than 48 hours before the function, the Hotel is to be advised of the exact number of guests to be set up for and served, which figure less 3% will then become your Guarantee, for which you will be charged, even though a lesser number attends.

20   Arranged by: _____

            Headwaiter: _____

            Executive Chef: _____

            5/18/79

DISTRIBUTING THE BANQUET STENCIL

In hotels doing large banquet business, the banquet stencil goes to many different departments. The list includes the director of food and beverage, the chef, steward, headwaiter, purchasing department, linen room, florist, food checker, checkroom, banquet auditor, information desk, superintendent of the building, and room service. The list varies from place to place. In smaller operations, perhaps fewer than a dozen copies will be needed. Even in the smallest kitchen, four or five copies of the banquet menu are needed to avoid unnecessary running around. The food receiving area must have one copy; the pantry station must have one; one must be placed where the meat is cut; one must be at the hot station; and a complete set, including all information, even that not directly concerned with the kitchen, must be available to the chef. Remember: paper is cheaper than confusion, and confusion is easily created when clear instructions are not generally available.

In larger kitchens where many copies of the stencil are needed, a distribution code is often printed on each copy of the stencil (see item 1 on Figure 9.1). In very large hotels, about 50 copies of each banquet stencil are made, and a separate stencil-room staff is needed to handle their reproduction.

THE GUARANTEE SHEET

Hotels that have many functions rooms send out a daily guarantee sheet that lists all functions taking place on a particular day and includes the latest attendance figures, referred to at that point as "guar-

Menu interior, dinner for La Confrérie des Chevaliers du Tastevin, March 1967. Unusual hors d'oeuvres preceed this springtime banquet.

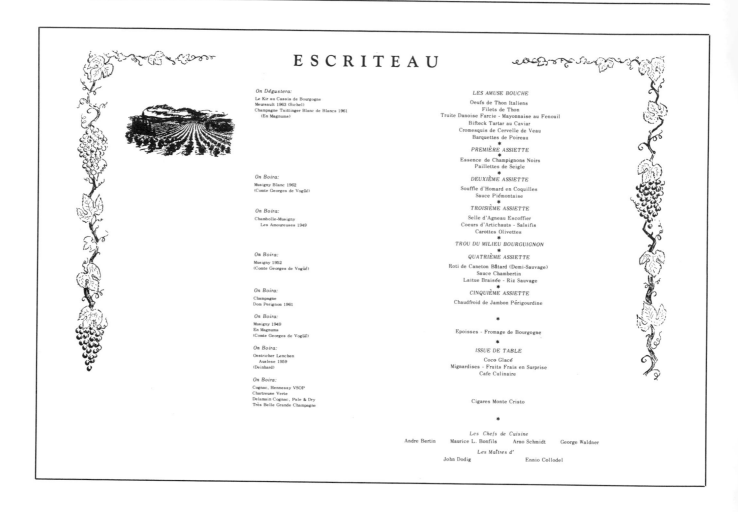

ESCRITEAU

On Dégustera:
Le Kir au Cassis de Bourgogne
Meursault 1963 (Sichel)
Champagne Taittinger Blanc de Blancs 1961
 (En Magnums)

On Boira:
Musigny Blanc 1962
(Comte Georges de Vogüé)

On Boira:
Chambolle-Musigny
 Les Amoureuses 1949

On Boira:
Musigny 1952
(Comte Georges de Vogüé)

On Boira:
Champagne
Dom Perignon 1961

On Boira:
Musigny 1949
En Magnums
(Comte Georges de Vogüé)

On Boira:
Oestricher Lenchen
 Auslese 1959
(Deinhard)

On Boira:
Cognac, Hennessy VSOP
Chartreuse Verte
Delamain Cognac, Pale & Dry
Très Belle Grande Champagne

LES AMUSE BOUCHE

Oeufs de Thon Italiens
Filets de Thon
Truite Danoise Farcie - Mayonnaise au Fenouil
Bifteck Tartar au Caviar
Cromesquis de Cervelle de Veau
Barquettes de Poireau
*
PREMIÈRE ASSIETTE
*
Essence de Champignons Noirs
Paillettes de Seigle
*
DEUXIÈME ASSIETTE

Souffle d'Homard en Coquilles
Sauce Piémontaise
*
TROISIÈME ASSIETTE

Selle d'Agneau Escoffier
Coeurs d'Artichauts - Salsifis
Carottes Olivettes
*
TROU DU MILIEU BOURGUIGNON
*
QUATRIÈME ASSIETTE

Roti de Caneton Bâtard (Demi-Sauvage)
Sauce Chambertin
Laitue Braisée - Riz Sauvage
*
CINQUIÈME ASSIETTE

Chaudfroid de Jambon Périgourdine

*

Epoisses - Fromage de Bourgogne
*
ISSUE DE TABLE
Coco Glacé
Mignardises - Fruits Frais en Surprise
Cafe Culinaire

Cigares Monte Cristo

*

Les Chefs de Cuisine
Andre Bertin   Maurice L. Bonfils   Arno Schmidt   George Waldner
Les Maîtres d'
John Dodig   Ennio Collodel

antees." This sheet is normally mimeographed on colored paper to make it distinct from the banquet stencil or the banquet menu. The guarantee sheet should also list the name of the group, the room in which it is meeting, the type of meal to be served, and the salesperson who sold the party. The color of the linen to be used can also be listed on the guarantee sheet as a reminder to the linen room.

The guarantee sheet usually is issued two days prior to the date of the scheduled event, and by that time all banquet salespersons are expected to have finalized (guaranteed) all attendance figures for their parties. These figures are taken from the diagram of the banquet room which is given to each host or hostess who is asked to indicate in writing on the diagram the number of tables needed and the expected attendance figures. Normally this is done three to four days prior to the function. Many operations allow a difference of 3 percent between the number of people noted on the diagram as expected to attend and the guaranteed number for which the client must pay, even if fewer guests actually attend the party.

Many operations allow the guaranteed figure to be lowered within 24 hours of the time the function is scheduled. Other operations require 48 hours notice, and there are still others that have no policy at all, allowing the guaranteed figure to be changed up to the last moment.

Guarantee increases are always welcome because they mean additional revenue. It should be pointed out, however, that large increases given at the last moment are difficult to handle in most places. When last-minute increases are permitted, the food and service for the group invariably suffer. To maintain the operation's good reputation and to bring in as much revenue as possible, the banquet salesperson must strive to get the best and most realistic guarantee figure possible.

When the bill is presented at the end of a party, it is unpleasant for a dispute to arise over the guarantee figure. Sometimes the payment of the whole sum is held up over disagreement about just a few covers. In such cases the cash flow of the establishment suffers. To avoid such misunderstandings, the policy of the establishment must be explained when the party is booked, and guarantee changes must be handled with great care.

In larger operations the banquet auditor reviews the guarantee figures charged by the banquet captains with the chef. This is because these figures represent money. Every cover charged for is revenue; every cover not charged for that should have been charged is lost revenue—also lost food and labor if the guarantee decrease was not recorded in time for the amount of food prepared to decrease accordingly.

Figure 9.2.   Guarantee memo.

To: Director of Food and Beverage, Chef, Steward, Headwaiter, Linen Room, Florist, Food Checker, Wine Room, Beverage Manager, Banquet Auditor, Superintendent of Service, Room Service, House Engineer

From: Mr. _____, Director of Catering
Tuesday, May 18, 19—

Guarantees:

Rooms	Linen	Salesperson
FRIENDS OF PENNSYLVANIA Reception, Luncheon 1234 Mississippi Ballroom	Gold	Anderson
SAVINGS BANK ASSOCIATION Reception, Dinner Dance 876 Mississippi Ballroom	House choice	Anderson
WESTWARD GROUP Luncheon 378 Mirror Room	Red napkins White tablecloths	Jones
PHILLIPPE SCHWARZ Wedding Dinner, Reception 256 Mirror Room	Blue	Trumbull

Sixth Floor Suites

COCA COLA Luncheon 54 Riverview	House choice	Trumbull
DOWNTOWN SAVINGS BANK Reception 79 Riverview	None	Freed
BLUE CROSS Dinner 90 Riverview	Gold/Blue	Houseman

Figure 9.2.   Guarantee memo (cont.).

CROWN ASSOCIATE Luncheon 27 Silver Salon	Red	Houseman
BABCO STEEL Luncheon 43 Oak Suite East	House choice	Trumbull

Arrangements by: Mr. _____, Director of Catering
May 16, 19—

Changes in the guarantee should be handled only by an authorized person, preferably by the same banquet salesperson who originally booked the party. If the attendance figure goes up at the very last minute (i.e., after the party has begun), the banquet headwaiter must be instructed to get written approval for the increase from the host. A simple preprinted form can be used to take care of such a situation. In smaller operations, a system of using different colored marking pens or felt tipped pencils is very effective. Every executive who may possibly be involved in changing guarantees selects a color and uses a pen of that color only for guarantee changes. With such a color code in use, the chef can tell at a glance who put a guarantee change through.

Of course, larger hotels need a much more formal system for guarantee changes. In some operations electro-writers are installed in the banquet office with terminals in the chef's office, the steward's office, and in the headwaiter's office. When transmitting guarantees over the electrowriter or over the telephone, the same method should be used at all times. The information given should be the day and date, the type of meal, the new guaranteee figure, and the room in which the function is to be held. The name of the group is, at this point, immaterial: on a given day, one company can have a number of functions going on in different rooms, but only one group can occupy a room at any given time. It is much more helpful to say "Monday, May 1, Luncheon, Ballroom, 523" than "Luncheon for Mr. Schwarz on Monday is 523." The difference in wording may seem insignificant, but when transmitting guarantee figures one cannot be too precise. For a sample guarantee memo, see Figure 9.2.

The person receiving the guarantee over the phone or over the electrowriter must also be instructed in how to record and document the change. Purchasing and staffing is directly based on the guarantees. Room changes and cancellations must be handled in the same fashion and with the same care as guarantee figures.

Menu, formal lunch in honor of British royalty. Note opening use of American place names, followed by dishes with a more continental tone.

MENU

BEDFORD STRIPED BASS SAUTÉ
With Gooseberries
Shenandoah Valley New Potatoes

*Callaway White Riesling
Estate bottled 1974*

ᨒ

FILET OF BEEF AND STRASBOURG PATÉ IN ASPIC
Chives Sauce
Pea Pods Vinaigrette

ᨒ

MACÉDOINE OF SEASONAL FRUIT
In Chocolate Shell

ᨒ

Waldorf-Astoria Macaroons and Tuiles

ᨒ

Demi Tasse

SETTING UP THE BANQUET STENCIL

How should the banquet stencil look? First, it should be filled out in the same detail for each event, regardless of whether the party is for 2000 or 15. Uniformity is the best guarantee that important information will not be forgotten. Many places use printed forms; others type a banquet stencil from scratch. Whatever the method, every banquet stencil must use exactly the same format and include all information pertinent to the party. In most cases, this will include the menu. For events such as dances, however, there is no menu but instead there are elaborate instructions concerning beverages, set-up, mechanical requirements, and other related concerns.

The salesperson booking the party issues the banquet stencil; (s)he is held responsible for all typographical errors and omissions. Don't blame the secretary if the banquet stencil reads 500 covers instead of 50. The salesperson must make sure that the banquet stencil is precise. Each banquet stencil should be initialed by either the banquet salesperson or her or his supervisor before distribution.

The banquet stencil must list the name of the group as well as the name of the person in charge (see items 2 and 3 in Figure 9.1) It is important for the banquet captain to know who can authorize guarantee increases and the banquet captain should never accept guarantee decreases. The name of the group used on the banquet stencil must correspond with the name used on the guarantee sheet. The reason for this is clear. If the Greyhound Association gives a luncheon in the Crystal Ballroom and a banquet stencil is sent out for that luncheon but the Guarantee Sheet lists the Bow Wow Club luncheon in the Blue Salon, the question immediately arises as to whether both groups are the same and the party has changed rooms, or whether an additional group has been booked but has been forgotten.

Next, the banquet stencil should list the type of function—luncheon, dinner, reception, dance, etc.—and the room the function is to be held in (see items 4 and 5 in Figure 9.1). Following that, the day and date of the event should be listed (see item 6 in Figure 9.1). These facts are very important and serve as a double check for all concerned with the event. To list: "Dinner on April 17" is not sufficient. Perhaps the client said April 7, or the secretary who typed the banquet stencil understood April 7. These things can happen and lead to disaster. Imagine a bridal party driving up to a country club and the manager saying: "I have you booked for tomorrow, Saturday, the twelfth. All weddings take place on Saturdays!" To avoid such a catastrophe both day and date should always be in writing.

To mention the day and date also helps the back of the house. Many kitchen workers do not pay too much attention to each day's date because their work is not date-oriented. But they will remember, "Wednesday is the big dinner" or, "Next Saturday, when we are busy in the Pool Room, the Fashion Show will take place!" Always put in both day and date.

Recording Service Time

The time for service selected for the party should be noted next (see item 7 in Figure 9.1). The estimated service time should be prominently featured on the first page of the banquet stencil. This is important to the kitchen. For formal banquets there may be a time when the doors will open, a time when the party for the dais marches in, a time when the invocation is said, a time when the first dance is danced, and so on. This time table is important for the headwaiter, for the band leader, for the electricians, and for other employees, and it belongs under "Extra Items and Arrangements" on the banquet stencil. What the kitchen must know is when the food must be ready.

If there is to be dancing between courses, this should be indicated on the stencil; if speeches are scheduled that will affect foodservice, the chef should be notified of the time they are to be given. When giving service time, be as precise as possible. Delays are always possible, and on some occasions, a dinner may even be advanced slightly. These things are unavoidable. But the chef cannot be expected to create a gourmet dinner and then have to keep it hot for hours on end because the banquet salesperson did not list the proper time.

Where a banquet operation is so extensive it requires serving a number of functions at different times during the day, proper timing is crucial. It is a waste of labor to send cooks to a satellite kitchen to help serve and then not need their services for hours. It is a waste of labor to hire dishwashers to arrive at 7 P.M. and then have no dirty dishes arrive until 10 P.M. Schedule information for each event must be available, and it must be right. The salesperson must, therefore, always work out an approximate time table with the host, then provide this information to the rest of the banquet operation by means of the banquet stencil. This schedule should be realistic and allow for the unforeseen, but it should also work to the advantage of all departments involved.

Setting Starting and Closing Times

In many efficiently-run operations, the banquet stencil mentions the approximate time of adjournment for an event. Selling banquets means selling space—a very valuable commodity. The more often the space can be sold, the more revenue will be realized. If a luncheon ends at 3 P.M. the room in which it was held can be sold for a reception at 5 P.M. and again for dinner at 7 P.M. Similarly, an early dinner can leave a room free for a late dance.

Another important aspect of the schedule is its role in energy conservation. Setting a proper starting and closing time for functions can often save on heat, lights, and air conditioning. Some operations even provide a checklist with the banquet stencil to be filled out by the banquet captain after the event ends. Such a list would include: lights turned out, air conditioner turned off, and similar energy-conserving practices.

Recording the Menu

At this point, the menu itself appears on the banquet stencil (see item 8 in Figure 9.1). It must contain any necessary extra instructions. For instance, when a reception is listed, the menu should state whether the food is to be served hot or cold, and whether it will be served from chafing dishes on a buffet or passed on platters by the service staff. Menu language itself is discussed in chapters 13 and 14. However, I would like to stress the fact that when preparing a menu for the banquet stencil, it is important to make sure the items listed on the menu are spaced so that reading the menu is easy.

Once the menu is written, price information must be considered (see item 9 in Figure 9.1). Some establishments list the menu price on each menu that is issued. Privately-owned places sometimes use a code or do not list the price at all. My experience has been that a menu code is the least-kept secret in the place. Very soon everybody knows how to read the code. I believe strongly that the price should be placed on the menu for all to see. Gratuities paid to the service staff are based on the selling price of the event, and the staff has a right to know how much money to expect. The chef is responsible for managing his kitchen in the most efficient manner, and he certainly should know what price the meal is bringing. Of course, this is a matter of individual policy to be set by the management.

Finally the banquet stencil should detail any special arrangements that the particular event will require. These details can range from quite simple, such as "coffee urns to be set up by 8:30 A..M" for a small breakfast gathering, to extremely complicated. In Figure 9.1, a banquet stencil for a major diplomatic reception and dinner, the details are fairly elaborate and all are very important. The plans for beverage service are covered (item 10) including budget, wine service, and drinks for entertainers. Set-up specifications are also provided, including the arrangement for collecting tickets (item 11), placing menus at the guests' places (item 12), room set-up and decoration (items 13 and 14), a number of items related to the group's entertainment plans (item 15), and security (item 16). The stencil then details arrangements made for payment of tax charges and gratuities (items

Menu interior, dinner to
celebrate the 60th anniversary of
the Long Island Culinary
Association, Inc., April 1978.
This menu features lovely
French and a pleasing meal.

Président
Matthew G. Ryan

Présidents Eméritus
Joseph D. Tarantino   William J. Spry

Exécutive Vice-Président   Vice-Président
Nathon Blom   Lee Tyre Sr.

Trésorier   Secrétaire
Vernon Jensen   Rick Brobmann

Sargents des Armes
Peter Benferamo   Carmine Granata

Directeurs
Eric Favières   Philip Panzarino
William Jenkins   Louis Donnard
Peter Berger   Francine Daubel

Chairman du Bal
Lee Tyre Sr.

Assistants
Marc Ross   Peter Berger
Peter Dickie   Raymond Riviera
Joseph Tarantino   Joe McKeon
Eric Favières   Rick Brobmann
Peter Benferamo   Louis Donnard
Carlo Bussetti   Carmine Granata
Philip Panzarino   Francine Daubel

Avante l'Oeuvre   Amuse Bouches

Première Assiette
Consommé Double Villeneuve
La Paillette d'Ore

Deuxième Assiette
Johanesberg   Les Délices de Sole Nantua
Reisling

Entr'acte
Le Sorbet à la Mirabelle

Troisièmme Assiette
Cabernet   Le Filet de Boeuf Charolais Argenteuil
Sauvignon   Sauce Bordelaise

Asperges Mimosa   La Tomate Farcie
Pommes Parisiennes

Quatrième Assiette
Le Fromage de Brie de Maux
Coeurs de Bibb Laitue au Vinaigrette

l'Apotheose
Champagne   La Bombe Glacée Panachée
Sauce aux Fraises

Liqueurs   Le Moka

Diécteur des Banquets   Chef de Cuisine
Alois Habjan   Heinz Aichen

Maître d'Hôtel   Chef Pâtissier
Sean Bowe   Fred Mayer

17 and 18), important factors to have in writing. It closes with a reiteration of the house policy on guarantees, (item 19) and closes with the signatures of the client, the salesperson who signed the client, the headwaiter, and the executive chef (item 20).

This is a lot of information to include, yet every bit of it is important. By providing a clear, comprehensive banquet stencil to all involved, the banquet department of any establishment takes a strong step towards the success of the banquet and the satisfaction of the guests.

Menu cover, Alan Chapel dinner,
February/March 1977.

For the Chef: How to Work with the Sales Staff

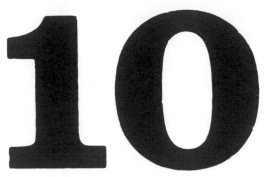

A healthy banquet department makes the difference between profit or loss for the foodservice departments in many establishments. A banquet department is healthy when it sells the available banquet space as often as possible for the highest price possible. The highest price does not necessarily come from the highest food check; it can also result from the combination of a very high liquor check and a relatively low food check, or it can come solely from a liquor check, providing the function brings the largest number of dollars possible to the bottom line. This is the catering director's chief responsibility.

WHO IS THE CATERING DIRECTOR?

Many chefs do not understand what is required in selling banquets. They see the catering director as a well-dressed individual who makes constant demands on the kitchen without understanding the problems the kitchen has. The catering director, or head of the banquet department, must be a super salesperson. Suave, charming and well-liked, moving among a large circle of friends—in the business community and on the social scene—yet possessing a terrific business sense in closing a deal: this is a portrait of the successful catering director.

Chefs must understand that a person's level of knowledge of gastronomy cannot be measured easily. There are as many food "experts" as there are people on earth. Who can honestly say what is right and what is wrong? When ordering banquets, customers often have preconceived ideas. It is the job of the catering director to give the customers what they want. This does not mean that the catering director should say yes to every wish. If it is not practical to produce a menu that meets the wishes of the host or hostess, the catering director should provide guidance, offer advice, and provide alternate suggestions. The successful catering director persuades the client that what can be provided with reasonable effort, at a satisfactory profit, is what the client wants. Still selling is a process of bartering. In the banquet business, a little concession made at the right moment by the salesperson can make the difference between getting a good piece of business or losing it.

THE IMPORTANCE OF COMMUNICATION

It is up to the chef to develop respect and rapport with the catering director, and to provide guidance to the catering staff. The catering director and staff, in turn, should be wise enough to accept the limitations in kitchen performance that the chef conveys to them. These limitations are dictated by the knowledge of the staff, and the availability

Menu interior, luncheon buffet,
November 1974. The clear
arrangement and uncomplicated
typeface make this an inviting
menu.

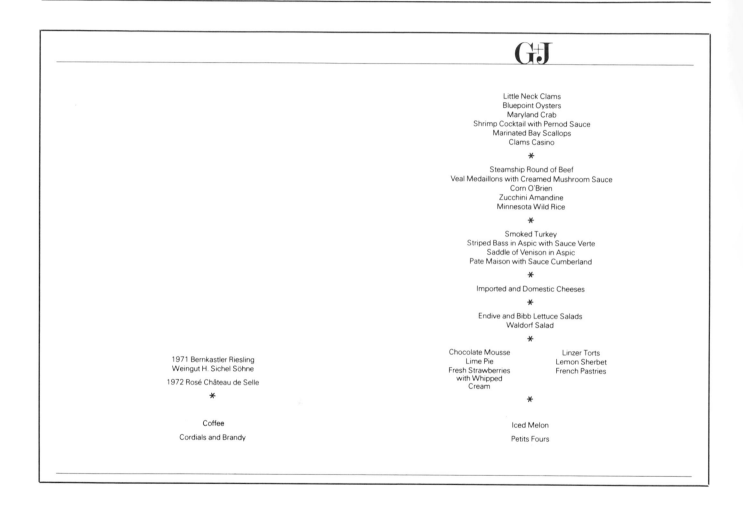

G+J

Little Neck Clams
Bluepoint Oysters
Maryland Crab
Shrimp Cocktail with Pernod Sauce
Marinated Bay Scallops
Clams Casino

✳

Steamship Round of Beef
Veal Medaillons with Creamed Mushroom Sauce
Corn O'Brien
Zucchini Amandine
Minnesota Wild Rice

✳

Smoked Turkey
Striped Bass in Aspic with Sauce Verte
Saddle of Venison in Aspic
Pate Maison with Sauce Cumberland

✳

Imported and Domestic Cheeses

✳

Endive and Bibb Lettuce Salads
Waldorf Salad

✳

Chocolate Mousse	Linzer Torts
Lime Pie	Lemon Sherbet
Fresh Strawberries	French Pastries
with Whipped	
Cream	

1971 Bernkastler Riesling
Weingut H. Sichel Söhne

1972 Rosé Château de Selle

✳

Coffee

Cordials and Brandy

✳

Iced Melon

Petits Fours

Menu interior, Alan Chapel
dinner. The lovely French is
simple enough for most readers
to understand.

A l'apéritif
toute petites fritures et Perrier Jouët Blason de France, 1969

———

pâté chaud d'anguilles, les deux beurres

*

salade de homard du Maine, de suprêmes de pigeonneaux
aux pourpiers et truffes noires

*

millefeuille d'epinards en branche et moules

———

ragoût de coquilles saint-jacques, d'huîtres
de pleine mer aux poireaux

*

gâteau de foies de canards baigné d'une sauce
aux petites crevettes

*

court-bouillon de red snapper aux petites légumes

———

rognon de veau, gratin de macaroni

*

filet d'agneau aux gousses d'ails,
petit paillasson aux courgettes et cerfeuil

*

tournedo poëlé, au beurre vert, cassolette d'aubergines et tomates

———

un fromage

———

crème glacée et sorbets
tarte au sucre et sablés

*

mousse de citrons verts et délicate gelée de mandarines
friands au miel et pralines

*

mousse au chocolat et brioche grillée chaude

———

moka, Brésil ou Colombie
et Marc de Bourgogne

of space, manpower, and equipment. The catering department should concentrate on making the best of the given situation.

Today, no large kitchen can produce any food item in all quantities at all times. Most kitchens can do a little better if there is some inspiration provided. The world is moving faster every day; new trends are born, new fads created; new ideas brought forward constantly. Most chefs are so busy solving the daily problems in the kitchen that they have no time to keep up with these new developments. The world is passing them by. The catering director, on the other hand, is in touch with the world and, as a result, can offer the chef suggestions and ideas. These should be considered with good will and in depth. Not all ideas are good, and not all of them are workable, but cooperation between the chef and the catering director will markedly improve the range of menus from the kitchen to the catering staff.

CONVERTING IMPOSSIBLE IDEAS

Often dinner committees or the hosting customer will have romantic ideas about food; they want a personal dining experience used as a model for a big dinner. The catering director and the chef, working together, must figure out how to provide a dinner that will please the customers even while it works well in the kitchen.

The chef will know that a dinner eaten in a charming bistro in Paris does not necessarily make a good banquet menu for hundreds of people. When that sort of demand is made on the catering director, the chef should use his or her authority to say no if the dish cannot be prepared properly. Keep in mind that a chef has authority only while keeping an open mind. No chef should say no automatically every time a new idea is presented or a time-honored routine in the kitchen is altered in the slightest way.

The chef should always be open-minded and business-minded, an equal partner with the catering director. No chef should become a silent martyr who says yes to the catering staff, then grumbles in the back of the house. If you are the chef, come forward with suggestions of your own. Welcome new ideas; say no when something cannot be done, then suggest an alternative that may be equally satisfactory. Remember, the buck stops in the kitchen!

Menu, dinner dance for the
Board of Advisory Trustees of
Iona College, March 1976. The
names of these dishes invoke
America and its colonies.

Dinner Menu

Clement Columbet
Burgundy
MARYLAND BAY SHRIMPS IN ARTICHOKE BOTTOM

THOUSAND ISLAND DRESSING

* * *

PENNSYLVANIA DUTCH WILD MUSHROOM SOUP

WITH CROUTONS

* * *

Clement Columbet
Chablis
BROILED HEART OF MASSACHUSETTS TENDERLOIN

CHESTNUTS AND CARROTS GLAZED WITH

VERMONT MAPLE SYRUP

LONG ISLAND O'BRIEN POTATOES

* * *

PILGRIMS SALAD

OIL AND CIDER VINEGAR DRESSING

* * *

OLD FASHIONED NEW YORK HOT APPLE PIE

PHILADELPHIA VANILLA ICE CREAM

* * *

COLONIAL COFFEE

CORDON BLEU DU SAINT ESPRIT

For the Sales Staff: How to Work with the Chef

Chefs are practical people. They deal with reality from the very first day they start to work in kitchens, and the reality of the kitchen dictates what work is done. A steak not put on the fire on time will not be cooked on time; an item not ordered will not be available. When a position in the kitchen crew is not filled with a suitable person, there will be a gap in the work force. When fifty chickens are put in the oven, fifty chickens will come out, and no amount of persuasion, double-talk, or cajoling will turn those chickens into roast beef.

Similarly, the chef will prepare only what the sales staff orders. When the menu calls for mushroom soup, mushroom soup will be served. For the banquet salesperson to announce an hour before the banquet begins that the person who prepared the banquet stencil made a mistake, that the customer changed his mind, or that the printer made an error, will not change reality. All these perfectly logical excuses will not turn mushroom soup into asparagus soup. Further, if the soup should have been asparagus, telling the chef "Do the best you can" is also unsatisfactory: it places the burden for solving the problem on the chef, when it belongs with those who prepared the menu and the stencil. When dealing with the chef, the sales staff should always remember: accurate communication is essential to success.

Good chefs are good organizers. Everything that is done in a kitchen requires physical work, and a good chef plans his activities and the workload of his crew meticulously. If, at the last minute, the catering director asks the chef to start all over again because somebody made a mistake, he or she cannot expect the chef to be very cheerful about it.

KEEP PROMISES REALISTIC

Menu cover, Cordon Bleu du Saint Esprit's fall banquet, October 1976. The society's official decoration forms a simple, striking design.

Salespeople can be evasive and unintentionally unrealistic. A verbal promise or a little concession given during the sales pitch may close the deal and make the customer happy, but can look like an enormous task to the chef when printed on the menu. Some catering directors are overly creative. They like to pull down a name from the sky or select a technical expression from an old cookbook and put it on the banquet menu to impress the client and staff. I do not want to discourage creativity or good selling, but I must remind the sales staff that dishes taken out of context or expressions not fully understood can easily lead to menu selections that throw the kitchen into chaos.

At times, when a menu is especially important, it is planned with great care to fit the occasion. The dishes may all be very difficult to produce properly, but the chef, knowing the importance of this dinner, makes a special effort to make this dinner a success. Forgetting

Menu, Cordon Bleu du Saint Esprit. A number of themes work together here—harvest bounty, national pride, bicentennial spirit—to form a well-orchestrated meal.

A BICENTENNIAL MENU

-o-

Strained Carolina Crab Gumbo

-o-

Emerald Dry
Paul Masson
California

Block Island Striped Bass Mousse
Bedford Clam Sauce
Puff Paste Diamond

-o-

Gamay Beaujolais
Paul Masson
California

Broiled Heart of Beef Tenderloin
Spice Wharf Pepper Corn Sauce
Glazed Turnip Roots and Carrots
Corn Fritters

-o-

Pilgrims Salad
Selection of American Cheeses

-o-

Waldorf-Astoria
Brut
California

Cinnamon Ice Cream Mound
In The Spirit of The Occasion

-o-

Baskets of Colonial Sweets

-o-

Ninny Broth

that this dinner was tailor-made for a specific occasion, other banquet salespersons will then pick out an item or two, maybe even more, and put them on the next rotary luncheon menu or the next ballroom dinner menu.

This is one sure way to irritate the chef and to ruin the relationship with the kitchen. It is like asking an olympic runner to break the world record every night. The next time a special effort is needed, the chef will not respond with great enthusiasm. This will not be done by a banquet salesperson who understands the chef's problems. This is why it is so important for the banquet sales staff to create a good working relationship with the chef.

CONSULT THE CHEF

One way to increase rapport with the chef is to encourage the chef to suggest ideas, and let the chef present them to important clients if schedules permit. However, that must be done with consideration and planning. Most kitchens today are so understaffed that few chefs can afford to spend time away. They certainly won't be very relaxed if they are required to sit in on a meeting while the committee talks about the golf outing, the latest trend in food, or the last trip to the vineyards of France. The chef must wonder whether the potwasher has come in to work, whether the purveyor has delivered the last crucial crate of chicken, and whether the frycook will remember to put the baking potatoes into the oven on time. In kitchens today, every minute is crucial. Keep this in mind whenever you deal with the chef.

UNDERSTAND THE DIFFICULT CHEF

Another characteristic often encountered among chefs is that, deep down, many chefs are shy. Because they are shy, some overreact at times, becoming belligerent or difficult. Most chefs prefer to stay behind the scenes. Often a chef will say yes to every request, regardless of how unreasonable it may be, just because it is so hard to say no. To exploit this tendency is unfair; doing so will ruin the relationship between the chef and the catering director. It is the catering director's responsibility to provide guidance and to lead the sales meeting even when the chef is present.

There is another kind of chef, who only sees the work involved in any suggestion and tends to discourage any changes from the established menu. This kind of chef definitely will not take a chance on more work without the assurance of additional benefits. One explanation of this attitude has to do with the monetary aspect of the kitchen versus the dining room. In New York city hotels, and probably in many other

Menu interior, 53rd dinner of the Lucullus Circle, January 1961. Well-chosen and pleasantly described accompaniments enrich this menu.

L'ESCRITEAU

1ère Assiette
LE CONSOMMÉ AUX OEUFS FILÉS

2ème Assiette
LA MOUSSE DE TURBOT DE LA MANCHE
AVEC LES NYMPHES À L'AURORE

PULIGNY MONTRACHET,
LES CHALUMEAUX 1957
Estate Bottled by Joseph Matrot
BATARD MONTRACHET 1957
Estate Bottled by Claude Ramonet

3ème Assiette
LE CHATEAUBRIAND À LA MÖELLE
AVEC LES CÉLERIS DE HOLLANDE
LES PETITES POMMES SOUFFLÉES

CHÂTEAU MARGAUX 1947
PAUILLAC
First Classified Growth
CHÂTEAU LATOUR 1947
PAUILLAC
First Classified Growth

l'Intermède
LA FRAMBOISE D'ALSACE

4ème Assiette
LES FILETS DE CANETON
À LA GELEE AU MADERE 1792
LA SALADE DE LAITUES D'HIVER

CHAMBERTIN 1957
EN MAGNUMS
Estate Bottled by General Rebourseau
NUITS ST. GEORGES,
LES VAUCRAINS 1937
Estate Bottled by Michelot

La Dorure
LES FROMAGES DE FRANCE

CHÂTEAU CALON-SEGUR 1945
ST. ESTEPHE
en Magnums — Third Classified Growth
CHÂTEAU HAUT BRION 1918
PESSAC
First Classified Growth

l'Apothéose
LES FRAISES CHANTILLY
AU GRAND MARNIER
LE GÂTEAU DES ROIS

CHÂTEAU D'YQUEM 1948
First Great Growth of Sauternes
CHÂTEAU DE RAYNE VIGNEAU 1928
First Classified Growth of Sauternes

HINE FAMILY RESERVE
GRANDE CHAMPAGNE
EAU DE VIE DE MARC MONTRACHET
Distilled by Julien Monnot

LE CAFÉ DES ILES

hotels and restaurants across the country, the dining room staff makes more money than the kitchen staff. In some New York city hotels, thanks to a union contract partial to waiters, payroll records reveal that a banquet captain makes more money than the executive chef. This covers his salary and recorded gratuities, not counting the gratuities only he knows about. Payroll records show that banquet waiters, working a ten-month season, make more money on the average than floor chefs, pastry chefs, and other key personnel in the kitchen. Again, I stress that this includes only the salary recorded on the books, not gratuities received in cash. In many hotels, the catering director, because he gets a percentage of banquet sales, makes more money than the executive chef.

The situation varies from operation to operation, and from state to state, but we can assume that in most cases the dining room staff makes much more money than the kitchen staff. This should be kept in mind by the hotel banquet director and by the owners of restaurants. Often, the chef and the kitchen staff are expected to make a special effort for a special occasion. The dining room staff is then handsomely compensated, while the kitchen staff does not even get a thank-you note.

To offset this unfair situation, one thing the catering director can do is to make the banquet office an efficient operation. This will help minimize kitchen problems. Catering directors should make it their business to show respect for and cultivate rapport with the chef, and work to develop similar relationships between the banquet sales office staff and the kitchen staff. Arrogant dictators have no place in the catering office.

THE EXPLORERS CLUB 74th ANNUAL DINNER

APRIL 14, 1978-GRAND BALLROOM-THE WALDORF ASTORIA, NEW YORK

Organizing Gourmet Dinners

Our public has become food-conscious over the years, and, as a result, gourmet dinners are proliferating. Many such dinners are organized by serious gourmet societies that have strict requirements for membership. Other gourmet societies require only love of food and the ability to afford fine meals. Other gourmet dinners are organized by fun-living people who just want a good time. Some gourmet societies make the study of wine from a particular region their purpose for existence, and the food at dinners planned by them is subordinate to the wines chosen for the occasion. One society keeps the ancient art of roasting the central focus of its dinners; another venerates French cuisine, and still another has been organized by women for women—chefs, restaurateurs, writers, and others—of outstanding gastronomic reputation.

Whatever the name of the organization, whatever the occasion for the dinner, gourmet dinners are almost never profitable. The question in planning one is how to limit monetary losses. Gains will still be reaped in publicity, image-building for the house, an educational experience and challenge for the staff, and the feeling of having done something to perpetuate gastronomy.

Throughout this book, there are examples of menus for gourmet dinners. A gourmet dinner is a happy marriage between wine and food in an ambience befitting the occasion. There can be gourmet picnics and gourmet luncheons, but if you strive for the epitome of gastronomy only a formal dinner will provide the proper setting.

Gourmet dinners should not be too large. How large they can be is a question of logistics, but to feed several hundred people "gourmet style" is impossible. I have prepared gourmet dinners for 40 or 50 persons, and I have provided gourmet dinners for as many as 250. The latter figure meant straining capabilities. In presenting a gourmet dinner, the staff must strive for perfection in food and service; that is difficult to do for so many people.

PROVIDE A LAVISH SETTING

The setting for a gourmet dinner should be elegant and lavish, with the best linen, china, silver, and glassware the house can muster. The table decorations should be seasonal flowers and fruit pieces, interspersed with fine silver. Make sure the table decorations are low enough to allow the guests to look at each other across the table. Also, remember that the flowers must not be fragrant: the aroma of food and wine should dominate the scene.

At true gourmet dinners, no ashtrays and no salt and pepper shakers are permitted on the table. No bread and butter is served at some dinners. I don't agree with this rule, but when it is enforced no

Menu cover, 78th annual dinner of the Explorers Club, April 1978.

155

Menu, the Explorers Club. The hors d'oeuvres here are indeed "exotic."

EXOTIC HORS D'OEUVRES

SEA SNAILS *donated by the Consul General of Canada*
CATALINA SQUID IN INK *donated by Willard Bascom*
SHANGRI-LA WILD BOAR *donated by Carlo Amato*
BROWN PELICAN SALAD
donated by the Cree Indian Tribe
WICHETTY GRUB SOUP *donated by Nixon Griffis*
MOUNTAIN LION MEATBALLS
MARINATED NOVA SCOTIA MUSSELS
courtesy of Mr. & Mrs. Coleman Williams
ELEPHANT STEW *donated by Peter Horn II*
MONGONUI LAMB *donated by New Zealand Board*
CAPE BUFFALO TONGUE CANAPE
donated by the Pen & Pencil Restaurant
EMU INFERTILE EGG OMELETTE *suggested by Milo Waldes*
TAPIR CHILE
CARIBOU TRIPE PROVENÇALE
MANTA RAY CURRY *donated by the Fish Factory Inc.*

DINNER MENU

MUSHROOMS AND HERBS
A LA LINNAEUS

WHITE RABBIT STEW WITH PRUNES

BOILED YUCCA

SHREDDED CARROT
AND ALMOND SALAD

SEMOLINA RING
WITH COMPOTE OF RHUBARB
AND STRAWBERRIES

TUILLES

COFFEE

"SHOULD WE EAT THE FISH?"

bread and butter plates are needed, either. At most gourmet dinners, water glasses are not allowed on the table; water is served by request only. The necessary number of wine glasses are put on the table before the meal begins, providing there is room. At some dinners as many as twelve wines are served, in which case more glasses are put out as used glasses are removed. Since wine glasses washed in dish machines often have a detergent smell, it is advisable to rinse glasses that have been machine-washed with bottled water, and then polish them with clean, lint-free cloths.

WINE SERVICE

The wine served must be handled very carefully. It is advisable to have one person in the back of the house assigned to handle and supervise the wine service to make sure that the proper wine is served at the right time. The proper temperature at which the wine should be served must also be observed.

Red wines should be opened ahead of time to allow the wine to breathe. The length of time required to bring the wine to the proper temperature varies from wine to wine. Very old wines can lose their aroma rapidly; opening such a wine too early can do irreparable damage. Other wine, in contrast, will improve tremendously when allowed to stand for an hour in the bottle. The desired temperatures and service procedures should be established at the wine and food tasting held prior to the dinner.

Some old wine will have sediment; such wine must be taken from the wine cellar and allowed to stand upright for a day or two to allow the sediment to settle. Decanting—pouring the wine into a carafe slowly, without disturbing the sediment—is difficult, and in most cases decanting will not be necessary if the waiters are instructed not to pour the bottle down to the very last drop.

When wine is served, the wine glasses should be filled sparingly. The gourmet wants to taste and test wine, not to get drunk. Wine for each course is always served before the food. This allows the wine to be on the table when the food arrives assuring that the hot food can be enjoyed with the proper wines. Often, two wines are served with the same dish to offer a comparison between different wines. After each course, the wine glasses used are removed, unless a guest would like to linger over the last drops. Wine labels must be shown to each guest but without making a big, time-consuming production of it. A gourmet dinner must be an enjoyable experience in all respects: if it takes five hours to eat a meal, the dinner will not be a success, because few people enjoy sitting at a table that long.

Menu interior, wine-tasting dinner for Les Amis d'Escoffier Society, October 1963. The number on the right allow the wines to be identified during the meal.

AVANT L'OEUVRE

BYRRH	*Le Caviar de Béluga sur pain Grillé*
CHABLIS CASSIS	*L'Esturgeon des Grands Lacs*
VERMOUTH CASSIS	*Le Saumon de la Nouvelle Ecosse*
SHERRY	*Les Petits Friands*
CHAMPAGNE	*Les Rissolées à la Russe*
	La Quiche Lorraine

* * *

LE MENU

Le Gumbo Claire Louisianne

* * *

White Wine   *La Paupiette de Sole*
à la Mode du Chef

* * *

Red Wine   *Les Cailles Souvarov*
Les Endives Flamandes

* * *

Red Wine   *Le Zéphyr de Volaille à l'Estragon*
accompagné de la Salad du Kentucky
à l'Huile Vierge

* * *

Le Fromage de Brie

* * *

Champagne   *La Mousse Pralinée*

* * *

Les Friandises

* * *

Liqueurs   *Le Café des Princes*

GEORGE W. FREES   ROBERT AUDELAN
Director of Sales and Catering   Le Chef des Cuisines

LES AMIS D'ESCOFFIER SOCIETY

Le Comité de la Bonne Bouche

Mardi, 1 Octobre 1963

SELECTIONS

WHITE WINE	1	2	3	4	5
RED WINE	6	7	8	9	10
RED WINE	11	12	13	14	

THE TASTING DINNER

Since the food and wine must match each other, tasting or sample dinners are often held. I have mixed feelings about sample dinners. Cooking is a creative process, and the meal cooked today will not necessarily be the meal cooked three weeks hence when the dinner is to be served. On the other hand, a sample dinner provides an opportunity to see how certain wines react with certain dishes. It gives the chef a chance to experiment. The tasting dinner is like a rehearsal in a theater; it offers a chance to correct the presentation before the final performance.

If a tasting dinner is planned, the reception food must not be available for the tasting, since it would be prohibitively expensive in time and labor. Only the main dishes or perhaps a controversial dish should be tasted to judge whether they will be compatible with the wine.

A menu and a wine list must be provided for the tasting. The wines to be tasted must be numbered. To keep track of all the wines, a sheet of paper containing circles the size of the wine glasses should be provided, one sheet for the white wines and one for the red wines. The circles on the paper should be numbered and the glasses put on the sheet. This makes it easy to pour the proper wine in the right glass, and for guests, during the tasting, to keep track of which wine is which.

Wine glasses should not be removed during the tasting because guests often like to compare the different wines, and also they may want to see how the wines behave when held in the glass for a period of time. For a wine tasting without food, dry french bread and a few pieces of cubed swiss or cheddar cheese should be provided. There should also be water on the table to rinse the mouth, and buckets to spit out wines, if necessary.

If wine and food are tasted together, the wine should be available first. The food can be served buffet style, so every guest can proceed at his or her own speed during the tasting. At the end, notes must be compared, and the proper combination of wine and food should be discussed.

At the discussion, the chef should always be invited, and the headwaiter should also be present. It takes a great deal of skill to serve a gourmet dinner properly, and the importance of gracious service must not be overlooked. A clear understanding between kitchen and dining room as to how food and wine are to be presented is needed. At times, it might be worthwhile to produce a small sample dinner for the service staff to familiarize them with the proper sequence of wine and food. It is not necessary to serve very expensive food and rare wines at this dinner. Closely related food will do to provide an opportunity for the service to be practiced.

Menu, dinner for La Confrérie de la Chaine des Rôtisseurs, January 1969. A Polynesian banquet, with reception hors d'oeuvres chosen to add a note of culinary history. Beverages carry out the Polynesian theme.

Les Intronisés

Joseph Amendola	Leopoldo Hirsch
Alfred H. Daniels	Harry J. McLaughlin, Cadet
LeRoi A. Folsom	Carl F. Roessler

Members and Guests

Mr. John H. Bogrette, Jr.	Mr. and Mrs. Robert A. Meyer
Mr. Maurice Bonfis	Mr. and Mrs. Charles S. Mueller
Mrs. Alfred H. Daniels	Miss A. E. Muir
Mr. and Mrs. Leonard P. Drabkin	Mr. and Mrs. Norman Holmes Pearson
Dr. and Mrs. Alvan Feinstein	Mrs. Natalie A. Robbins
Mr. and Mrs. Dennis N. Garvey	Mrs. Carl F. Roessler
Mr. and Mrs. Reuben A. Holden	Miss Sara Rosenberg
Mr. and Mrs. Howard Jacobs	Mr. and Mrs. Jacob Rosenthal
Mr. Alphonse S. Marcello	Mr. and Mrs. Arthur Sachs
Mr. William A. J. Marino	Mr. John E. Smith
Mr. Ronald McDaniels	Mr. and Mrs. Robert F. Thompson

Mr. Joseph P. Tonetti

Polynesian Dinner
TROPICAL DELECTABLES

Reception

Moet & Chandon Imperial Brut (Schieffelin)

THE ORIENTAL INFLUENCE

Pork Chiao Tse   Tiny Egg Rolls

Beef, Lamb, and Seafood Teriyaki

Crisp Wonton

Wan Fu "Chinese Wine"

FROM THE PORTUGUESE ANCESTORS

Curried Meat Turnovers   Chicken Satés

South Pacific Pineapple Wine

THE HISPANO–PHILIPPINE HERITAGE

Seviche De Pescado   Platanos Fritos

NATIVE KAU KAU

Lomi Lomi Salmon Steaming Lau-Lau Rumaki

Polynesian Punch

Glacéd Pineapple "Do It Yourself Wikiwiki"

Dinner

Soup of Avocado and Coconut

Johannisberger Klausergarten Estate Graf Schoenborn 1965 (Sichel)

Island Abalone served with a Pungent Ginger Sauce

Lime Nectar & Papaya to Refresh your Spirits

Chateauneuf du Pape Blanc, 1966, Rochette (Kobrand)

An Original by "Hale Hanat" as executed on Papeete

Pinot Rosé d'Alsace, 1966, Jerome Lorenze

Crisp Honey-Flavored Duckling Baked in Melon

Nasturtium Leaves, Bamboo Shoots and Radishes Tossed in Sesame Oil

Mme. Tsou's Sesame Rolls

Barsac, 1961, Sichel

Sweet Little Surprises from The South Pacific

Ginger Brandy, Garnier

Kauna Coffee of the Islands

Chefs de Cuisine	Maitres d'Hotel
Arno Schmidt	Dennis Lee Powell
Jean Nicolas	Richard E. Saenz

Confrérie de la Chaîne des Rôtisseurs

Menu, 194th meeting of the
Wine and Food Society, Inc.,
December 1970. An authentic
Portuguese banquet, including
specialties flown in from
Portugal.

EMENTA · MENU

VINHOS · WINES

**LEACOCK MADEIRA
SERCIAL SECO**
dry fine madeira

SIP PORTO SECO
dry apéritif porto

**ESPUMANTE NATURAL
ROYAL BRUT**
natural sparkling wine

**VINHO VERDE
CASAL GARCIA**
green wine

SERRA BRANCO
white wine

DÃO GRÃO VASCO TINTO
red wine

**PORTO VINTAGE
NIEPOORT 1944**
vintage porto

ACEPIPES VARIADOS
hors d'oeuvre

> **SANTOLA NO CARRO**
> *spider crab in "carriage"*

> **LAGOSTINS DE CASCAIS**
> *crayfish from cascais*

> **LINGUIÇA**
> *portuguese sausage*

PEIXE
fish

> **CALDEIRADA À FRAGATEIRA**
> *"riverboat" stew*

SOPA
soup

> **CALDO VERDE**
> *green soup*

CAÇA
game

> **PERDIZ CONVENTO DE ALCÂNTARA E
> ERVILHAS COM PAIO**
> *partridge in the style of "Alcântara Convent"
> and peas cooked with pork sausage*

QUEIJOS
cheeses

> **SERRA · AZEITÃO · CASTELO BRANCO**

DOCE
dessert

> **TOUCINHO DO CÉU**
> *"bacon from heaven" almond dessert*

CAFÉ PORTUGUÊS
portuguese coffee

Menu interior, honorary dinner of the Culinary Institute of America, January 1975. An elaborate reception buffet preceeds this banquet.

Réception		*Diner*

PREMIÈRE ASSIETTE

L'Essence Provencale Bien Chaude
Paillettes Waldorf-Astoria

Taittinger Brut La Francaise
Kobrand Corporation

Saucissons Chauds, Assortis

1973 Bereich Bernkastel
H. Sichel Sohne

Surprise de Fromage

DEUXIÈME ASSIETTE

Chateau Bouscaut 1970
Austin, Nichols & Co., Inc.

Ragout d'Escargots, Ville Bernier

Lugana 1972
Ruffino
Schieffelin

La Mousse de Truite Fumée
en Gelee
Les Oeufs de Caille au Nid
Sauce aux Fines Herbes

Cuissot de Venaison, Rôtie

Jambon Persillé

TROISIÈME ASSIETTE

Gravad Lax

Chateau Cos d'Estournel 1969
Julius Wile

La Longe de Veau Poelée
au Rosemarin
Salpicon Forestière
Courgettes Florentine Gratinées

Galantine de Canard, Salade d'Oranges

Biftek Tartare aux Champignons Marinés

ISSUE DE TABLE

Lucca Augen

Cote Rôtie 1970
Domaine Gerin
Schenley Imported Wine Company

Les Fromages d'Amerique et
de la Belle France
La Corbeille des Raisins
Muris au Soleil

Roulade de Boeuf, Institut Culinaire

Bundnerfleisch Mit Birnen

LE BOUTEHORS

La Charlotte Reinette
La Sauce au Grand Marnier

Mousse de Foie de Volaille

CAFÉ

La Pouyade-Grande Champagne
Jean Fillioux
Kobrand Corporation
Pippermint Get
B & B Liqueur D.O.M.
Julius Wile Sons & Co.

Fantaisie Amphitryon

Le Café des Montagnes

Garde Manger Instructors
Frederic Sonnenschmidt, Coordinator
Stephen Beno

Students
Group 309

Chef de Cuisine
Arno Schmidt

Maitre d'Hôtel
Guenther Noeth

Director of Catering
William Grimley

Wine and Food Selection

When selecting wines for a gourmet dinner or regular banquet, if the guest does not specify a specific wine or wines from a certain region, be open-minded. California produces excellent wines and recently fine wines have become available from New York and Ohio. Until now, French wines have dominated the banquet scene. Fine wines are imported from many other countries, and it might be interesting for a group to try something different for a change. Some years ago I suggested to a renowned gourmet society that they serve an Austrian wine at one of their dinners, and the wine was a great success.

Food selected for a gourmet dinner must be light. Heavy fried food, thick soups and sauces, and gaseous vegetables must be avoided. Portions must be small; starch must be used sparingly. People should not feel stuffed after having eaten a gourmet dinner; rather, they should feel pleasantly satisfied. Portion size is also most important. If you usually serve small portions, make them even smaller. The plates, naturally, must be in proportion to avoid having the portions look skimpy. If the dinner plate is 12 inches in diameter, you cannot put a tiny piece of meat and a small garnish on it and have it look well.

Some chefs stay away from tomatoes because the acidity will kill the taste of fine wine. The same is true of very sour dressings. Endive and artichokes are also suspect because they have a slight bitter taste. The cheese tray should be interesting but should not feature cheeses with a strong smell.

The reception before a gourmet dinner should be like the overture of an opera—a taste of what will come during the evening. Little food should be served, enabling the guests to enjoy the big dinner to follow. Still, the reception food can be interesting and slightly educational. There are many ways of accomplishing this: offer a selection of four to six interesting light soups served in small cups from a buffet, or a selection of two or three varieties of smoked fish plus one meat dish. There could be a choice of six different pates, some with game if the season is right, others with fowl, and some made with seafood. There could be a selection of several kinds of oysters flown in from different parts of the country to give the guests the opportunity to taste a Cape Cod oyster and then compare it with a Chincoteaque or Malpeque oyster.

At the reception for a gourmet dinner, the only liquor served is sherry, champagne, or white wine. Hard liquor is never served at such a reception.

Menu, testimonial dinner at the Plaza Hotel, May 1970. Note the elaborate description of the final course.

Avant l'Oeuvre

Pernod, Vermouth Cassis
Dubonnet, Byrrh
Canadian Club et G. & B.

AMUSE-BOUCHE

Première Assiette

Germiny Royal Frappé

·◉·

Deuxième Assiette

Vins
La Doucette Pouilly Fûmé
Château du Nozet 1967

Gratin de Langoustines des Côtes d'Armorique
Cardinal

·◉·

Troisième Assiette

Beaujolais - Villages
Nuits St. Georges
(Côte d'or) 1967

Rognonnade de Veau des Maîtres-Queux
Endives Braisées à la Moelle
Petites Carottes au Beurre
Pommes Dauphine

·◉·

Entr' Act

Granité des Trois Epis

·◉·

Quatrième Assiette

De la Fromagerie
Brie, Boursault et Roquefort de France
Accompagnés des Feuilles des Cavernes du Kentucky
Parfumées à l'Huile Vierge et au Citron
Flûte Maison

·◉·

L'Apothéose

Champagne
Mercier

La Cassata Fantaisie
présentée par le Maître Pâtissier
La Toque entourée de Sucreries
Le Café Noir . . . comme le diable
et brûlant . . . comme l'amour
Cognac - Liqueurs

Chefs des Cuisines   *Directeur des Banquets*   *Maître d'Hôtel*
ANDRE RENE   BART MOORE   ANTONIUS PAPPAS

Brigade
Sous Chef: JOSEPH TROMBETTI
Chef des Banquets: JEAN-CLAUDE NEDELEC
Chef Pâtissier: JOSEPH TARANTINO

CONCLUDING THE GOURMET DINNER

A gourmet dinner is an exhibition of good taste. Cordials, little sweets, and demi-tasse coffee are always served after a gourmet dinner. Years ago, it was customary to pass cigars after such a dinner. Many people find this practice objectionable today, and we have to leave this decision up to the host. I do not smoke and would hate to sit next to somebody smoking, their smoke drifting into my face.

During these concluding enjoyments, the accolade to the chef should be presented. Normally, the host says a few words and the chef, resplendent in a clean uniform, is called in and congratulated. Even if the dinner is not an unqualified success, the chef should be called in and thanked. The chef, in turn, should call his or her closest colleagues who worked on the dinner: the sous chef, the banquet chef, and the pastry chef. Then the director of catering should be summoned, who, in turn, should call on the headwaiter to take a bow. At this point, a waiter should be standing by with the necessary number of champagne glasses, and the crew should toast the host or hostess and the party.

Few people realise the amount of thought, anxiety, and plain hard work that go into planning and executing a successful gourmet dinner. I have seen chefs who were physically exhausted to the point of collapse after a dinner. Ways and means should be explored to reward the chef for such extraordinary effort. A nice letter of congratulation, a few bottles of wine sent to his or her house, or perhaps an invitation to the chef and his or her spouse for the next dinner of the gourmet society are suitable tokens of appreciation.

The English used here is so descriptive that the menu is as elegant as any written in French.

The Fare

COCKTAILS

*Persian Caviar
and the Fruits of the Seas and the Lakes*

·

FINO SHERRY

*A Bisque of the Oysters
of the Atlantic*

·

PULIGNY-MONTRACHET, 1953
ESTATE BOTTLED BY SAUZET

*Canadian Pacific Salmon
with a Nantua Sauce*

·

MUSIGNY, 1952
ESTATE BOTTLED BY
ADRIEN

*Saddle of Spring Lamb
from the Salt Meadows of Kentucky
A Gratin of New England Marrow Squash
and Maryland Tomatoes
Small Roasted Potatoes*

·

Apple Brandy Sherbet

·

CHÂTEAU PETRUS 1945

*Goose Liver with Truffles
as prepared in Strasbourg
Filets of Long Island Duckling*

·

CHÂTEAU LA GAFFELIERE-
NAUDES 1937

Brie Cheese of France

·

CHÂTEAU
D'YQUEM 1942

*A Charlotte of Mohawk Valley Apples
with it's Garniture*

·

CHÂTEAU DE MARSAN
PRIVATE RESERVE
ARMAGNAC VIEILLE CURE

Haitian Coffee

Writing Menus in English

13

What eye-catching packaging does for the retail business, the language on the menu does for banquet sales. A properly presented, well-written menu that has a special flair tells the host or hostess that the planned event will be long remembered by those who attend. The menu should suit the occasion and tell the truth. The language should not sound too expensive or elegant if the meal is to be simple. It should not be too complicated if the majority of the guests are rather unsophisticated. The menu should tell the client what the guests will be served.

A menu tells people what they will get to eat. The basic reason for writing a menu is to communicate that information. Menu language should be a little poetic, perhaps even a bit mysterious. Artful menu language adds excitement to the occasion. At the same time, the language should be precise enough to be clearly understood by the client and the chef. A menu is a promise in writing, and there is nothing more embarrassing than having to explain to the client or to the chef that something written on a menu does not mean what it appears to mean. For both legal and ethical reasons a menu must be truthful.

To comply with the above guidelines, foreign words should be avoided wherever they can be replaced with suitable English words, words that are the equivalent in beauty and flair. All too often foreign words—usually French—are used as a crutch to confuse the guest and to add meaningless embellishment to the menu. The practice supposedly makes the menu elegant. This is nonsense. In my estimation, English is the best language to use in writing menus for English-speaking audiences. English is so rich in words that a suitable English word can usually be found to replace a French term.

GIVE A MENU EYE APPEAL

Before discussing the actual choice of words for the menu, let us review the appearance of the menu. To ensure that all people involved understand how the meal will be served, each course should be clearly separated from the next. This can be achieved by lines, asterisks, some repeated motif, or simply the ample use of space. Whatever items are to be served together at one time should be listed together. If at all possible, enough words should be used in describing menu items to indicate the relative importance of certain courses. This will not be the case if the main course is given only a short, two-word description while the accompanying vegetables take up three long lines.

For clarity and appearance, a certain amount of poetic license in the use of capitalization and punctuation is permitted on menus. Usually, all nouns are written using a capital letter, while every line on the menu uses a capital letter for the first word. Starting a new line on the

Figure 13.1.   "Tired" words to avoid in your menus.

My advice on the following menu terms is too avoid them whenever possible. Too frequent use has made them overly familiar. The good menu writer will find other, more intriguing ways to express their meaning, and will do so in English.

Tossed	Maison
Laced	Center cut
Fresh	Du jour
Supreme	Delicate
Almondine	Garni
Milkfed	Chopped sirloin
Succulent	Doré (golden brown)
Maraschino cherry	Half broiled
Demi	Au beurre
On tasse	Parfait
En tasse	Style
Glace	A la mode

menu with words like "with" or "and" should therefore be avoided. If foreign words must be used, they should be spelled correctly and not anglicized. (See the next chapter for a list of frequently misspelled foreign words.)

SELECT WORDS WITH CARE

A list of English and foreign nouns, expressions, and verbs that I believe should be banned from menus appears in Figure 12.1. This list is subjective, reflects my taste, and can be argued about endlessly. I have also deliberately left it up to you, the reader, to find substitute words for the words you shouldn't use.

Special attention should be paid to descriptive words in menu writing. You must strive to remain credible even as you avoid sounding comical. I have seen some rather comical expressions on menus. One that comes to mind is "Beer battered Shrimp" which makes me think that these happy shrimp were lying in beer until "battered."

The word fresh is especially tricky. We hope—and assume—that in a fine kitchen everything is fresh. However, we also know that not everything can be fresh at all times. How fresh is fresh? If the dish was prepared yesterday, is it still fresh? What about fresh-frozen—does this exist at all? Menu use of the word fresh can also come in conflict with truth-in-menu laws. I recommend omitting the word fresh from menus as much as possible, using it only to identify merchandise that is often frozen but seasonally available fresh. One such example would be asparagus when it is in season. Fresh could also be used to describe certain berries or perhaps a special fish flown in from a faraway place. But even in these cases, the use of the word fresh can be avoided. "The very first Asparagus" sounds fine on a menu, providing it is true. "Season's green Asparagus" also indicates freshness to most people.

ADD GEOGRAPHICAL NAMES

Geographical names, such as live crayfish from Louisiana, North Atlantic halibut, Chesapeake Bay shad and roe, and Lynnhaven oysters, are marvelous additions to menus. Attention must be paid to be sure that any claim to a geographic origin can be substantiated, however. A geographic name can also indicate a certain style of preparation, a certain cut of meat, or a certain spice. These terms provide considerable leeway which, exercised with caution can make a menu more distinctive yet not misleading to the public.

New York strip steak does not come from New York city nor from New York State. However, it is always a steak cut from the sirloin, or shell, of beef. On the other hand, Virginia ham is a certain type of ham produced in a number of southern states, but in especially large numbers in Virginia. A relatively salty, cold smoked ham covered with pepper, it looks and tastes different from other smoked hams. Smithfield is a town in Virginia where this delicious ham is produced, and it would be unfair, misleading, and perhaps illegal to serve as Smithfield ham an odd ham that happened to be on hand.

There is also Virginia-style baked ham. This can be any ham baked with brown sugar, molasses, spices, and perhaps fruit. Incidentally, the word style used this way should be avoided, if at all possible. Maybe in the above case we could use such a description as glazed baked ham, colonial baked ham or Monticello baked ham, (making reference to the refined tastes of Thomas Jefferson).

ADD COOKING TERMS

You can also mention a cooking process on a menu to make it read well, but be careful not to sound ridiculous. Hickory smoked is an old cliche from the supermarket. What about using cold smoked or honey cured? Words like baked, marinated, glazed, simmered, poached, roasted, grilled, broiled, and boiled are popular. Certain desirable characteristics that are expected in a specific food can also be mentioned on the menu. "Crisp Duckling Breast with tiny Grapes" is a good example of this style.

Menu, dinner for the American-Irish Historical Society. Place names and menu selections highlight the evening's Irish theme.

MENU

*Fluffy Pasty with
Jugged Venison in Claret Wine*

⚜

PINOT CHARDONNAY

*Shannon River Salmon
Broiled with Prawn Butter*

⚜

Irish Mist Sherbet

⚜

CABERNET MERLOT

*Boned Squab Stuffed with Pate
and Penny Loaves
Sauce Flavored with Port
Tiny Sprouts*

⚜

LAURENT PERRIER
CHAMPAGNE

*Bibb Lettuce Salad
Normandy Brie Cheese
Jacob's Crackers*

⚜

*Hot Charlotte of Apples and Currants
Whipped Ennis Cream*

⚜

Dried Fruits

⚜

Demi Tasse

When using cooking terms on the menu, make sure they are understood by all who will be reading them. Sauté means to cook quickly in fat, preferably by gently tossing the product being cooked. You cannot sauté anything in sherry wine or in mushroom sauce. Broil means to cook something that is about portion size under or with dry heat. The product must be covered with some sort of fat to prevent drying out the surface, unless the item being broiled has a very fatty skin. The broiled product is always served dry with a suitable sauce either on the side or around it. You cannot have a broiled fish glazed with Mornay sauce. If you want to cook fish and sauce together, and if you want the surface to brown, the proper terminology to use in describing the dish on the menu is baked.

Careless mistakes can creep into menu writing, as on this menu listing "Planked Chopped Sirloin Steak broiled with Mashed Potatoes." As a cook, I visualized the chopped steak smeared with mashed potato and put under the broiler—not an appealing picture. Making a verb out of a noun must also be avoided in menu writing. Expressions like parsleyed potatoes, sherried seafood, and herbed scrambled eggs should not be used.

Meat on the Menu

Special attention should be paid in making references to meat grades and meat cuts. USDA grades—prime, choice, good and so on—are not interchangeable. Meat identified by these terms must be USDA graded. A certain amount of freedom is permissible when describing meat cuts, although you should remember that, in banquet terminology, words like roast rib of beef, filet mignon, rack of lamb, tenderloin, lamb chop, loin chop and others are well established and cannot be interchanged.

Veal is available under a number of name brands. These brand names can be used if desired. Chops and cutlets must be solid pieces of meat, not chopped. The word steak implies 100 per cent meat; chopped steak means meat without any filler or extender.

There is also confusion about the terms spring lamb and baby lamb. Spring lamb is lamb born in the spring, as late as April or May, in which case it may not reach the market until as late as August. Baby lamb is a very small lamb, having a maximum weight with the pelt, on, of 35 lbs. Since the yield from a baby lamb is small, it is not an item to use for banquets.

Many menus use the word capon indiscriminately. Capon is a castrated male bird that is specially fattened and, therefore, rather large. Roast capon can be a fine speciality in an elegant restaruant, but the size and price of the bird make it impractical to serve capon breast for

With its theme of seafood, this menu from La Chaîne des Rôtisseurs of New York features a distinctive variety of oysters. Note the range of beverages, from pinot Chardonnay to "moonshine."

OYSTER MENU
BAR & RESTAURANT

LA CHAINE DES ROTISSEURS
NEW YORK CHAPTER
Presents
A Dinner of American Beverages and Seafood
November 13, 1975

Honored Guests

PAUL BOCUSE	JEAN TROISGROS	FRANÇOIS BISE	ALAIN CHAPEL	LOUIS OUTIER

Oysters:
Malpeque, Belon (Maine), Wellfleet, Cotuit, Blue Point,
Kent Island, Chincoteague, Apalachicola
Mondavi Fumé Blanc

Sautéed Tongues and Cheeks of Codfish
Spring Mountain Sauvignon Blanc

Bay Scallops and Mussels in Mustard Vinaigrette
on Fresh Leaf Spinach
Heitz Pinot Blanc

Maryland Crab Cake
Freemark Abby Pinot Chardonnay

Philadelphia Snapper Soup

Maine Lobster from Spruce Harbour
Michelob Beer

Chateau Saint Jean Johannisberg Riesling 1974
Selected Late Harvest

Fortified Big Mac

Coffee
Georgia Moonshine

Hosts: Roger Yaseen
Jerome Brody
Bailli of New York: William Meyer

banquets. Squab is the culinary term for pigeon, so to avoid misunderstanding the words squab chicken should not be used to describe a small chicken.

There is a world of difference between shrimp and scampi. Shrimp come in all sizes, and very large ones can be called Jumbo, like the famous elephant of Barnum and Bailey and Ringling Bros. Circus fame. Large shrimp can be split and broiled with garlic and oil in the same way that scampi is prepared in Mediterranean countries. A scampi is a crustacean with a pale pink body, a meaty tail, and very slender claws. Scampi used to come from the Adriatic Sea, but are imported today from all over the world and described as Icelandic Lobster tails, langostino tails, or Danish lobster tails.

Trade Names

Certain trade names have almost become household words although they still remain the property of companies or of producing cooperatives, and this must be kept in mind when writing menus. The Roquefort Cheese Manufacturers are constantly watching to see that blue cheese dressing is not called Roquefort dressing when mentioned on menus. Jello is a trade name owned by General Foods Company. Unless their product is used, the word gelatin should be used on the menu.

Plural or Singular?

Menus are always directed to an individual diner. This simple rule makes it easy to decide when to use the plural and when to use the singular on a menu. The plural is used for strawberries, because the guest will get more than one. It is "Baked Potato" or sliced "Beefsteak Tomato," but "Cherry Tomatoes" are sprinkled over a salad. For a number of words in common use on menus, like fried fish or beef stew, there is no plural.

Sauce or Gravy?

There is a distinct difference between sauce and gravy and that difference should be understood by the menu writer. A gravy is always part of a specific cooking process. When roasting or pan frying meat, the resulting pan juices are thickened and served as gravy. The best known example is giblet gravy, served with turkey. Gravy has an old-fashioned, home-cooking sound and does not make a very elegant impression. A sauce can be made independently from the dish it is served with, for example, tomato sauce, Hollandaise sauce, or strawberry sauce. Sauces indicate a more elegant presentation for the food they accompany.

Menu, spring dinner for Les Amis d'Escoffier, April 1976. This was one page of an eight-page menu. Three other pages are reproduced here. Together they provide a detailed portrait of the banquet served that evening.

La Reception

Taittinger La Francaise Brut
Cordon d'Alsace Willm 1973
Benmarl Seyval Blanc 1974
Sercial Madeira, Solera of 1860

Fantaisies - Chaudes et Froides
    Palourdes Escoffier
    Huitres à la Moutarde
    Tartelette au Welsh Rabbit

Fumé à l'Institute:
    Saumon
        Esturgeon
    Caviare de Saumon
    Poire d'Avocat aux Crevettes

Le Diner

Club Dry Amontillado

Clos des Mouches 1973

Chateau Petit Village 1964

Corton Clos du Roi 1962

Asti Spumante Fontanafredda

Benedictine
Chartreuse V.E.P.
Courvoisier V.S.O.P.
Framboise

Soupe à la Queue de Boeuf Amontillado

Les Homards Lafayette
Riz Pilaf

Les Pintadeaux au Genièvre
Les Pommes de Terre Fondantes
Les Petits Pois à la Française

Le Soufflé au Parmesan
La Salade Escarole aux Fines Herbes

Le Trocadéro Lafayette

Le Café des Gourmets

Reception description, spring
dinner for Les Amis d'Escoffier,
April 1976. Note the opening
line that sets the stage for the
evening.

This dinner replicates the first grand dinner of Les Amis d'Escoffier Society of New York, which was held in the Jantzen Suite of the Waldorf Astoria on 30 March 1936.

La Reception ~ Description

Palourdes Escoffier
Fresh clams are opened, dotted with butter, finely chopped shallots, minced chives and piquant Escoffier Sauce, then cooked quickly in a hot oven.

Huitres à la Moutarde
Oysters are rolled in golden mustard, wrapped in bacon and a cloak of bread crumbs, then skewered and grilled.

Tartelette au Welsh Rabbit
Cheddar cheese is melted with ale, mustard, and cayenne pepper to make the traditional Welsh Rabbit, then spooned steaming onto small pastries.

Fumé à l'Institute: Saumon et Esturgeon
Salmon and sturgeon prepared by Institute students in our own smokehouse and served on Melba toast - an Escoffier invention.

Caviare de Saumon
Because relations with Russia were strained in 1936, many American epicures took to eating the logical substitute for Black Sea caviar, native salmon eggs, this afternoon served as a canape with herbed (watercress, chervil, chives, and spinach) butter.

Poire d'Avocat aux Crevettes
In 1936, Americans were just discovering the avocado! Today, it is marinated in white wine and lemon juice before topping with tiny shrimp nestled in a sauce made of mayonnaise, horseradish, ketchup, Madeira, brandy, mustard, dill and paprika.

Dinner description, spring dinner for Les Amis d'Escoffier, April 1976. Historic notes are woven in among inviting descriptions of the food to be served.

Le Diner - Description

Soupe à la Queue de Boeuf Amontillado

Although clear, this oxtail soup is very rich in flavor, made even more so with a discreet lacing of the accompanying Sherry.

Les Homards Lafayette
Riz Pilaf

Maine lobster is lightly steamed then removed from the shell, the coral reserved, then sauteed lightly with carrots, celery, leaks and garlic. After flaming with cognac, the mixture is dampened with white wine and fish stock, then tomatoes (and tomato sauce) with thyme, bay leaves, tarragon, salt, pepper, and cayenne pepper are added. Simmering intermingles the flavors, and the cooking medium is enhanced with heavy cream, butter and lobster coral to create a smooth sauce, emrobing the lobster. Tonight it's served on a bed on rice pilaf with a garniture of truffles rather than in the half shell.

Les Pintadeaux au Genièvre
Les Pommes de Terre Fondantes
Les Petits Pois à la Française

Young, tender, guinea hen, seasoned with Juniper butter and a lightly spiced pork forcemeat, is served with shaped baked potatoes and tiny peas cooked with lettuce, butter, onions, and salt, then finished with sugar, chicken consomme, parsley and chervil.

Le Souffle au Parmesan

Because of its holding power, Parmesan presented few problems in slow transatlantic shipping of the 1930's. For this reason, it was popular to make it the chief ingredient in souffles which would serve as the cheese course at fine dinners.

La Salade Escarole aux Fines Herbes

Curly endive is swathed in zesty dressing liberally sprinkled with the Chef Garde Manger's choice of herbs.

Le Trocadéro Lafayette

Ice cream with Kirsch-infused strawberries is hidden between two layers of crispy puff pastry, slathered with sweetened whipped cream and decorated with more strawberries.

Wine descriptions, spring
dinner for Les Amis d'Escoffier,
April 1976. Well-written
descriptions inform the guests
and heighten expectations.

Les Vins ~ Description

Ces vins etaient selectionnés par le Comité de la Bonne Bouche qui les ont goutés et, pour prendre une décision completement égale, les ont choisis sans savant leurs noms. [These wines were selected by the Comite de la Bonne Bouche who tasted them with the lobster and the guinea hen and, to make a completely fair decision, chose them without knowing their identities.]

Taittinger La Française Brut Champagne, in Magnums, Imported by Kobrand Corp.
An elegant sparkling wine made from the first pressing of the Champagne region's finest red and white grapes, a predominance of the latter making for distinctive lightness and delicacy.

Cordon d'Alsace Willm, 1973, Imported by Julius Wile Sons & Co.
Blended from the Sylvaner, Riesling and Traminer grapes, cousins of those grown farther Northeast in the Rhine Valley, this gracious wine from France is somewhat prouder and heartier than its German counterparts.

Benmarl Seyval Blanc 1974, Produced by Benmarl Vineyards, Marlboro, NY
The French viniculturist Seyve-Villard never revealed the parents of this hybrid grape which is grown so successfully here in the Hudson Valley.

Leacock Sercial Madeira, Solera of 1860, Imported by Julius Wile Sons & Co.
From the white Sercial grape comes this golden, highly perfumed wine of Madeira, an uncommon combination of rich, aromatic scent and sharp, dry taste.

Duff Gordon Club Dry Amontillado, Imported by Renfield Importers
Moderate in both dryness and coloration, this Sherry is noted for its characteristic cleanliness and nuttiness, breathing 'Spain' with each taste.

Clos des Mouches 1973, Shipped by Jos. Drouhin, Imported by Dreyfus Ashby & Co.
A product of Burgundy's Cote de Beaune in the township Beaune, and of the Chardonnay grape, this premier cru wine is noted for its ampler than average body and great elegance.

Chateau Petit Village 1964, Shipped by Gineset, Imported by Kobrand Corp.
Containing more of the Cabernet Sauvignon grape than is usually found in other wines of Pomerol, this wine is very full-bodied and has a big bouquet, notably reminiscent of violets, a bouquet released by the decanting sometime before service.

Corton Clos du Roi 1962, Shipped by Jos. Drouhin, Imported by Dreyful Ashby & Co.
Another Cote de Beaune wine - from the north end - this is round, lush, and rich, with the characteristically powerful bouquet of its principal grape, the noble Pinot Noir. Decanted just prior to service.

Asti Spumante Fontanafredda, Imported by Schenley World T. & I.
This sparkling wine, produced in the Piedmont region of Northwestern Italy, carries with it the honey-like sweetness and rich bouquet of the Muscat grape.

Benedictine, Imported by Julius Wile Sons & Co.
First developed in 1510 as a medicine to ease the fatigue, and raise the spirits, of weary monks, this sweet liqueur is flavored with a secret combination of herbs, plants, and fruit peels.

Chartreuse V.E.P., Imported by Schieffelin & Co.
Sometimes called the world's most mysterious liqueur, this herb and plant flavored elixer was developed by Chartreusian monks, who age a small part of their production in a special cellar, offering it as Chartreuse V.E.P. only after time has worked its wonders upon it.

Courvoisier V.S.O.P., Imported by W. A. Taylor
Aged in limosin oak for at least five years, this noble product of white grapes is flavorful but even better known for the potent bouquet which fills the snifter to the brim.

Framboise, Produced by G. E. Massenez, Imported by Dreyfus Ashby & Co.
Fresh raspberries are gathered, fermented, and distilled, then the resultant fruit brandy is quickly bottled so that none of the berries' fragrance will be lost. Here served frozen for added refreshment.

Figure 13.2.   Sample menu for February.

Vichyssoise

****

Lobster Newburgh

Rice Pilaff

****

Loin of Lamb Chops

Asparagus* Hollandaise Sauce

Au Gratin Potatoes

****

Avocado Salad

****

Baked Alaska

****

Coffee

Sunday, February 12, 1978

Special Names

Years ago French chefs gave names to the garnishes that were served with dishes. All of these names have a story behind them. Some names are geographical names; some are names of regions famous for certain cooking styles. In the United States, we do the same thing today, except that we generally use words related to our own products. It would be foolish to call asparagus soup Potage Argenteuil because our asparagus would probably come from California, not from Argenteuil, a suburb of Paris. As a matter of fact, I think very little asparagus is grown there now, so even in France the name is outmoded.

Other garnishes honor famous personalities of their times, spectacular events such as battles won, and well-known restaurants; one even honors a racehorse. This custom makes fascinating culinary history, but using such names indiscriminately does not help to make menus easier to understand. The purpose of a menu is to communicate. Sprinkling the menu with names that have no meaning to the reader does not make sense.

On the other hand, words describing certain garnishes, cooking methods, as well as foreign expressions used in discussing food have become part of menu language and can be used with caution. The words Maitre d'Hotel, Meunière, Jardinière, or Boulangère are known in many parts of the country; they should be used in menu descriptions if the dish is prepared in a manner that corresponds to the name used on the menu. Keep in mind, though, that a needless mixture of languages should be avoided in menu writing, unless the menus are directed to an ethnic group. Good taste and the desire to communicate should always be the guiding rules.

UPGRADING A MENU

Figure 13.2 shows a menu printed some time ago. It was used and read by hundreds of guests. In addition to some questionable choices on the menu (see chapter 7, Basic Rules of Menu Construction, for clues on how to spot items that could be improved) the menu language was poorly chosen. Nor was the menu proofread well; it contains a misspelled word. The menu has no flair and no romance, although the meal surely must have cost a lot of money. Even if the food was good, the guests did not get the total experience they deserved. Good food should be introduced by a good menu.

Let's see how we can upgrade this menu. We will cause no increase in cost to the establishment, nor will we break any truth-in-menu laws. Moreover, none of our changes should sound corny. Let's begin with the soup. Vichyssoise can be served hot or cold. Let's assume that this time the soup was served cold. Why not mention that fact on the menu? To add a little extra interest, we might also mention chives—the customary garnish for vichyssoise.

Lobster Newburgh seems to be a rather brief and unexciting description for such an expensive dish. It would be more impressive to list it as Lobster sauté Newburgh. This would be quite appropriate since in the preparation of this dish the lobster pieces are sautéed in butter before the sherry wine and cream are added. It could also be listed as Creamed Lobster Newburgh, but, since this menu has a great deal of cream, it might be wiser not to emphasize. Lobster Newburgh Amontillado would be a permissible description, if genuine Amontillado sherry from Spain was used in it, or if another famous brand of sherry were to be used, that name could be featured. For this menu, however, I prefer Lobster sauté Newburgh because the next course is a broiled item.

Rice Pilaff does not read well to me. In French, the proper term would be Riz Pilaw or Riz Pilaf. In English, however we use the terms

Figure 13.3.   **Revised menu for February.**

Iced Vichyssoise sprinkled with Chives

****

Lobster sauté Newburgh
Pilaff Rice

****

Broiled Loin Lamb Chop
Tarragon Butter
Season's new Asparagus
Sauce Hollandaise
Potatoes au gratin

****

Avocado Half on Romaine Lettuce
Oil and Vinegar Dressing

****

Vanilla and Chocolate Baked Alaska
Melba Sauce

*****

Coffee

Spanish Rice, Yellow Rice, Baked Rice, **and so on. I think** Pilaff Rice **is more suitable for this menu.**

The menu listing for the main course is quite strange. I suspect that every guest was served only one chop, because the menu is quite substantial and loin lamb chops are rather large. To indicate some contrast with the preceding course, it would be a good idea to mention the fact that the chops are broiled. So I would change the menu to read Broiled Loin Lamb Chop. If the chef planned to add a little butter to the broiled chops, either as Butter Maitre d'Hotel, which is butter mixed with parsley, lemon juice, and spices, or butter with chopped tarragon added (and I think with lamb the latter would be best) I would like to add a line reading: Tarragon Butter **under the listing for the chop.**

Why there is an asterisk next to the asparagus is a mystery. There was no footnote on the menu. In fact, there should never be footnotes on menus. I suspect that this asterisk was just one of these little things somebody added without too much thought.

The menu was served in the middle of February. Since the menu was obviously an expensive one we can assume that fresh asparagus was served. Consequently, it certainly could have been listed as Season's new Asparagus. Hollandaise sauce is a well-known accompaniment for asparagus. In addition, in this country the sauce is so universally recognized as part of French cuisine that we can properly list it as Sauce Hollandaise. I personally prefer to see the sauce listed right alongside the asparagus on the menu. Somehow, seeing it listed that way gives me, personally, a nice mental picture of green asparagus with luscious yellow hollandaise sauce. Graphically, however, it looks better to list the sauce under the asparagus.

With the Au gratin potatoes entry, the word order has been reversed and not to advantage. It does not look well to begin a menu listing with Au. In addition, the expression au gratin is not as important to the diner as the fact that potatoes are to be included. For that reason I would suggest Potatoes au gratin.

I am not completely happy about using the words au gratin since they bring more French to the menu. However, the existing options may not be elegant enough. Potatoes baked with Cream and Cheese unfortunately emphasizes cream and also sounds too plain for this menu. Browned Potatoes is not specific enough. That could mean hashed brown potatoes, which would mislead the guests. The best choice seems to be Potatoes au gratin.

Avocado Salad is also a listing with no extra appeal. Probably every guest was served a half avocado on some lettuce. Why not mention that on the menu and heighten the guest's expectations? Also, why not describe the dressing? At the least, there would be oil and vinegar dressing. Let's mention it on the menu.

Baked Alaska does not convey much to the guest. Let us add the flavors used, and, since a suitable sauce was probably served with the baked Alaska, our version of this menu will mention the flavor of the sauce as well

Figure 13.3 shows the revised menu. It would not cost any more than the old menu, but it probably could be sold for a dollar more.

Figure 13.4 shows another menu fairly typical of those used in banquet operations. It is passable but not exciting. Supreme, as we all know, means the highest; the word came from French cuisine in which the breast of a bird or the top fillet of a flat fish is described as supreme.

Figure 13.4. Typical banquet menu.

Supreme of fresh fruits

****

Vegetable Soup en tasse

*****

Half broiled Chicken

Vegetables au beurre

Potatoes

****

Tossed Salad

****

Strawberry Parfait

****

Coffee

Our equipment manufacturers invented the supreme cup, a three piece service utensil that should be filled with ice and used to serve fruit cocktail or seafood. Since the stand is rather high, the word supreme was applied to the utensil; eventually the word was also used to describe foods served in it, hence the listing Supreme of fresh fruits. The whole set-up is very old-fashioned, and the word supreme does not tell today's customer much about a dish. As previously pointed out, the inherent pitfalls exist in using the word fresh, so that word is out too.

Half broiled Chicken in menu descriptions has always irked me. Is the chicken cooked medium like a steak? Obviously that couldn't be done. Why then use the expression: Half broiled? This entry must be changed to be clarified.

Vegetables au beurre is another poor menu listing. If possible, we should let our guests know what kind of vegetables we serve. If we offer the freshest vegetables on today's market, that practice should be noted on the menu. In addition, why use the French term au beurre? We should also describe the potatoes to be served, if possible.

Figure 13.5.   Revised typical menu.

Medley of cut Fruits on Ice

****

Garden Vegetable Soup with
Chick Peas

****

Broiled Chicken Half
Herb Butter
Zucchini and Cauliflower
Tiny Oven Roast Potatoes

****

Seasonal Salad

****

Frozen Strawberry Mousse in Glass

****

Coffee

****

Tossed is used too frequently in connection with salad. Incidentally, I have never, ever seen any body in this country tossing the salad in a commercial kitchen!

The word parfait is French and means perfect. Ingredients of the finest quality—egg yolks, sugar, cream, and fruit pulp—are whipped into a fluffy mixture that is the perfection of the ice cream chef's art. This mixture frozen and served elegantly is a parfait. There is nothing exciting about the version too often encountered in which some ice cream has been portioned into tall glasses, topped off with some whipped cream, and then called parfait. If we can create an excellent dessert, let's do it. If we do it well, it deserves a more exciting listing than parfait.

Figure 13.5 shows the rewritten menu. As before, a little rewriting has not changed the meal ordered, nor increased the cost to the catering organization. Rewriting has improved the allure and appearance of the menu, though, and may have increased its marketability as well.

Menu, Waldorf-Astoria
Distinguished Alumni Dinner,
November 1977. An excellent,
uncomplicated autumnal meal.

MENU

PETITE MARMITE HENRI IV

* * *

POUILLY FUME
"CHATEAU DU NOZET"
LADOUCETTE FRERES
1973

WEAKFISH NORMANDE

* * *

FREEMARK ABBEY
CABERNET SAUVINGON
1969

BALMORAL GROUSE PIE
CELERY IN CELERY
BRAISED CHESTNUTS

* * *

AUTUMN SALAD
BOUCHERON AND BELLE BRESANNE CHEESES

* * *

BOGGS LIQUEUR

CRANBERRY GRANITE

* * *

CHOCOLATE MACAROONS

* * *

COGNAC AND PORT

DEMI-TASSE

ESTABLISHING MEANINGS FOR MENU TERMS

Before concluding this chapter, I would like to emphasize the importance of using understood terms on all menus. Menu language is a technical language similar to the technical language used in other trades. Unlike the technical terms used in other trades, however, menu terms are less precise. Since a banquet menu is a written order, given to the chef's department and to the purchasing department, it is of paramount importance that all parties involved interpret the terms used in the same fashion. This is especially important in larger banquet operations where a number of people write menus and sell banquets. If everybody involved in banquet sales is allowed to invent names and dishes or interpret culinary terms at will, endless confusion will result. One salesperson describes a dish to a client in one way, and next door another salesperson describes the same dish altogether differently, and then, in the end, the chef will cook a private version of the dish!

To prevent this, menu term meetings should be held for all sales personnel and the chef in which the exact meaning of each term is established. The term and its meaning should then be written down and this information distributed to all salespeople.

The importance of precision in the choice of menu terms is clearly illustrated with the vegetable, beans. Many operations serve whole string beans for banquets. Others use French cut beans, others use short cut beans, and there are also wax beans on the market. As you can see, a bean is not just a bean, and if banquet salespersonnel are allowed to use any name that comes to mind for beans, the confusion can be endless.

The same is true of sole. There is genuine imported Dover sole, domestic fresh fillet of sole, frozen imported fillet of sole, rex sole, grey sole, lemon sole, and Boston sole. There may even be further local varieties. A salesperson who sells broiled fillet of rex sole in New York can confuse a lot of people. Menu language is the poetic link between the culinary art and the guest. Good menu language is poetry, but it must be meaningful poetry that draws a true picture of what is to be served.

Menu, dinner, January 1938.
The writer of this menu
delighted in French, as can be
seen especially in the lovely
descriptions of the last two
courses.

Assortiment de Bonnes Choses Chaudes
et Froides Servies en Antichambre
avec les Apéritifs

Menu

Potage Bonne-Femme

Chablis Milly 1929

Mousse de Sole au Champagne avec
le Cardinal des Mers Polignac

Poitrine de Volaille au Beurre Noisette
Petits Pois Frais a l'Étuvée
Pommes de Terre Chatelaine

Pommard
Côte d'Or 1929

Parfait de Foie Gras de Strasbourg
sur Jambon de Virginie à la Gelée Rosée

Il Sera servi en Même Temps
Une Bonne Salade d'Automne
Bien Mélangée avec de la Délicieuse Huile
d'Olive de Provence

Biscuit Glace aux Perles de Lorraine
Fraises au Suc de Framboises

Cognac

Mille Feuilles

Café

Cigares
Cigarettes

Hotel Pierre
New York

Samedi, le 8 Janvier, 1938

Writing Menus in French and Other Languages

To one who knows French people, it often seems nothing is more sacred to them than the French language. Following closely in importance are the art of French gastronomy and the description of its creations in the correct culinary French terms. Yet culinary French is so often abused outside France that it is the exception, not the rule, when one finds a well-written menu in the French language. Even in newspaper articles about French gastronomy, in advertisements for French cuisine, and in some cooking schools, French is used inaccurately.

The reason for the general misuse of French in reference to gastronomy is that culinary French is a technical language that must be learned. Words cannot always be translated literally into English. In addition, French grammer is quite different from English grammer and is, in ways, more complicated. This chapter cannot teach you how to write beautiful menus in French, but it will tell you things to watch out for and mistakes to avoid.

French is the most beautiful culinary language I know. In this chapter you will see several examples of well-written French menus. These menus sound marvelously poetic in French, but often seem ridiculous when translated literally into English. This, of course, would be true of many translations. The names for various foods change from country to country so much that translations made with the use of a limited dictionary can easily become inaccurate, even silly.

I remember an occasion when someone tried to translate a standard American room service menu into French. Soon he came to the popular American breakfast selection, French toast, and with the help of a little pocket dictionary translated it as Toast a la Française. That was meaningless of course, because French toast properly translated is Pain perdu or lost bread. Actually, this is a lesser-known dessert in France; our French toast would never be served as a breakfast item in France. This example shows why a solid knowledge of French culinary terms is essential.

HOW TO LEARN CULINARY FRENCH

French-English dictionaries only sometimes identify the culinary meanings of French words. If the culinary meaning is not included among dictionary definitions, the menu writer must look further for the information. Such knowledge can be acquired by working in fine French restaurants here or abroad. I know a prominent American-born chef who learned to speak French fluently in New York City hotel kitchens. Needless to say, he also mastered the meaning of French culinary terms. For those who cannot work in a French kitchen, the

Menu (reproduced same size),
September 1959. A classical
French menu.

Menu

Tartelette Maisonette

———

Le Borschock au Madère
Paillettes Diablées

———

La Poularde Poëlée au Champagne
La Mousseline Forestière Gratinée
Céleri au Beurre Fines Herbes

———

Les Feuilles Vertes Melangées

———

L'Ananas Voilé à l'Orientale
La Corbeille de Friandises

Café Moka

La Maisonette   *Jeudi le 10 Septembre 1959*

best way to acquire the necessary knowledge of the language is to get hold of cookbooks, culinary encyclopedias, or culinary dictionaries that are written in French. Two excellent resources are A Repertoire de la Cuisine, **Dupont et Malgat, Paris, and** LaRousse Gastronomique, **Librairie Larousse, Paris. The dictionaries should give English meanings. Read the cookbooks over and over again, using the encyclopedias and dictionaries as references, until you understand the meaning of the terms used.**

Grammar for French Menus

To use French properly in menu writing, you have to learn certain facts about French grammar. A person who has taught French can help you with this, but do not expect him or her to translate the whole menu for you; a teacher would not know the proper technical or culinary terms needed to describe the various dishes. Here then are a few basic rules of French grammar especially useful when writing menus.

French nouns have gender: they are either masculine or feminine. A noun's gender is indicated by the article that precedes it. Le (the) in front of a noun indicates masculine gender; la (the) indicates feminine gender. It is essential that you know the gender of a noun because, when used together, nouns, adjectives, and verbs, must be in agreement in gender and number (i.e. singular or plural). A feminine plural noun requires adjectives and verbs that have feminine plural endings. Verbs used must be in the correct tense. Since food, when ready for service, has already been prepared, the past tense must be used for the verb describing how the food was prepared. Grilled ham would be jambon grillé.

Figure 14. provides a list of frequently used French words as well as some words in other foreign languages, with the gender of each noun indicated.

Here are some examples of how the noun/gender/adjective agreement works. In French, the word for butter, beurre, is masculine. The word for sauce, sauce, on the other hand, is feminine.

Beurre vert **means green butter.** Sauce verte **means green sauce.** In translating green sauce, the letter e has been added to the adjective for green, vert, **because the adjective refers to a feminine noun,** sauce. **This rule is basic and is not difficult to apply if you know whether the noun is masculine or feminine. Another example would be** consommé blanc—blanc **means white, or simple.** Consommé you recognize already. Since the noun consommé **is masculine, the masculine form is used for the adjective** blanc. **For** la carte blanche **(which, in its simplest translation, means the white card)** carte **is feminine in gender, and** blanche, **the feminine form of** blanc **must be used with it.**

Menu, dinner of Les Amis d'Escoffier Society. This menu provides English listings after the French; note that terms such as "timbales" are assumed to be understood in both languages.

Menu

AVANT DE PASSER À TABLE

*Pink and White
1943 Mailly Champagne
Waldorf Sherry*

HUÎTRES DE PECONIC BAY, BLUE POINT ET CAPE COD ET LES CLAMS SUR GLACE

FANTAISIES AU FROMAGE

(Peconic Bay, Blue Point, Cape Cod oysters and clams on the half-shell,
simple cheese appetizers)

le Dîner

LE CONSOMMÉ DOUBLE AUX PERLES

PAILLETTES DIABLÉES

(Double Consomme with golden straws, Diablé)

*Chassagne-Montrachet 1947
Clos des Ruchottes
Magnums*

LA TIMBALE DE FRUITS DE MER NANTUA

(Timbales of Seafood)

*Château Talbot
1933 Magnums*

LE TOURNEDOS AUX CÈPES

POMME DAUPHINE   ASPERGES DE CALIFORNIE

(Tournedos of Beef with cepes)
(Dauphine potatoes — Fresh asparagus with butter)

LE TROU CHAMPENOIS

(Champagne Sherbet)

LA TERRINE SAINT HUBERT

SALADE DE SAISON

(A Waldorf specialty with field salad)

Château Coutet 1943

LE GÂTEAU ST.-HONORÉ

*Godet Cuve 51,
Montesquiou Armagnac
Private Reserve,
Vieille Cure*

DEMI-TASSE

CIGARS

ERNEST TREYVAUD, *Chef des Cuisines*

When the plural is used in French, it is usually indicated by adding the letter s to the noun. There are exceptions to the rule, but they do not occur frequently on menus. Again, the adjective must be in agreement. Haricots verts means string beans, or literally translated, green beans. You may have guessed already that because the noun haricot is masculine, the adjective vert has to be spelled without the e on the end. Unfortunately, when singular nouns start with an h, it is difficult to tell whether they are masculine or feminine, since when le or la are used to precede them, the vowel is omitted, and le or la becomes l' followed by the noun. In the above case it would be written l'haricot, if it referred to a single bean. When a noun is plural, whether the gender is feminine or masculine, the is translated as les. Since few people are ever served a single string bean for a meal, string beans would always be written in French as les haricots verts. White beans would be called, of course, les haricots blancs. Some feminine nouns in the plural end in es: a good example is les fines herbes, the fine herbs.

Verbs for Menu Writing

Verbs on menus are usually put in the past tense, as noted earlier, because the dish has already been prepared. The past tense is normally indicated by adding an e with an accent to the verb. The French language utilizes three different accents and the rules governing their use are quite difficult. Fortunately, accents are not used on capital letters in menus, and this offers a tidy way out for the inexperienced menu writer. However, a menu written completely in capital letters might be a little awkward, and it might be better, with the help of a dictionary, to place the necessary accents in their proper position.

Gateau doré means cake baked to a golden brown. Le gateau is masculine and, therefore, doré, the masculine form of the past participle is used. La sole dorée, sole with a golden brown appearance, of course, requires a feminine ending for the verb. The French verb dorer has a culinary meaning, to golden.

When the noun used is plural, the adjectives and verbs must agree. Le champignon, being masculine, when plural would be written with a verb with a masculine and plural ending. Les champignons grillés is the way to write grilled mushrooms. Les pommes soufflées are the famous potatoes fried at different degrees of heat until they blow up like little balloons. La pomme, potato, is feminine, so the menu item becomes les pommes, potatoes, with the verb soufflées added in the past tense, with a feminine plural ending.

Menu for the 2nd annual dinner
of the Braniff International
Board of Chefs, December 1977.
Inconsistency in the use of
capitalization and accents mar
this menu's French.

SECOND ANNUAL DINNER
BRANIFF INTERNATIONAL BOARD OF CHEFS

WALDORF ASTORIA,
SUITE LOUIS XVI
December 4, 1977

A LA RECEPTION

Champagne Brut   Les Delices De Canards
Pouilly Fuissé 1976   Aux Herbes De Provence
Ou Au Cassis
  De DiJon   Les Ramequins a la Suisse

LE MENU

La Petite Marmite a la Moelle En Tasse
Les Paillettes Dorées

Dézaley L'Arbalete   MeliMelo de Saumon Au Citron Vert
Premier Cru 1975

Le Carré d'Agneau Du Près Salé
      a l'ail Doux

Brouilly Chateau   Les Primeurs
  De Lachaize 1975

La Salade De Kentucky Endives Et Noix
Chambolle-Musigny Les Fromages De France
    1970
La Poire Nicoleau
Creme — Brulée

Friandises
Le Café De Colombie

Liqueurs

Executive Chef
Arno B. Schmidt

ADDING ACCOMPANIMENTS TO MENUS

Most of this grammar lesson is over, but a little more must be explained. When one item is served with another the word used to link the two words must agree in gender and number with the accompanying item. A good example is our famous roast beef or boeuf (masculine) rôti au Jus. Le jus means juice, any kind of juice; au means with. The roasted rib is served in its natural juice and that is written au jus, which is translated in culinary language to in its own juice. If the noun in question is feminine, the connecting words are a la. For example, creamed spinach would be epinards à la crème.

When the noun is plural, the connecting word aux is used, whether the noun it accompanies is masculine or feminine. For example, salade aux crevettes means salad with shrimps, while choux de bruxelles aux marrons means brussels sprouts with chestnuts. Care must be taken to use the correct plural form of the accompanying noun. Certain words do not have a plural in either English or French. Crème (cream) is a good example. Whether you use one pint or one hundred gallons, crème will always stay singular and, consequently, will be preceded by à la. There are not too many such exceptions but they must be memorized. In most cases, words that do not have a plural form in English do not have one in French either. Most garnishes in French cuisine are feminine and singular, such as à la Boulangère, à la Jardinière, and à la Parisienne.

There is still one more grammatical rule to learn before we go on to practical examples. This one covers the use of the word de which, in most cases, means of. You would write queue de boeuf for tail of the bull or oxtail. Filets de Sole means fillets (plural, because in this dish every guest gets more than one fillet) of sole. The word sole is singular because sole in this dish, although singular, is understood to mean quantity. When serving the fish whole, the reference can become plural. For example, a buffet menu can describe les soles grillés.

The word de can also have a plural form des, which is not, however, always used. In the term purée de marrons, chestnut purée, de is correct as it here means made of. The word for chestnuts must be plural, because a single chestnut is not enough to make purée, but the verb for puréed remains singular because only one purée is made. We say corbeille de fruits, which means fruit basket. A basket filled with several kinds of fruit, however, is a corbeille des fruits. A plateau de fromage is the cheese tray itself. A plateau des fromages is a tray filled with several different cheeses. When the steward is cleaning all the cheese trays, he is preparing the plateaux de fromage (an x rather than an s is used here to make the word plural; this is done when the noun ends in au). The noun plateaux is made plural because more than

Figure 14.1.   **Simple French menu with American dishes.**

Velouté de Champignons

****

Poulet sauté aux Aubergines

Nouilles gratinées

****

Tarte aux Pommes

Café

Figure 14.2.   **Easy-to-translate French menu.**

Melon glacé

****

Velouté d'Asperges vertes

****

Côte de Boeuf rôti au Jus

Haricots verts au Buerre noisette

Pomme au Four

****

Salade verte avec Tomate

****

Omelette Norvegienne

Cerises flambées

au Cognac

****

Petits Fours

****

Café

one platter is being cleaned. Cheese remains singular, because it serves as a collective noun.

It is very important not to confuse de with du and de la. Du is used in connection with masculine nouns. Legumes du jour are the vegetables available that day; potage du jour is the soup of the day. Often careless menu writers write vegetables de jour which, of course, is wrong. When nouns are feminine, the accompanying expression is de la. For instance, the special of the house is spécialité de la maison.

DOUBLE-CHECK WRITTEN MENUS

I hope this short lesson in French grammar has not been too boring. Keep this book handy when you have to write menus in French. Remember, too, to always give the finished menu to a French-speaking person to double-check for errors. It is always easier to find the mistakes in somebody else's work.

After the menu has been returned from the printer, proofread it very carefully. Most printers are not used to printing French menus, and typographical errors are frequent. Remember to check details such as capitalization.

It is perfectly correct to start every line on the menu with a capital letter, and to use a small letter to begin all other menu words with the exception of proper names or nouns. On the other hand, a little poetic freedom is permitted and many menu writers start all words with capital letters.

SAMPLE FRENCH MENUS

Now let us examine some examples, beginning with easy menus that can be translated with the help of a good French-English dictionary. Figures 14.1, 14.2 and 14.3 provide some examples of simple menus written in French. They are not typical "French" menus consisting of classical French cuisine, but rather present American—Continental cuisine. In Figure 14.4, however, some French culinary terms were used, which, to most of our guests, would be meaningless. It is written in poor culinary French and uses terms that are very difficult to understand. Yet this menu appeared in an ad for a cooking school!

Many names for garnishes appear on this menu. Such names are part of the culinary heritage, but it is very difficult to judge just by reading the menu whether a name is legitimate or has just been invented for the occasion. In chapter 13, I caution against the use of names which are meaningless to the banquet guests. The case would be different with menus written in French because a certain number of these names belong on French menus.

Figure 14.3.   **Sample French menu—elegant yet understandable.**

Consommé Viveurs

****

Mousse de Sole
Sauce Cardinal
Fleuron doré

****

Selle de Veau pôelée au Madere
Champignons à la creme
Epinards en branches aux Croutons

****

Salade de la Saison
Plateau de Fromages

****

Bombe Nesselrode

****

Petits Fours

****

Café

Figure 14.4.   **Advanced French menu using obscure terms.**

Potage Carmen
Filets de Sole St. Tropez
Suprêmes de Volaille farcis Bearnaise
Veau de Marengo
Crêpe au Fraises
Mousse à la Caroube

Figure 14.5.   Sample menu in very difficult French.

Velouté Carmen

****

Rouget Trouvillaise

****

Filet de Boeuf Godard

****

Les Haricots verts avec Champignons emincés sautés au Beurre

****

Salade Jockey Club

****

Charlotte Plombières

****

Café

Let's start our review of this menu with the first line: Potage Carmen. It is a well-known French soup, often listed on menus as Velouté Carmen, when the soup is thickened with egg yolks, or Crème Carmen, when cream is added. Filets de Sole St. Tropez is the next item listed. Although the term does exist legally, a cooking school would be advised to select a better known garnish.

The entry Suprêmes de Volaille farcis Bearnaise puzzles me. Suprême means the most elevated part of something, in this case chicken. The most elevated part would be the breast, so the listing must mean stuffed breast of poultry (chicken). Assume that every guest gets only one breast. Therefore, the singular Suprême de Volaille farci would, I think, be more appropriate. Next, there is a question about the word Bearnaise. Obviously, sauce Bearnaise is meant. This sauce is normally served with grilled items. If the chicken is to be grilled, it should be indicated on the menu. Better wording would be Suprême de Volaille grillé, Sauce Bearnaise.

Veau de Marengo is not clear at all; it does not mean that the veal came from Marengo. Rather the garnish being referred to is classic and goes back to a chicken dish called Poulet sauté Marengo, invented

Menu, testimonial dinner at the Biltmore Hotel, May 1968. A lovely spring menu, written in expert French.

RÉCEPTION

Buffet   Appéritifs   Clam Bar

M E N U

Le Consommé Parisien

⁓

La Mousse de Turbotin Bercy

⁓

Les Vins:
Pouilly Fumé Ladoucette 1961   Le Sorbet au Citron du Testimonial
Appellation Controlée

⁓

La Selle d'Agneau du Chef Gonneau
Les Asperges Fraîches en Branches
La Sauce Hollandaise à la Menthe

⁓

Mouton Cadet 1961   La Salade Biltmore à la Sauce Vinaigrette
Appellation Bordeaux Controlée   Le Fromage de Brie de Meaux

La Bombe Individuelle Jeanne d'Arc
aux Fraises Glacées

⁓

Champagne Moët et Chandon   Les Macarons "Solange"

⁓

Liqueurs   La Demi-Tasse de Café

Manager des Banquets   *Maître d'Hôtel*   *Exécutif Chef des Cuisines*
Paul J. Wuyckens   Harold Harris   A. McDowell

in Napoleon's time. The name for this garnish can also be applied, though to a lesser degree, to veal stew. The correct French term would be Sauté de Veau Marengo. It may seem a bit confusing, because the term sauté is being applied to a stew, but, it is correct.

Crêpe au Fraises is easy to correct. Since more than one strawberry goes into a pancake, and since, when crêpes are served, there are almost always two crêpes to a portion, the proper listing would be Crêpes aux Fraises.

Mousse à la Caroube is another dish I could not find in my reference books. Again, I cannot claim that it does not exist, but at least it is not one of the better known desserts.

Figure 14.5 presents another menu that could profit from rewriting. As can easily be seen, that menu could have been written in Chinese as far as the basic purpose of a menu, to communicate with the guest, is concerned. It is always important when writing menus in French to create menus that are beautiful and a little mysterious, but they must also be understandable to the majority of people who will read them.

A menu should not read like a recipe. The vegetable listing Les Haricots verts avec Champignons eminceés sautés au beurre means green beans with sliced mushrooms cooked in butter. That gives a lot of unnecessary information and does not read well. The simple line Haricots verts aux Champignons would have been sufficient. The same dish can also be described more elegantly by writing Haricots verts à la Forestière, meaning in the style of the forester's wife who, supposedly, cooks her dishes with the mushrooms readily available to her.

Use of Articles

Whether or not to use articles in menu writing is also very controversial. Very formal menus often start with the proper article in front of the noun, as in Le Potage Mulligatawny. The menu in Figure 14.6, served to a gourmet society, was written this way. As you can see, the menu is needlessly cluttered with articles. The lack of grouping of dishes belonging and served together is also objectionable. A menu like this one reads poorly and leaves the guest confused rather than enlightened. (Since we are discussing only the use of language in this chapter, I will reserve comment about the choice of dishes. I would like to point out, however, that probably only one stuffed tomato was served to each guest, and for this reason the dish should have been listed in the singular on the menu, La Tomate farcie.)

Figures 14.7 and 14.8 present exceptionally well-written menus prepared by a chef in New York City. They undoubtedly represent the best in contemporary French menu writing in our country.

Figure 14.6.   **Using articles in French menu-writing.**

La Tortue Verte Lady Curzon

****

Le Filet de Sole Veronique aux Fleurons

****

Le Suprême de Faisan Gastronome

****

Le Sorbet de Citron

****

Le Tournedos Bayard

****

Les Tomates farcies

****

Les Pommes de Terre Chateau

****

Les Epinards flambés

****

Les Fromages varies

****

Le Soufflé au Chocolat

****

La Sauce Sabayon

****

Les Petis Fours glacés

****

Le Cappuccino

****

Les Grandes Liqueurs

****

Figure 14.7.   **An excellent French menu.**

Le Buffet Choisi des Créations du Maître
Pour la Joie et le Régal des Convives de la Soirée

****

Suivant cet Agréable Prélude

****

PREMIERE ASSIETTE
L'Essence de Queue de Boeuf Lucullus
Paillettes Dorées Croustillantes

****

DEUXIEME ASSIETTE
Le Turban de Mousse de Sole
Barre   Garni de Fruits de Mer au Whiskey
Muscadet 1975   Asperges Blances de Californie

****

INTERMEZZO
Granité au Calvados

****

TROISIEME ASSIETTE
Le Coeur de filet du Charolais en Croûte
Ginestet   Sauce Perigourdine
St. Emilion 1973   La Bouquètiere de Legumes de la Saison

****

LA DORURE
Une Bonne Salade d'Automne
Accompagnée d'un Brie à Point

****

L'APOTHEOSE
La Bombe Anniversaire
Taittinger   Au Parfum de Praline

Figure 14.7.   **An excellent French menu (cont.).**

Brut La Française   Entourée de Mont-Blanc
                                     Sabayon Mousseu au Kirsch

                                     ****

                                     Les Mignardises du Maître
                                     L'Essence du Bresil en Demi-Tasse

                                     ****

Figure 14.8.   **Another well-written French menu.**

                        Première Assiette:
                            La Petite Marmite Henry IV
                        Deuxième Assiette:
Muscadet   La Mousse de Sole Aux Fruits de Mer
Barres Freres   Sauce Nantua
                            Fleurons Dorés

                        Intermezzo:
                            Le Granité Surprise

                        Troisième Assiette:
Beaujolais   La Côte de Veau Sautée Mascotte
Marguisat Beaujolais   Sauce Perigourdine
Villages 1976   L'Artichaut Florentine
                            La Pomme aux Amandes

                        La Dorure:
                            Le Bibb Lettuce, Fines Herbes
                            Accompagnée de Brie de France

                        L'Apothéose:
Moet Chandon   La Bombe Isle de France
Brut Imperial 1973   Entourée de Vacherin
                            Aux Abricots Farcis
                            Sauce Nougatine
                            Les Petits Fours Royales
                            Café des Princes

Figure 14.9.   **Mistakes in French menu-writing.**

Menu for a Burgundian Christmas Dinner

Aperitif
Le Kir Au Chablis
Les Petits Cornets de Jambon du Morvan
(Little filled Trumpets of Burgundian Ham)
Les Escargots à la Mode de Bourgogne
(Snails in White Burgundy)

White:
1972 Chevalier-Montrachet,
Les Demoiselles

****

White: Les Homards au Meursault
1969 Meursault,   (Lobsters poached in White Meursault)
Perrieres

****

Red: Rôti de Gigot de Marcassin au Chambertin
1969 le Chambertin   (Roast Leg of Wild Boar with Hunter's Sauce)
1969 Beaune,   Haricots verts
Boucherottes   Petits Oignons au Four
                             Purée de Marron

****

Red: Salade verte à la Dijonaise
1970 Nuits-St. Georges, (Green Salad with Mustard Vinaigrette)
Les Boudots   Plateau des Fromages Assortis
1970 la Tache,   (Board of Mixed Cheeses)
Domaine de la Romanée-Conti

****

La Bûche de Nöel
(Yule Log)
Les Poires à la Bourgognon
(Pears with Cassis in Red Burgundy)

****

Marc de Bourgogne   Le Café

Menu interior, dinner for La Confrérie des Chevaliers du Tastevin, 1970. The caligraphy is as beautiful to look at as the French is to read.

À BOIRE

Dom Pérignon Brut 1962 en Magnums

Clos des Mouches 1967
Domaine Joseph Drouhin

Chevalier-Montrachet "Les Demoiselles" 1966
Domaine Louis Jadot

Musigny 1962
Domaine Comte Georges de Vogüé

Chambertin "Clos de Bèze" 1953
Domaine Louis Jadot

Château Corton Grancy 1962
Domaine Louis Latour

Taittinger "La Française" Extra Sec

Marc De Bourgogne
Domaine de la Romanée - Conti

POUR L'INITIATION
Clos Vougeot 1957
Sélectionné par les Jurés-Gourmets de la
Confrérie des Chevaliers du Tastevin
de la Cave de Murray Ward

RÉCEPTION
Les Huîtres de Marennes et Belon
Caviar Impérial d'Iran
Petits Friands du Chef

DÎNER
Consommé Xavier

Mousse de Turbot Truffée, au Meursault
Jack Garland

Noisette d'Agneau Printanière
Pâtisson Farci de Céleri
Purée Crécy
Barquettes de Groseilles en Gelée

Suprême de Caille Vendangeuse
Mousseline de Jambon Dijonnaise

Les Bons Fromages de France

Vacherin de la Confrérie

Café Noir

Raymond Bompart
Directeur de la Restauration

Val Vaillancourt
Maître d'Hôtel, Banquets

Richard Hepperle
Assistant Maître d'Hôtel, Banquets

Jack Crash
Chef des Cuisines

Michel Cardon
Chef des Banquets

An example of a well-written
French menu that avoids the use
of accents.

Avant l'Oeuvre

Dans le "Fountain Court" sera servi un choix d'aperitifs
accompagne d'un buffet froid et chaud compose de:

On Boira:

Saint Raphael
Dry Sack Sherry
Cinzano
Chablis Cassis

Saumon Fume de la Nouvelle Ecosse
Esturgeon des Grands Lacs
Jambon de Parme
Dinde Sauvage
Escargots Bourguignonne
Saucisson en Croute
Quiche Lorraine
Galantine de Volaille

Puis, on se rendra dans la Grand Salle de Dance pour se
mettre a table, et Savourer les mets Suivants

Menu

Le Consomme au Fumet de Faison Nemrod
Avec les Fines Pailettes Dorees

nous passerons ensuite aux

Chablis Cruse

Quenelles de Brochet en Croustade Provencale
Garnies de Moules et Crevettes Roses

on continuera par

Saint Emilion

Les Noisettes d'Agneau Paillard
Avec les Petits Pois a la Francaise
Et Les Endives Braisees

un petit intermede de musique

pendant que l'on attend

Le Fromage de Brie
Et la Salade aux Fines Herbes

et maintenant, le dessert

Moet & Chandon
White Seal

Sur Socle Lumineux le Turban Praline
Rempli de Fraises au Kirsch d'Alsace

Les Petits Fours

pour aider la digestion un bon
Moka

FRANK X. FISHER
Food and Beverage Manager

MAURICE GONNEAU
Executive Chef des Cuisines

Menu, gala banquet honoring the Queen and Prince of Denmark, May 1976. Visually striking in its simplicity, this menu is also unusual for the Danish emphasis of its cuisine.

Menu

de Terry Camborio Sherry	*Les Crevéttes du Groenland* *et* *Le Caviar Danois*
	Le Carré de Porc Croustillant *Pommes au Caramel* *Choux Rouge Braise*
Champagne Pommery	*Les Fromages du Danemark*
	Le Soufflé Glacé "Cherry Heering" *Sauce aux Mûres*
	Le Gatêau "Kransekage"
Peter Heering Liqueur	*Le Moka*

A FEW FINAL NOTES

Remember that well-written French menu descriptions often sound ridiculous when translated into other languages. The sherbet course called la Neige des Alpes parfumée à la Framboise would sound unappealing, even silly, if translated into English. Another example of the poetic freedom French menu-writing provides is the listing le Café bien chaud. This uses colloquial rather than text-book French grammar, another illustration of the fact that, if you master a language, you can use it more freely.

The menu in Figure 14.9 was composed by a connoisseur of Burgundian wines. He knew his wines very well but not his culinary French. First of all, we note a minor mistake that has crept into the listing of the fish course. Lobster should be singular because nobody would have been served two lobsters at a big dinner like that. On menus for very formal dinners, the use of the plural is acceptable to indicate abundance. A more serious error is Rôti de Gigot de Marcassin au Chambertin. Gigot almost always means leg of lamb or leg of mutton. To use this word to describe a leg of boar is incorrect. The sequence of words also could be improved. The entry would be better if written as Cuissot de Marcassin rôti, Sauce au Chambertin. The English translation under the French text is also misleading. Hunter's Sauce is Sauce Chasseur, but the French indicates only a red wine sauce made with Chambertin wine.

Some of my other corrections for this menu would be Purée de Marrons—Marrons in the plural—is better because the purée would have to be made from more than one chestnut. Also, Salade verte à la Dijonaise is a nice little touch indicating the use of the famous Dijon mustard in the dressing; however, la Dijonnaise is spelled with a double n.

As this menu demonstrates, it is not easy to write menus in French correctly, but it can be done if you take the time and effort. In the menus reproduced throughout this book there are numerous gourmet dinner menus written in French. Also included in appendix D is a list of the correct spellings for difficult foreign words. This list must be used with caution because some word endings must be changed to agree in gender or number with other words in the phrase. Always have a menu proofread by someone fluent in the appropriate language. Still, the list should be helpful for your menu writing.

Ethnic Menus

Occasionally, when a menu must be prepared for an ethnic group, it is permissible to write the menu description for a particular dish in a foreign language other than French. Specialities from foreign countries often cannot be translated without losing flair. In addition, the majority of the attending guests can usually be expected to know the item by its original name.

Correct spelling is essential; it is advisable to check with a person fluent in the particular language or to consult a good dictionary before the menu is printed. The precise composition of the dish should also be checked. Otherwise there may be error, as frequently happens in the case of the well-known German dish, Hasenpfeffer. This is routinely translated as rabbit stew, yet, when prepared in Germany, it is a stew made with hare, not with rabbit.

When using foreign words, it is advisable to mention on the menus the country the dish has come from, such as Spanish Paella with Chicken and Seafood or German Sauerbraten with Savoy Cabbage. Foreign words should not be anglicized. String beans Almondines is neither an English nor a French term. A needless mixture of foreign languages should be avoided. If a menu for a Greek group starts with Greek Avgolemono Soup, and continues with Greek Salad with Feta Cheese, all other items on the menu should be either English or Greek; no French or German expressions, should be mixed in. An exception to this rule would be a dinner organized for the United Nations or similar organization. Then, each course could correspond to a particular country, with that dish written in the appropriate language.

Again, whatever language you use, the desire to communicate with your guests in the pleasantest and most appealing manner should be your criteria when writing menus.

Menu, dinner for La Société Culinaire Philanthropique, March 1964. A simple yet elegant French menu.

Le Menu

Dubonnet	LA PETITE MARMITE HENRI IV
	* * *
Riesling	LES FILETS DE SOLE GLACÉS
	SAUCE CHAMPAGNE
	FLEURONS
	* * *
Pommard Clos de la Commaraine	LE FILET DE BOEUF AU MADERE
	LES ENDIVES BRAISÉES
	LES POMMES OLIVETTES
	* * *
	LA SALADE DE SAISON
	A L'HUILE D'OLIVE VIERGE ET JUS DE CITRON
	LE FROMAGE DE BRIE, LE ROQUEFORT
	* * *
Piper Heidsieck	LES ORANGES A LA TSARINE
	LES PETITS FOURS
	* * *
	LE CAFE DES PRINCES
	* * *

LE MAÎTRE DES CUISINES
EUGENE SCANLAN

APPENDIX A
Sample Form Letters

(Date)

(Name of Person)
(Company Name)
(Address)
(City/State/Zip)

Dear (Name of Person):

Just a short note to thank you (once again) for selecting (name of operation) for your (Type of Function) which is to be held (Date) in our (Name of Function Room).

It is indeed an honor to have this pleasure, and I can assure you that we will provide your guests with cuisine and service second to none.

At a later day I will be in touch with you concerning the menu and arrangements although, in the meantime, if I can be of assistance to you in any way, please do not hesitate to contact me.

With kindest personal regards, I remain

Cordially yours,

(Name of Manager)
(Title)

(Initials)
(File #)

(Date)

(Name of Person)
(Company Name)
(Address)
(City/State/Zip)

Dear

We appreciate having had the privilege to serve (Name of
Group) for its (Type of Function) on (Date of Function).

Looking forward to next year, we have entered the following
tentative reservation for your consideration:

> (Name of Group)
> (Day/Date/Year)
> (Type of Function)
> (Function Room)
> (Time)
> (Attendance)
> (Rental - if any)

To serve as your definite confirmation, please sign and
return the enclosed copy of this letter, within two weeks,
with a deposit check in the amount of ($). If you should
cancel the above function and we are able to re-book this
space, the deposit, less an administrative charge of 1% of
the contract price, not to exceed $50, will be returned to
you; however, if we are unable to re-book this space, the
entire amount of the deposit will be retained by the Hotel
as liquidated damages.

You can be sure that no efforts will be spared to please
you in every way. Please feel free to call should you have
any questions.

Sincerely yours,

(Name)
(Title or Dept.)

(Initials)
Enclosure
(File #)

(Date)

(Name of Person)
(Company Name)
(Address)
(City/State/Zip)

Dear

You will be interested to learn that the next Annual (Type of Function) of the (Name of Group) will be held at (name of operation) on (Day/Date/Year).

Should you wish to have your (Type of Function) prior to the (Dinner ?), we are holding the following tentative reservation:

> (Name of Group)
> (Day/Date/Year)
> (Type of Function) (in connection with Ballroom Annual)
> (Function Room)
> (Time)
> (Attendance)
> (Rental - if any)

To serve as your definite confirmation, please sign and return the enclosed copy of this letter, within two weeks, with a deposit check in the amount of ($). If you should cancel the above function and we are able to re-book this space, the deposit, less an administrative charge of 1% of the contract price, not to exceed $50, will be returned to you; however, if we are unable to re-book this space, the entire amount of the deposit will be retained by the Hotel as liquidated damages.

You may be sure that no efforts will be spared to please you in every way. If you have any questions, please feel free to call.

Sincerely yours,

(Name)
(Title or Dept.)

(Initials)
Enclosure
(File #)

(Date)

(Name of Person)
(Company Name)
(Address)
(City/State/Zip)

Dear

It is our pleasure to confirm the following change of date
for the (Name of Group - Type of Function):

>   (Name of Group)
>   (Type of Function)
>
>   CHANGE DATE TO:
>
>   (Day/Date/Year)
>   Instead of (Previous Day/Date/Year)
>   (Function Room)
>   (Time)
>   (Attendance)
>   (Rental - if any)

We are happy to be able to make this change for you. To
serve as confirmation, please sign and return the enclosed
copy of this letter.

You can be sure that no efforts will be spared to please
you in every way. Should you have any questions, please
call.

Sincerely yours,

(Name)
(Title or Dept.)

(Initials)
Enclosure
(File #)

(Date)

(Name of Person)
(Company Name)
(Address)
(City/State/Zip)

Dear

It is our pleasure to acknowledge the following definite
reservation:

> (Name of Group)
> (Day/Date/Year)
> (Type of Function)
> (Function Room)
> (Time)
> (Attendance)
> (Rental - if any)

To serve as your confirmation, please sign and return the
enclosed copy of this letter, within two weeks, with a
deposit check in the amount of ($). If you should can-
cel the above function and we are able to re-book this
space, the deposit, less an administrative charge of 1% of
the contract price, not to exceed $50, will be returned to
you; however, if we are unable to re-book this space, the
entire amount of the deposit will be retained by the Hotel
as liquidated damages.

You can be sure that no efforts will be spared to please
you in every way. Please feel free to call if you have any
questions.

Sincerely yours,

(Name)
(Title or Dept.)

(Initials)
Enclosure
(File #)

(Date)

(Name of Person)
(Company Name)
(Address)
(City/State/Zip)

Dear

It is our pleasure to acknowledge the following definite
reservation:

> (Name of Group)
> (Day/Date/Year)
> (Type of Function)
> (Function Room)
> (Time)
> (Attendance)
> (Rental - if any)

To serve as your confirmation, please sign and return the
enclosed copy of this letter, within two weeks, with a
deposit check in the amount of ($). This deposit is
subject to the standard terms and conditions attached.

We are also enclosing the Proposed Menu and Arrangements
for your function. At your convenience, please sign and
return the original copy, indicating choice of menu and
making any changes or notations you wish. At a later date,
we can finalize details.

Be assured that no efforts will be spared to please you in
every way. Feel free to call if you have any questions.

Sincerely yours,

(Name)
(Title or Dept.)

(Initials)
Enclosure
(File #)

(Date)

(Name of Person)
(Company Name)
(Address)
(City/State/Zip)

Dear

It is our pleasure to acknowledge the following definite
reservation:

> (Name of Group)
> (Day/Date/Year)
> (Type of Function)
> (Function Room)
> (Time)
> (Attendance)
> (Rental - if any)

To serve as your confirmation, please sign and return
the enclosed copy of this letter, within two weeks, with
a deposit check in the amount of ($). This deposit is
subject to the standard terms and conditions attached.

The Final Stencilled Menu and Arrangements for your function
are enclosed. After you have reviewed these, indicate your
acceptance by signing and returning the designated copy.

You can be sure that no efforts will be spared to please
you in every way. Feel free to call if you have any
questions.

Sincerely yours,

(Name)
(Title or Dept.)

(Initials)
Enclosure
(File #)

(Date)

(Name of Person)
(Company Name)
(Address)
(City/State/Zip)

Dear

Enclosed are two copies of the Diagram for the (Function Room) to assist you with your seating plans for the (Group Name and Type of Function) taking place on (Date).

One copy of this diagram should be returned to our office not later than 48 hours before the function, at which time the final guarantee will be established.

Please call three days before the (Type of Function) to advise the approximate number of persons you expect, and to let me know when you will bring in the diagram.

Sincerely yours,

(Name)
(Title or Dept.)

(Initials)
Enclosure
(File #)

(Date)

(Name of Person
(Company Name)
(Address)
(City/State/Zip)

Dear (Name of Person):

Enclosed are the final Stencilled Menu and Arrangements
for the (Type of Function) of (Name of Group/Guest) taking
place on (Date of Function).

After you have carefully reviewed these, indicate your
acceptance by signing and returning the designated copy.

We have also enclosed two copies of the Diagram for the
(Function Room) to assist with your seating plans.

One copy of this diagram should be returned to our office
not later than 48 hours before the function, at which time
the final guarantee will be established.

Please accept our assurance that no efforts will be spared
to ensure the success of your (Type of Function).

Sincerely yours,

(Name of Manager)
(Title)

(Initials)
Enclosure
(File #)

(Date)

(Name of Person)
(Company Name)
(Address)
(City/State/Zip)

Dear

To date, we have not received your signed confirmation
for the following reservation:

> (Name of Group)
> (Day/Date/Year)
> (Type of Function)
> (Function Room)
> (Time)
> (Attendance)
> (Rental - if any)

Due to the many requests we are receiving for accommodations
during this period, and to avoid possible misunderstandings,
please sign the enclosed duplicate of your letter of confirmation and return it, within one week.

Thank you very much for your attention to this. Please call
if you should have any questions.

Sincerely yours,

(Name)
(Title or Dept.)

(Initials)
Enclosure
(File #)

(Date)

(Name of Person)
(Company Name)
(Address)
(City/State/Zip)

Dear

We are sorry to learn that you are unable to continue with your plans for:

> (Name of Group)
> (Day/Date/Year)
> (Type of Function)
> (Function Room)
> (Time)
> (Attendance)

Accordingly, we have cancelled the above reservation.

With reference to your deposit, if we are able to re-book this space, the deposit, less an administrative charge of 1% of the contract price, not to exceed $50, will be returned to you; however, if we are unable to re-book this space, the entire amount of the deposit will be retained by the Hotel as liquidated damages.

We look forward to being able to serve you in the future and would be delighted to hear from you.

Sincerely yours,

(Name)
(Title or Dept.)

(Initials)
(File #)

(Date)

(Name of Caterer)
(Address)
(City/State/Zip)

Dear

Enclosed is the final Menu for the (Type of Function)

IN HONOR OF:

      or   (Name/s)

  FOR:

to be held on (Day/Date/Year) in the (Function Room).

If you have any questions, please let me hear from you.

Sincerely yours,

(Name)
(Title or Dept.)

(Initials)
Enclosure
(File #)

(Date)

(Name of Person)
(Company Name)
(Address)
(City/State/Zip)

Dear

Enclosed is the Printer's Copy of your menu for the
(Name of Group - Type of Function) taking place on (Day/
Date) in the (Function Room).

Please have your printer return one proof copy for our
records and to note possible corrections.

Sincerely yours,

(Name)
(Title or Dept.)

(Initials)
Enclosure
(File #)

(Date)

(Name of Person)
(Company Name)
(Address)
(City/State/Zip)

Dear

Thank you for your very kind and thoughtful note.

It was a pleasure working with you and I hope you will
be back at (Name of Operation) very soon.

Sincerely yours,

(Name)
(Title or Dept.)

(Initials)
(File #)

(Date)

(Name of Person)
(Company Name)
(Address)
(City/State/Zip)

Dear

WHAT HAVE WE DONE TO OFFEND YOU?

Are you aware that your organization has not held an event at (Name of Operation) since (Date)? Did something occur to cause this long absence? If so, please let us know.

If not, consider this an invitation to review our facilities. A personal tour is unbeatable for visualizing your functions taking place in our Hotel, or allow us to send our brochure which describes all meeting and banquet accommodations.

We hope to see you back at (Name of Operation) soon.

Sincerely yours,

(Name)
(Title or Dept.)

(Initials)
(File #)

(Date)

(Name)
(Address)
(City/State/Zip)

Dear

Thank you for your letter of (Date) regarding advertising
in your forthcoming (Type of Publication).

Throughout the year we receive a great number of requests
for advertisements. Rather than risk displeasing any of
our friends through a seeming display of favoritism, our
policy is, of necessity, to refuse them all.

Please be assured of our interest in your fine organization,
and understand our position in this matter.

Sincerely yours,

(Name)
(Title or Dept.)

(Initials)

Menu interior, the Waldorf-Astoria Distinguished Alumni Dinner, November 1975. Menu descriptions celebrate great moments in the organization's past.

PEACOCK ALLEY

Japanese Hors d'Oeuvres

As served to
Their Imperial Majesties, The Emperor and Empress of Japan
October 6, 1975

•

SOUP KITCHEN

Savoring with Chef Arno Schmidt

Key West Turtle Soup
General MacArthur's Favorite

•

CONRAD SUITE

Memorabilia of The Waldorf-Astoria

Sandeman Dry Sherry
Oscar's Choice
October 1, 1931

CHABLIS, 1972
BARTON AND GUESTIER
often recommended by
René Black

CHATEAU GRAND-PUY DUCASSE, 1949
MIS EN BOUTEILLE AU CHATEAU
as presented to
Mr. Conrad N. Hilton
on the Twenty-Fifth Anniversary
of his purchase of
The Waldorf-Astoria
on October 19, 1949

LAURENT PERRIER
Extra Dry
Esteemed by
Fio Del Agnese

REMY MARTIN
preferred by
Barron Hilton

CONRAD SALON

Poached Striped Bass
Sauce Champagne
Garnished with Truffles and Crayfish
Golden Fleurons
As served to
Her Majesty, Queen Elizabeth II
October 21, 1957

•

Boneless Partridge a la Conti
Choice of Les Amis d'Escoffier
January 31, 1938
—
Roquefort Mousse and Fall Pears
as enjoyed by
The Duke and Duchess of Windsor

•

Crown of Coconut Sherbet
with Flaming Brandied Chestnuts
At a Dinner Honoring
His Excellency, Carlos P. Romulo
Minister of Foreign Affairs
Philippine Republic
October 14, 1975

•

PRESIDENTIAL SUITE

Demi Tasse
Accompanied by
The Waldorf-Astoria Famous Macaroons

Executive Chef	*Director of Catering*	*Director of Food and Beverage*
ARNO B. SCHMIDT	RUDY W. MAZZONELLI	GUENTER H. RICHTER

APPENDIX B
Banquet Waiter Rules from the Waldorf-Astoria Hotel

THE WALDORF-ASTORIA

THIS SET OF RULES HAS BEEN ISSUED AT EVERY ROLL CALL FOR MANY YEARS, BUT IT APPEARS THE POINTS MENTIONED HAVE BEEN AT TIMES IGNORED. PLEASE READ EVERY SENTENCE CAREFULLY. VIOLATIONS WILL BE BROUGHT TO YOUR ATTENTION.

Your assignment to this job is based on the belief that you are a competent waiter. To maintain the long standing reputation, we expect you to respect the hotel rules and regulations. We want you to know that we realize you are a very important link in our department. To keep that link firm, PLEASE LIVE UP TO OUR REQUIREMENTS.

In order to establish a close employee-employer relationship, a meeting which you are requested to attend will be held periodically before a function. The purpose of the meeting will be to discuss ways and means to improve our service, along with other operational problems.

Grievances or other union problems will NOT be discussed at these meetings.

BANQUET SERVICE

1) Be on time—ready to work.
2) If you are unable to report for work as scheduled, it is important that you notify the Headwaiter's office early enough so that arrangements can be made to cover your assignment.
3) Make certain to have a clean uniform, corkscrew, pen, and above all, a neat appearance.
4) You are required to wear your name badge, in the prescribed manner at all times when in uniform; no a la carte checks will be issued without badge.
5) After checking in, first report for duty at your station. Instructions are detailed on the menu in the pantry of the room you are working in.
6) Check your set-up, silver, china, glassware, and linen, to be sure they are clean and spotless.
7) Water, Wine, Highball Glasses are to be picked up by their stems or outside face.

CONDUCT OF SERVICE

Keep calm, with your mind on your work; never argue in any dining room. For safety, avoid unnecessary haste to prevent breakage and, above all, accidents to yourself or to your fellow worker. Please be extra careful, particularly in crowded areas to avoid "spills."

SERVICE

Use tray or underliner for everything. All food and ice must be handled with Service Silver.

In order to obtain the main course from the chef, you must present a "Roast Slip" to the chef. This slip must be the original and must indicate:

Date . . . .
Function . . . . Example: Breakfast/Luncheon
Table Number . . . .

Number of Guests at your Table ....

Your Name ....

The Duplicate must be turned in to the Captains.

Please be accurate—your "Roast Slip" will be checked to determine if it is filled out properly and in correct amounts.

The serving of Soup, Salad, Roast, Vegetable, and Dessert MUST BE SERVED FROM THE LEFT SIDE OF THE GUEST ONLY. That means ten (10) stops for a table of 10 guests. Service and clearing procedure as follows:

1) Clear off the Fruit Course or other cold first course.
2) Take only 10 or 12 soup plates for your own table.
3) Serve the soup for your table and pass the Croutons.
4) Clear off Soup Plates and set up plates UNLESS FISH IS SERVED.
5) Put on your own salad plates.
6) Serve the Salad, unless the Salad is a separate course.
7) Put on your own Hot Plates and remove some of the empty salad plates.
8) ALL BEVERAGE GLASSES TO BE PLACED AND SERVED FROM THE RIGHT.
9) TO SERVE THE ROAST: The Chicken Breast should face the Guest; NOT THE LEG. The Roast Beef Bottom—NOT THE TIP should face the Guest. ALL MEATS ARE SERVED FIRST—with your Partner following with the vegetables. Remember—Potatoes are served on the Upper Left Corner of the plate and Vegetables on the Upper Right of the Plate. When serving Asparagus Spears, Broccoli, Salsifis— the Tips face the Guest—NOT the Stems.
10) After your Roast is served, pass Rolls and Butter around—Refresh Ice in Water Glasses and RE-PLACE all used Ash Trays.
11) Clear off the Roast Plates.
12) Return with a Tray and clear off all B and B, Salad Plates, and Salt and Pepper! UNLESS you have a Salad and Cheese Course in which case, the B and B Plate and the Salt and Pepper remain on table.
13) One Waiter brings in Dessert Plates and Dessert Silver—while the Partner brings in all the Coffee Cups, Sugar, and Teaspoons.
14) Each Partner serves his own Dessert. Separate Service Silver for Ice Cream and Sauce.
15) Each Waiter serves his own Coffee—WITH UNDERLINER—THIS IS MOST IMPORTANT; serves Cream and PASSES THE PETITS FOURS.
16) Each Waiter clears off his own Dessert Plates—Passes the Coffee once more, and asks the Guests if he can be of any further service. Candles and Number Stands are removed unless instructed otherwise.

Additional pads of Roast Slips can be obtained from Headwaiter's Office.

General Service Instructions

All items are to be served! Water glasses are to be filled all during the service. PLEASE keep ash trays clean. Except as indicated above,—before serving the dessert, clear off B and B plates, salt and pepper shakers, empty glasses, relishes, etc., and by all means—Remember to Crumb the Table.

CLEARING OFF:	Not more than 10 Silver Cups at a time to avoid breakage and spillage. Do not overload your tray. Separate china and glassware. No trucks or room service tables are to be used for set-up or clearing off in the Ballroom.
	Room Service tables to be used for service on tiers only. Salt and Pepper shakers are to be removed SEPARATELY. Please do NOT place shakers with Soiled Dishes.
	ON DINNER DANCES ONLY—Round Trays are to be used. NO ROLLING TABLES.

GENERAL RULES

COURTESY AND POLITENESS: It is the most important asset in our line of business—and costs nothing—a little effort. As a good salesman, at the arrival of guests, find out in a polite way if any beverages are needed—such as a cocktail, highball, wine, or cordial with the coffee. Before presenting the check, the additions have to be made by the cashier. All beverage checks C.O.D. unless approved by station captain. If tickets are to be collected, do so at the beginning of the service. If a guest does not have a ticket or requests any change of food, call the Captain. Never refuse a request and never say "NO." Clean your table before leaving the room (as much as can be done). Before the checking out, you must turn in your check to the Cashier. The change must always be returned. DO NOT ASSUME THAT THE CHANGE IS A GRATUITY.

SIDE JOBS: SIDE JOBS ARE PART OF YOUR JOB AS A WAITER. PLEASE BE AWARE OF YOUR ASSIGNMENTS AND DO NOT SHIRK YOUR RESPONSIBILITIES.

CLOSING: Any Waiter who obtains a substitute closing waiter without prior clearance from the Headwaiter's office or the Charge Captain will be considered "Walking Off" the job and, as such, treated accordingly.

The Waiter who obtains the substitute AND the Waiter who is substituting WILL NOT BE PAID CLOSING WAGES since both men are involved in assignments which are illegal and unauthorized. Since the diagram becomes a payroll record, No one is permitted to alter or substitute names on the diagram. ONLY the Charge Captain or a representative of the Headwaiter's Office may make changes on the diagram.

ACCIDENTS, ILLNESS, SAFETY:	If you should become ill or involved in an accident while on duty, please report to your captain who, in turn, will refer you to the Assistant Manager on duty in the Lobby.
	SAFETY SHOULD BE UPPERMOST IN YOUR MIND AT ALL TIMES. PREVENTING AN ACCIDENT IS WORTH EVERY EFFORT. ACCIDENTS ARE EXPENSIVE . . . SOMETIMES PAINFUL.
	If you are absent from work for five days or more due to illness, you are required to report to the Personnel Department. Before being permitted to return to work, you must bring a note from your doctor stating the nature of your illness and that you may return to work.

IF YOU CANNOT REPORT FOR WORK DUE TO ILLNESS, you are requested TO NOTIFY THE HEADWAITER'S OFFICE IN SUFFICIENT TIME SO THAT A REPLACEMENT FOR YOUR JOB ASSIGNMENT CAN BE MADE.

YOU WILL NOT BE ASSIGNED TO ANOTHER JOB WHETHER IT BE THE SAME DAY OR THE FOLLOWING DAY UNTIL YOU NOTIFY THE OFFICE AGAIN THAT YOU ARE WELL AND AGAIN AVAILABLE FOR WORK.

REMOVAL OF FOOD: IT HAS ALWAYS BEEN THE POLICY OF THE HOTEL TO FORBID THE REMOVAL OF MEAT OR OTHER FOOD FROM THE HOTEL. NO PASSES WILL BE ISSUED TO ANYONE FOR SCRAPS OF FOOD OF ANY TYPE EVEN IF IT APPEARS THAT THE FOOD WILL BE DISCARDED.

TELEPHONES: Employees are requested to use the telephones in the Service Area to make their private telephone calls. It is embarrassing to see employees using telephone booths in guest areas while guests are patiently waiting to make a call. REMEMBER . . . the guest cannot use the telephones in the service area, but an employee can. WE THINK THIS IS FAIR.
Please do not have friends or relatives call you on the telephone except in case of emergency.

LOCKERS: Observe the locker room rules as posted. Make every effort to keep the place clean. Your locker is only intended for storing your clothing and uniform.
DO NOT LEAVE JEWELRY OR OTHER VALUABLES IN LOCKERS.

RESTRICTED AREAS: Please do not loiter in the vicinity of the kitchen area near the chef's bulletin board. Waiters are not permitted to use the housemen's storeroom as a rest area.
While entertainment is in progress in a dining room and you are requested to leave the room . . . please do so. Viewing entertainment from the tiers, even if the tiers are not occupied by guests, is not permitted.

When assigned to a particular room to perform your duties, you are expected to remain in that room. Please do not pay "visits" to another room where you are not assigned.

SMOKING: Smoking is not permitted in dining rooms, pantries, and other designated area. There are certain areas in the hotel where smoking is permitted.

GAMBLING:	NO GAMBLING IN ANY MANNER OR FORM IS PERMITTED.
LINEN:	When you are assigned to "close," please make every effort to see that no foreign matter such as silverware, journals, etc., are returned with the soiled linen.
	Clean, unused linen is to be returned to the linen room in a separate truck. Do not mix clean and soiled linen.
SPILLS:	Every effort should be made to avoid spills. We realize that at times it cannot be avoided. All "spills" however must be reported to the captain.

SERVICE OF ALCOHOLIC BEVERAGES:

Alcoholic Beverage Sales to Certain Persons
As you know, the New York State Liquor Authority has a strict law regarding the sale of alcoholic beverages to minors and, in addition, to other persons to whom the sale of liquor is prohibited. The Law reads as follows:

No person shall sell, deliver, or give away, or cause or permit or procure to be sold, delivered, or given away any alcoholic beverages to:

Any minor, actually or apparently, under the age of 18 years.

Any intoxicated person or to any person actually or apparently under the influence of liquor.

Any habitual drunkard known to be such to the persons authorized to dispense any alcoholic beverages.

REMOVAL OF ITEMS FROM TABLES:

The following procedures pertaining to removal of any articles from the dining room tables, such as souvenirs, favors, gifts or personal items, etc., are to be followed:

1) None of the above-mentioned articles are to be at any time removed while a guest is seated at a table.

2) When clearing, if these articles do remain on the table, they are NOT to be taken to the locker room for personal use. They are to be directed to the Headwaiter's office. The name of the Waiter will be placed on the article and it will be sent to the Lost and Found Department.

3) After a period of 90 days has elapsed and the article has not been claimed, it will then become the property of the finder.

ALCOHOLIC BEVERAGES:

Opened bottles left on tables by guests may be picked up only by the waiter servicing that table. The waiter must report to the captain the approximate amount and brand and he in turn will make a list for the headwaiter's office. The waiters have 24 hours to obtain a pass from the Headwaiter's office in order to take such bottles out of the hotel. Therefore, no alcoholic beverages may be kept for more than 24 hours, in the lockers, nor can it be used in the Hotel, or given to any other employee for his consumption.

1. Carry with you at all times your identification card as you may be called upon to identify yourself.

2. Enter and leave the building by the Employee's Entrance (when coming on and going off duty). The Employees' Entrance is located on 50th Street just off Lexington Avenue.

3. It is important that your time card be punched in and out when you arrive or leave from work. When you finish work, please punch out promptly. Loitering will not be tolerated! Never leave or enter the hotel except through the Timekeeper's Entrance. All other exits are not to be used. You are not permitted to punch in or out for any other employee.

4. Employees authorized to eat in the Employees' Cafeteria will please confine their eating to that area only. No food or kitchen equipment shall be carried out of the kitchen.

5. Do not chew gum, rattle change, or count money while on duty.

6. Any change in home address or telephone number is to be reported to the Personnel Department immediately, as well as to your supervisor.

7. It is the Management's right to examine all parcels carried by Employees in or out of the hotel. It is requested that you leave personal packages at home or check them with the Timekeeper of the Hotel. Packages may be carried out of the hotel only if the employee has obtained a pass from his-her department head, but still would be subject to inspection.

8. Theft is grounds for immediate dismissal.

9. Employees are not permitted to sell merchandise of any sort, lottery tickets, or anything else on our hotel property.

10. Fighting or wrestling of any type will not be tolerated.

11. Employees must confine their presence in the hotel to the area of their job assignments. It is not permissible to roam the hotel at will or to visit in other parts of the hotel, or to leave the hotel without permission of your department head. Sleeping on the job or willful shirking of duties are grounds for immediate dismissal.

12. Willful destruction of hotel property is grounds for immediate dismissal.

BANQUET HEADWAITER

Menu, United Nations luncheon. Italicized notes increase readers' understanding and accent the international theme.

Menu

SOUPA AVGOLEMONO
(Rice and Egg Soup from Greece)

~

POLLO HONDURENA
(Chicken Saute, Honduras Style)

ENGLISH SPUDS

TOMATO DOLMASI
(Baked Stuffed Tomato from Turkey)

~

AMERICAN SALAD GREENS
Danish Blue Cheese Dressing

~

SAVARIN AU RHUM
(Rum Cake from France)

~

COFFEE
(From Haiti)

Prix Fixe
$4.75

Wednesday
October 24, 1962

APPENDIX C
Sample Banquet Stencils

Sample 1.   Coffee break order form.

A.M. COFFEE BREAK SELECTION

_____Gallons of Coffee $____per gallon

_____Half Pints of Milk $____each

_____Quarts of Freshly Squeezed Orange Juice $____per quart

_____Gallons of Tea $____per gallon

_____Assorted Butter Danish Pastries $____each

_____Pound Cake, _____Raisin Cake $____each slice

P.M. COFFEE BREAK SELECTION

_____Gallons of Coffee $____per gallon

_____Half Pints of Milk $____each

_____Gallons of Tropical Fruit Punch $____per gallon

_____Bottles of Cola and Seven-Up $____each

_____Gallons of Tea $____per gallon

_____Assorted Cookies $____per pound

____% of Food and Beverage Sales will be added to your account, of which____% will be distributed to waiters, waitresses, and, where applicable, bus help and/or bartenders engaged in the function, and____% to supervisory, sales, and other banquet personnel. The current state sales tax is also applicable.

Date of function:_____Time of function:_____

Organization:_____Room:_____

Sample 2.   Banquet stencil for small breakfast meeting.

Wednesday, May 24, 19—	The Blue Grass Club
The Tapestry Room	Executive Committee
Time: 7:00 AM Coffee Service	Breakfast Meeting
7:30 AM Breakfast	Attendance: 17 to 20 guests
9:20 AM Adjournment	Mr. Walter Seed, in charge

Breakfast Menu

at 7:00 AM sharp:

One (1) gallon of coffee

Charge: $____per gallon

at 7:30 AM:

Freshly squeezed Orange Juice

****

Scrambled Eggs

Bacon Strips

Hashed Brown Potatoes

****

Brioche and Croissants

Marmalade, Butter, Fruit Preserves

****

Coffee or Tea

Charge: $____ per person

Extra Items and Arrangements

Beverages: None.

Room Set-up: In Tapestry Room set tables in "T" Shape for 14, two (2) places at the Head, six (6) on each side. In Pink Salon set table for six (6).

Special Service Note: Hot coffee must be available at 7:00 AM sharp. Please clear table after breakfast service, meeting will follow immediately—adjournment by 9:20 AM.

Decorations: Linen. Blue

Candles. With shades, complimentary.

Floral. None.

Mechanical: None.

Tax: Sales tax to be added to account.

Gratuities: ____% of Food and Beverage Sales will be added to your account, of which____% will be distributed to waiters, waitresses, and, where applicable, bus help and/or bartenders engaged in the function, and____% to supervisory, sales, and other banquet personnel.

Guarantee: Not later than 48 hours before the function, the Hotel is to be advised of the exact number of guests to be set up for and served, which figure will then become your Guarantee, for which you will be charged, even though a lesser number attends.

Arrangements: _____

Headwaiter: _____

Executive Chef: _____

May 1, 19—
NC-001095
O   MK   MP   GM   B1   B2   BQT   PAS   IC   SR   PD*

*Distribution Code: this will vary from operation to operation. Here it indicates: Office, Main Kitchen, M.P. Kitchen, Garde Manger, Butcher 1, Butcher 2, Banquet Chef, Pastry Chef, Ice Cream Chef, Store Room, Purchasing.

Sample 3.

Banquet stencil for large luncheon—575 guests.

Friday, May 14, 19—   Sons of Blarney
Star Room and Riverview Room   Reception and Luncheon
Time: 12 Noon Guest of Honor   Attendance: 575 guests
       Reception   Ms. Rose Kelly, in charge
       1 PM Luncheon
       4 PM Adjournment

Reception Menu

No Food Service

Luncheon Menu

Irish Leek Soup

****

Roast Leg of Lamb

Braised Kale

Browned Tiny Potatoes

****

Rock of Cashel Trifle

****

Oatmeal Cookies

****

Tea or Coffee

Charge: $____per person

Extra Items and Arrangements

Time:	Guest of Honor Reception	
	Star Room (60 guests)	12:00 Noon
	No beverage service	
	Luncheon	
	Riverview Room	1:00 PM
	Adjournment	4:00 PM

Control: Waiters to collect tickets.
One (1) six-foot (6′) committee table in corridor.

Checkroom: Tipping by each guest.
Guest of Honor—charge to master account based on 60 guests.

Beverages: None.

Room Arrangements: Per special diagram. Set round tables of ten (10) guests each.
Double dais opposite entrance.

Decorations: Linen. Gold.
Candles. With shades, complimentary.
Floral. Own arrangements.

Mechanical: Radio room. Provide mike for lectern, complimentary.

Banners: None.

Flags: U.S. and Irish flags.

Tax: Exempt.

Gratuities: ____% of Food and Beverage Sales will be added to your account, of which____% will be distributed to waiters, waitresses, and, where applicable, bus help and/or bartenders engaged in the function, and____% to supervisory, sales, and other banquet personnel.

Guarantee: Not later than 48 hours before the function, the Hotel is to be advised of the exact number of guests to be set up for and served, which figure less 3 percent will then become your Guarantee, for which you will be charged, even though a lesser number attends.

Arrangements by: _____

May 2, 19—

BT 7-04578

Sample 4.

Banquet stencil for modest-sized Kosher reception and dinner—100 guests.

Saturday, May 6, 19—
Napoleon Suite
Time: 9:00 PM Reception—
        Foyer
        10:00 PM Dinner—
        Dining Room

Private Party in Honor of Mr. Rosenblatt
Reception and Dinner
Attendance: 100 guests
Ms. Sara Schwartz, in charge

Reception

During the reception, we will pass Butler Style on small silver trays and in bi-metal pans the following hot hors d'oeuvres and cold canapes

Hot:

Miniature Pirojkes

Medallions of Veal with Mushrooms en brochette

Goujonettes of Sole in Sesame Seeds

Cold:

Turkey Amandine Spears

Smoked Bundnerfleische around Melon

Razor-thin sliced raw Filet of Beef wrapped around freshly grated horseradish

On each bar, we will have an elegantly arranged bouquet of Crudité with Guacamole dip

Charge: $____per person

****

Dinner Menu
Cold Poached Salmon en Gelee on a large leaf of Boston Lettuce
Garniture of Parisienne Vegetable Salad and a half-lemon wrapped in
gauze
Cucumber Dill Sauce to be Passed
Special note: First course to be served a la Russe on caterer's own
crystal plate

****

Completely Boned and Skinned Breast of Capon in Champagne Sauce
with Morilles
Wild Rice and Pignoli Nuts
Fresh Asparagus with Mock Butter Sauce
Special Note: the main course to be served English style. Waiter to
present tray to the guest with serving fork and spoon. Guest will remove food himself from the platter

*****

Salad of Kentucky Bibb Lettuce, Endive with Fresh Vinaigrette
Dressing with Dijon Mustard
Special Note: Salad to be served as a separate course on a cold fish plate.
Waiters to serve English style.

*****

Individual Rocher
Grapefruit Sherbet
Extra Large Driscoll Strawberries with stems on, Sugar Coated and
presented on an oval silver platter on a white linen napkin

LeRoux Creme de Cassis to be passed in the bottle.
Special Note: Waiters to serve sherbet. Strawberries to be served En
glish style with serving fork and spoon on the platter.

****

Lange du Chat
Demi Tasse

Special Note: Gold set-up plate and gold glasses.

Charge: $____per person

Mashgiach Charge:$_____

Distribution Code:

O   MK   MP   GM   B1   B2   BQT   PAS   1C   SR   PD

Under Dietary Law Supervision of: Hills of Judea Caterers

Extra Items and Arrangements

Time: Reception

                     Foyer   9:00 PM

                     Dinner

                     Napoleon Suite   10:00 PM

Checkroom: $____per person, added to the account with a "No Tipping" sign displayed.

Control: By invitation only.

                  Escort cards to be arranged on the marble table in the hall. Do not cover with lace.

Beverages: Two (2) bars and bartenders, charge $____ each to serve assorted cocktails and highballs. Cocktails at drink prices, highballs at bottle prices.

                  With the fish, we will serve Carmel Sauvignon Blanc at $____ per bottle.

                  With the main course, we will serve Carmel President's Sparkling Wine at $____per bottle.

                  With the dessert, we will serve Carmel Sauterne at $____per bottle.

Special Note: Tulip champagne glasses to be used for sparkling wine.

Gratuities: ____% of Food and Beverage Sales will be added to your account, of which____% will be distributed to waiters, waitresses, and where applicable bus help and/or bartenders engaged in the function, and____% to supervisory, sales, and other banquet personnel.

Tax:	____% to be applied.
Decorations:	Linen. New white.
	Candles. Three (3) tall white tapers in silver holders on each table.
	Floral. On each table in attractive baskets anemones in all colors. Also include white roses and coordinated tulips. Charge $____ each. For the Reception Area: Three (3) very special arrangements of cut flowers to include rubrum lilies, baby orchids, and other exotic flowers, charge $____each.
Room Set-up:	Foyer. Reception style—bar on east and west end.
	Napoleon Suite: 10 round tables of 10 guests each, according to special diagram. Baby grand piano in center.
Special Note:	Waiters to wear black jackets, no aprons.
	Wine stewards to wear red jackets.
	Captains in regular dinner suits.
	All waiters to wear white gloves.
Service Requirements:	One (1) waiter for each table.
	One (1) wine steward for every three (3) tables.
	One (1) Captain for every four (4) tables.
	Maitre d'hotel, Mr.____ and assistant headwaiter, Mr. ____ also to be in attendance.
Mechanical:	Radio room. Standing mike and lectern to be available.
Flags:	American and Israeli flags to be available.
Piano:	To be available in Napoleon Suite.
Guarantee:	Not later than 48 hours prior to the function, the Hotel is to be advised of the exact number of guests to be set up for and served, which figure will become your Guarantee, for which you will be charged, even though a lesser number attends.

Arrangements: _____

Headwaiter: _____

Executive Chef: _____

May 3, 19—

Sample 5.   Banquet stencil for modest-sized reception—125 guests.

Tuesday, May 16, 19—   The Fund for CWC
Library and Astor Suite   Reception Attendance: 125 guests
Time: 5:30 PM Reception   Mr. Yah Hue Sho, in charge
        8:00 PM Adjournment

Reception in Library
From an attractively skirted buffet and using silver chafing dishes we will serve an excellent selection of cold Canapes and hot Hors d'Oeuvres consisting of:
Hot:
Tartelettes of Crabmeat
Clams Casino
Mushroom Caps Florentine
Batter-fried Shrimp, Pungent Sauce
Tiny Skewers of Beef, Lamb, and Pork
Chicken Tidbits in Soy Sauce
Duckling Tidbits
Won-Tons

Cold:
Canapes of Smoked Salmon
Melon Balls and Prosciutto
Deviled Eggs
Liver Pate on Toasted Brioche
Cornets of Salami

Special Service Note: Provide 2/3 hot hors d'oeuvres, 1/3 cold canapes.
Charge: $____per person
Arrangements by: _____
March 6, 19—
Extra Items and Arrangements

Checkroom: $.60 per person added to the account with a "No Tipping" sign displayed.

Control: Set one (1) committee table with two (2) chairs outside entrance to the _____ room.

Beverages: Provide two (2) bars and bartenders, charge $____each, to serve premium brand highballs and cocktails at bottle rates. Kirin Beer and Suntory Whiskey to be available. All charges to be added to the master account and we have established a $____per person beverage budget, not to be exceeded without the permission of Mr.____. Corkage of $____each for six (6) bottles of Suntory.

Room Arrangements: According to special diagram.

Decorations: Linen. White.

Candles. Provide five-armed candelabras for the buffet tables with 18″ tapered candles, complimentary. Provide shaded candles for all cocktail tables, complimentary. Use white shades.

Floral. One (1) screen at $____. Arrangement for receiving line and on buffet table. Also four (4) boutonnieres. Total $____.

Mechanical: Radio Room. One microphone, complimentary. All additional microphones at a charge of $____each.

Electrician. To spotlight all buffet tables and highlight all floral work, $____per spotlight, two total.

Announcer: $____to be provided.

Overtime: In accordance with our union regulations, overtime must be paid to our employees if the time of the function extends over three (3) hours for luncheon, or over four (4) hours for dinner, or after 2:00 AM, if the facilities are not vacated. The overtime rate is $____per person, per hour or any part thereof.

Tax: ____% sales tax added to the acount.

Gratuities: ____% of Food and Beverage Sales will be added to your account, of which____% will be distributed to waiters, waitresses, and, where applicable, bus help, and/or bartenders engaged in the function, and ____% to supervisory, sales, and other banquet personnel.

Guarantee: Three days prior to the function, kindly notify the Hotel as to the approximate number of guests expected. Not later than 48 hours prior to the function, your diagram must be returned to the Hotel and we are to be advised of the exact number of guests to be set up for and served, which figure less 3 percent will then become your Guarantee, for which you will be charged, even though a lesser number attends.

Arrangements by: _____

Headwaiter: _____

Executive Chef: _____

XC 0-09875

Sample 6.   Banquet stencil for large reception and dinner—1200 guests.

Thursday, May 27, 19—	The Gulf Coast Society
The Mississippi Ballroom Suite	Annual Reception and Dinner
General Reception-South Foyer	Attendance: 1200 guests
and North Foyer	Mr. Edward Jones, in charge

6:30 PM General Reception—No Food Requirements
6:30 PM Guest of Honor Reception—Bourbon Room—No Food Requirements
5:30 PM Press Reception—Riverboat Room
7:40 PM Dinner Service—Ballroom
9:40 PM Adjournment

Dinner Menu

Artichoke Hearts
Chopped Pimento and Mushrooms a la Grecque
(Pre-Set)

***

Roast Sirloin of Beef, Two slices each
Sauce Bordelaise
Potatoes Anna
Fresh Asparagus in Lemon Butter

***

Bibb Lettuce, Watercress, and Endive
With Cherry Tomatoes
Lemon and Oil Dressing

***

Open Face Apricot Tart
With Chantilly Cream

***

Petits Fours
Coffee and Tea

Charge: $____per person

Distribution Code:

O   MK   MP   GM   B1   B2   BQT   PAS   1C   SR   D

Extra Items and Special Arrangements

Special Note: 1. Dinner Service: 1 hour & 10 minutes.
     2. Do not remove table numbers.
     3. Serve salad with main course.

Arrangements: _____

Headwaiter: _____

Executive Chef: _____

Time:		
	Press Reception—Riverboat Room	5:30 PM
	General Reception—South Foyer and North Foyer	6:30 PM
	GOH Reception—Bourbon Room	6:30 PM
	Open Doors—Ballroom	7:10 PM
	Dais Guests enter Anthem and invocation to follow	7:30 PM
	Dinner Service	7:40 PM-8:50 PM
	Speeches	8:50 PM
	Adjournment:	9:40 PM

Control: Tickets to be collected at tables by waiters, except dais.

Checkroom: Flat rate of $____to be added to account with a "No Tipping" sign displayed.

Beverages: General Reception—South Foyer and North Foyer. (Approximately 1,000 Guests.) Provide eight (8) bars and bartenders, charge $____each. Serve assorted cocktails at $____per drink and assorted highballs at $____to $____per bottle. Mixers at $____per quart. Use Name Brands including, Dewar's White Label, Jack Daniels, and Canadian Club. Domestic white wine also available. Dry sherry and assorted fruit juices. Beverage Budget: $____ per person, do not exceed without approval of Mr. _____ or Mr. _____.

Press Reception—Riverboat Room, 5:30 PM. Provide one (1) bar and bartender, charge $____. Serve same as above.

GOH Reception—Bourbon Room.
(Approximately 350 Guests).
Provide three (3) bars and bartenders, charge $ each. Serve same as above.
Beverage Budget: $____ per person, do not exceed without further approval.

Bars to close at 7:15 PM sharp! Only exception:

One (1) bar in south foyer, to close at 7:30 PM for late comers.

During dinner, serve Bin # 8211, Pinot Noir, Jordan, at $____ per bottle, two (2) bottles per table, added to the account.

All other beverages a la carte. No other beverage added to the account unless approved in writing by Mr. _____ or Mr. _____.

Room Arrangements:	Jade Corridor.

Jade Corridor.
Provide one (1) long 18 ft. table with six (6) chairs. One (1) door opened to South Foyer for entry. One (1) 6 ft. table at entrance to room. One (1) 6 ft. table at entrance to bridge area of room and salon. One (1) 6 ft. table at entrance to North Foyer.

South Foyer.
South bar open. Set double bar at north end. Cocktail tables and chairs, vanderbilt style.

North Foyer.
Set bar at east side. Cocktail tables, vanderbilt style.

Green Salon.
Set double bar on east side and double bar on west side. Cocktail tables and chairs, vanderbilt style.

Bourbon Room.
Set one (1) bar on east side and one (1) bar on west side. Two-tiered dais line-up with chairs at north end. Cocktail tables and chairs.

Riverboat Room.

Set one (1) bar on west side. Cocktail tables and chairs.

Grand Ballroom.

Two-tiered dais on stage, apron out. Round tables of 10 guests each per special diagram including first and second tier.

Decorations:	Linen. Red cloths with red napkins; Dais all white
	Candles. Five-armed silver candelabras with five (5) 18″ white tapered candles at $.75 each on each table.
	Floral. Own arrangements.
Mechanical Require-ments:	Amplification. Provide dual lectern mike for dais, no charge.
	Stand microphones in Bourbon Room and Green Salon. Captain's use, no charge.
	Electrician. Stage switchboard operator, charge $___. Provide one (1) spotlight and operator, charge $___. Provide four (4) outlets in royal box for projector.
	Carpenter. To set stage, apron out.
	Upholsterer. No special requirements.
Banners and Flags:	U.S. and _____ flags on poles each side of stage.
Dinner Pro-grams and Seating Lists:	Program and seating list distributed from control tables by committee.
Security:	Own arrangements with Hotel Security Department.
Tax:	Exempt.
Gratuities:	___% of Food and Beverage Sales will be added to your account, of which ___% will be distributed to waiters, waitresses, and, where applicable, bus help and/or bartenders engaged in the function, and ___% to supervisory, sales, and other banquet personnel.
Guarantee:	Three days prior to the function, kindly notify the Hotel as to the approximate number of guests expected. Not later than 48 hours prior to the function, your diagram must be returned to the Hotel and we are to be advised of the exact number of guests to be set up for and served, which figure less 3 percent you will be charged, even though a lesser number attends.

Arrangements: _____

Headwaiter: _____

Executive Chef: _____

May 24, 19—

LC-820702

Sample 7.   Banquet stencil for moderate-sized buffet breakfast—250 guests.

Monday, May 8, 19—	XYZ Corporation
Blue Salon, Wedgewood Room,	Buffet Breakfast
and Mirror Room	Attendance: 250 guests
Time: 7:30 AM Breakfast	Mr. Jack Jones, in charge
9:30 AM Adjournment	

Buffet Breakfast

From two attractively decorated buffets, one located in the Wedgewood Room and one in the Blue Salon, we shall serve the following:

Assorted Juices including
Orange, Grapefruit, Tomato, Apple and Prune

****

Sliced Bananas, Whole Strawberries,
Seasonal Melon Wedges

****

Scrambled Eggs
French Toast
Hashed Brown Potatoes
Grilled Sugar-Cured Ham
Link Sausages
Rashers of Bacon

****

Assorted Cold Cereals
Milk, Cream, and Half-and-Half

****

Assorted Danish Pastries
Brioche and Croissants
Assorted Rolls and Muffins
Marmalade, Butter, Fruit Preserves

****

Coffee, Tea, and Milk

Charge: $____ per person

Arrangements: _____

Headwaiter: _____

May 1, 19—

NH-007321

Extra Items and Arrangements
Beverages: None.
Control: Informal seating.

Checkroom:	Not required as guests are staying in the hotel.
Room Arrangements:	Wedgewood Room. Buffet in center for 100 guests.
	Mirror Room. Round tables of 10 for 100 guests.
	Blue Salon. Buffet on east wall for 150 guests. 17 round tables of 10 each for remainder of group.
Decorations:	Linen. Blue.
	Candles. None.
	Floral. None.
Mechanical:	None.
Gratuities:	____% of Food and Beverage Sales will be added to your account, of which ____% will be distributed to waiters, waitresses and, when applicable, to bus help and/or bartenders engaged in the function, and ____% to supervisory, sales, and other banquet personnel.
Tax:	____% sales tax added to your account.
Guarantee:	No later than 48 hours before the function, the Hotel is to be advised of the exact number of guests to be set up for and served, which figure less 3 percent will then

become your guarantee for which you will be charged,
even though a lesser number attends.

Arrangements
by: _____

May 1, 19—
NH-007321

Menu interior, dinner for La Confrérie des Chevaliers du Tastevin.

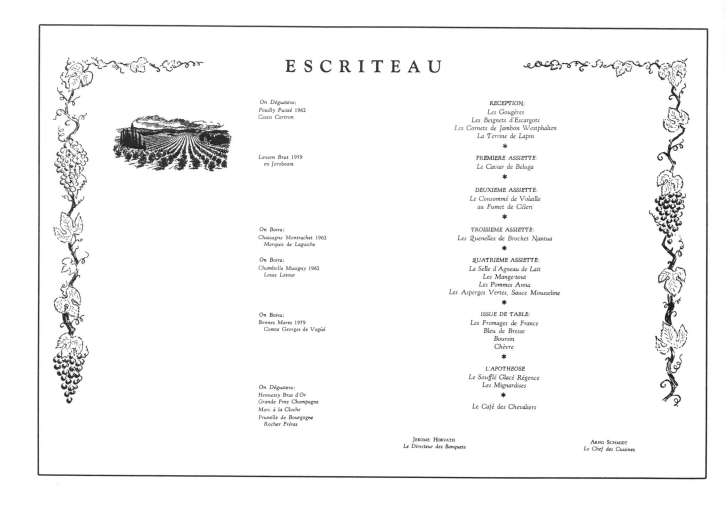

ESCRITEAU

On Dégustera:
Pouilly Fuissé 1962
Cassis Cartron

Lanson Brut 1959
en Jeroboam

On Boira:
Chassagne Montrachet 1962
Marquis de Laguiche

On Boira:
Chambolle Musigny 1962
Louis Latour

On Boira:
Bonnes Mares 1959
Comte Georges de Vogüé

On Dégustera:
Hennessy Bras d'Or
Grande Fine Champagne
Marc à la Cloche
Prunelle de Bourgogne
Rocher Frères

RECEPTION:
Les Gougères
Les Beignets d'Escargots
Les Cornets de Jambon Westphalien
La Terrine de Lapin
＊

PREMIERE ASSIETTE:
Le Caviar de Beluga
＊

DEUXIEME ASSIETTE:
Le Consommé de Volaille
au Fumet de Céleri
＊

TROISIEME ASSIETTE:
Les Quenelles de Brochet Nantua
＊

QUATRIEME ASSIETTE:
La Selle d'Agneau de Lait
Les Mange-tout
Les Pommes Anna
Les Asperges Vertes, Sauce Mousseline
＊

ISSUE DE TABLE:
Les Fromages de France
Bleu de Bresse
Boursin
Chèvre
＊

L'APOTHEOSE
Le Soufflé Glacé Régence
Les Mignardises
＊

Le Café des Chevaliers

JEROME HORVATH
Le Directeur des Banquets

ARNO SCHMIDT
Le Chef des Cuisines

APPENDIX D
Spelling Guide for Menu-Writing

The following spelling guide is not meant as a dictionary but rather as an aid for someone composing a menu but unsure about the correct spelling of certain words. I have included the gender of nouns and also the plural forms where needed. Where only the plural form of a word is used on menus, I have only included the plural form in the following list.

As a further help to menu writers, I have added some frequently used methods of preparing particular dishes with their proper spelling to emphasize the importance of the proper spelling of verbs used on the menu to describe food preparation.

A list of frequently misspelled words also appears at the end of chapter 13. Some of these words are English, others come from foreign languages, and all are often found on menus, often misspelled. This list cannot in any way claim to be complete. You may want to add to it as your own menu writing experience increases. Keep these lists as a growing resource for menu composition.

Soups

Le consommé	Clear consomme
Le consommé double	Double consomme
La crème	Cream soup
Le potage	Soup
Le pot au feu	Strong consomme of meat, poultry and vegetables
La petite marmite	Elegant clear consomme of meat, poultry and vegetables
La soupe	Old fashioned thick soup
La soupe à l'oignon	Onion soup
Le velouté	Velvet smooth soup made with stock and roux

Sauce (Sauce is feminine: la sauce, la sauce Bernaise.)

Bearnaise	Egg yolk and butter emulsion with tarragon and spices
Bechamel	Cream sauce
Bigarade	Bitter orange sauce
Bordelaise	Red wine sauce with shallots and marrow
Bourguignonne	Well-reduced red wine sauce made with Burgundy wine
Cardinal	Lobster sauce
aux champignons	Mushroom sauce

Chaud-froid blonde	White garnishing sauce
Chaud-froid brune	Brown garnishing sauce
Gribiche	Cold sauce with chopped pickles and herbs
Choron	Bearnaise sauce with tomato
Duxelles	Chopped mushrooms and ham sauce
à l'estragon	Tarragon flavored
Grand veneur	Game sauce
Cumberland	Cold red currant sauce
Hollandaise	Egg yolk and butter sauce
Madère	Madeira-wine-flavored sauce
Mornay	Cream sauce with cheese and egg yolks
Nantua	Pink crayfish sauce
Perigourdine	Truffle sauce
Poivrade	Pepper sauce
Poulette	White sauce with mushrooms, shallots and stock
Tomate	Tomato sauce
Raifort	Horseradish sauce (hot or cold)
Verte	Cold green sauce
Vinaigrette	Pepper, oil, and vinegar sauce (cold)

Meats

L'agneau (masculine, singular)	Lamb
L'agneau de lait (masculine) (singular)	Baby lamb
Le baron d'agneau	Whole back and legs of lamb
La blanquette d'agneau	White lamb stew
Le carré d'agneau	Rack of lamb
Le carré d'agneau rôti persillé	Roast rack of lamb flavored with parsley and garlic
La cervelle d'agneau	Lamb brains
La côtellette d'agneau grillée	Broiled lamb chop
L'epaule farcie (feminine)	Stuffed lamb shoulder
Le gigot d'agneau persillé	Leg of lamb with garlic and parsley
Le gigot d'agneau rôti	Roast leg of lamb
La noisette d'agneau	Boneless lamb chop
Les noisettes d'agneau sautées	Panfried boneless lamb chops
Sauté d'agneau	Brown lamb stew
La selle d'agneau rôtie	Roast saddle of lamb

Boeuf (masculine, singular)	Beef
L'aloyau (masculine, singular)	Shell strip and filet, sirloin
Le boeuf braisé à la mode	Braised beef with calf's feet and vegetables
Le boeuf braisé	Braised beef
Le chateaubriand	Double or triple size, center cut, tenderloin steak
Le contre-filet	Sirloin (shell strip)
La côte de boeuf rotie	Rib of beef (roast beef)
L'emincé de boeuf (masculine)	Shredded beef
L'entrecôte de boeuf (feminine)	Sirloin steak
L'entrecôte de boeuf grillée	Broiled sirloin steak
Le coeur de filet de boeuf	Filet mignon (center cut)
Le filet de boeuf	Beef tenderloin
Le filet de boeuf froid	Cold beef tenderloin
Le filet mignon	Small filet mignon
Le filet de boeuf rôti	Roast beef tenderloin
Les medaillons de boeuf	Small filet mignon (plural)
Les tournedos de boeuf (masculine)	Small filet mignon (plural)
Les tournedos sauté	Small filet mignon sauted
Ragout de boeuf (masculine)	Beef stew
Porc (masculine, singular)	Pork
La ballotine d'épaule de porc	Stuffed pork shoulder
Le carré de porc	Pork loin
Le carré de porc fumé	Smoked pork loin
Le carré de porc rôti	Roast pork loin
Le cochon de lait	Suckling pig
La côte de porc	Single pork chop
Les côtes de porc braisées	Braised pork chops
Les côtes de porc grillées	Broiled pork chops
Le filet de porc	Pork tenderloin
Le foie de porc	Pork liver
Le jambon à la choucroute	Ham and sauerkraut
Le jambon en croute	Ham baked in crust
Le jambon frais rôti	Roast fresh ham
Le jambon froid à la gelée	Ham in aspic
Le jambon fumé	Smoked ham
Le jambon braisé au Madere	Braised ham in madeira wine
Le jambon persillé	Cold ham dish that has been flavored with parsley

Le jambon glacé de Virginie	Glazed virginia ham
Le veau (masculine, singular)	Veal
La blanquette de veau	White veal stew
Le carré de Veau	Rack of veal
La cervelle de veau	Calf's brain
La côte de veau	Veal chop with bone
La côte de veau à la duxelles	Veal chop with mushroom puree
L'épaule de veau (feminine)	Veal shoulder
L'épaule de veau poelée	Potroasted veal shoulder
L'épaule de veau rôtie	Roast veal shoulder
L'escalope de veau (feminine)	Veal cutlet
L'escalope de veau panée	Breaded veal cutlet
Le filet de veau	Veal tenderloin
Le foie de veau	Calf's liver
La fricassee de veau	White veal stew
Le fricandeau de veau	Veal bottom round
La longe de veau	Veal loin
La noisette de veau	Small boneless veal chop
La paupiette de veau	Veal bird (singular)
La poitrine de veau	Breast of veal
La poitrine de veau farcie	Stuffed breast of veal
Les ris de veau (masculine, plural)	Sweetbreads
Les ris de veau braisés	Braised sweetbreads
Les ris de veau grillés	Broiled sweetbreads
Les ris de veau poelés au màdere	Sweetbreads simmered in madeira wine
Le rognon de veau	Veal kidney
La rognonnade de veau	Loin roast with kidney
La selle de veau	Whole veal saddle
La tête de veau	Calf's head

Poultry

La volaille (feminine, singular)	Poultry
L'aspic de volaille	Chicken in aspic jelly
La ballotine de volaille	Stuffed chicken leg
Le chapon	Capon
Le consommé de volaille	Chicken consomme
Le coq au vin	Chicken sauted in red wine
La crème de volaille	Cream of chicken soup
La cuisse de poulet	Chicken leg

L'eminé de volaille (masculine, singular)	Shredded chicken
Les foies de volaille (masculine, plural)	Chicken livers
La galantine de volaille	Chicken galantine
La mousse de volaille	Chicken mousse
Les mousselines de volaille (plural)	Individual chicken mousse
La poularde	Poularde (fattened pullet)
Le poulet (masculine, singular)	Broiler chicken
Le poulet grillé	Broiled chicken
Le poulet à l'estragon	Chicken with tarragon
Le poulet rôti	Roast chicken
Le poulet sauté	Chicken sauteed
Poulet en chaud-froid	Chicken in cold chaud-froid
Poulet sauté au Champagne	Chicken in champagne sauce
Le poussin	Baby chicken
La salade de volaille	Chicken salad
Le suprême de volaille	Cicken breast
Le canard (masculine, singular)	Duckling
Le caneton (masculine, singular)	Duckling (elegant French)
L'aiguillette de caneton	Thin duckling breast slices
Le suprême de caneton croustillant	Crisp duckling breast
Le caneton braisé aux navets	Duckling with turnips
Le caneton rôti à la bigarade	Duckling with bitter oranges
Le caneton rôti à l'orange	Duckling with oranges
Caneton rouennaise à la presse	Pressed Rouennaise duckling
Caneton montmorency	Duckling with cherries
Pigeonneau (masculine, singular)	Squab (pigeon, young)
Pigeonneaux (plural)	Squabs
Dindonneau (masculine, singular)	Tom turkey
Le dindonneau farci aux marrons	Turkey stuffed with chestnuts
La dinde (feminine, singular)	Hen turkey
Oie (feminine, singular)	Goose
L'oison (masculine, singular)	Young goose, gosling
Le foie gras (masculine, singular)	Goose liver

L'escalopes de foie gras en gelée	Goose liver slices in aspic
Parfait de foie gras	Goose liver parfait (available canned)
Pâté de foie gras (masculine, singular)	Goose liver pâté

Game Birds

La caille (feminine, singular)	Quail
Cailles (feminine, plural)	Quails
Cailles à la vigneronne	Cold quail with grapes (culinary meaning)
Cailles aux nids	Quails in nests
Cailles en cocotte	Quails in cocotte
Cailles désossées	Boned quails
Cailles farcies	Stuffed quails
Canard sauvage (masculine, singular)	Wild Duckling
Le salmis de canard sauvage	Wild duckling stew
Dinde sauvage (feminine, singular)	Wild turkey
Faisan (masculine, singular)	Pheasant
Faisane (feminine, singular)	Hen pheasant
Le faisan en plumage	Pheasant adorned with feathers
Le faisan en volière	Pheasant in flight (adorned with feathers, culinary phrase)
Le faisan rôti	Roast pheasant
Le suprême de faisan	Pheasant breast
La terrine de faisan	Pheasant terrine
Le faisan souvarov	Pheasant baked with truffles and foie gras
Gelinotte (feminine, singular)	European grouse
Perdreau (masculine, singular)	Partridge
Perdrix (masculine and feminine, singular)	Old partridge (culinary meaning)
Perdreaux (masculine, plural)	Partridges
Chartreuse de perdreau	Vegetable mold with partridge
Perdreau en chartreuse	Partridge in vegetable mold
Perdreau aux choux	Partridge in cabbage (cabbage as plural is French culinary usage)

Game

Chevreuil (masculine, singular)	Roebuck
Le cuissot de chevreuil	**Leg of roebuck**
Venaison (feminine, singular)	Venison, game in general
Lapereau (masculine, singular)	Wild rabbit
Lapin (masculine, singular)	Domestic rabbit
Lievre (masculine, singular)	Hare
Le Civet de lièvre	**Hasenpfeffer (hare stew made with blood)**
Le rable de lièvre	**Saddle of hare (back)**
Marcassin (masculine, singular)	Young boar
La cuisse de sanglier	**Boar leg**

Fish and Shellfish

Alose (feminine, singular)	Shad
Alose grillée	**Broiled shad**
Les oeufs d'alose	**Shad roe**
Les oeufs d'alose grillé	**Broiled shad roe**
Anguille (feminine, singular)	Eel
Anguille frite	**Fried eel**
Anguille fumée	**Smoked eel**
Anguille grillée	**Broiled eel**
Roulade d'anguille	**Stuffed eel**
Bar Rayé (masculine, singular)	Striped bass
Barbue (feminine, singular)	Flounder
Brochet (masculine, singular)	Pike
Cabillaud (masculine, singular)	Codfish
Morue fraiche (feminine, singular)	Scrod (fresh)
Carpe (feminine, singular)	Carp
Coquilles Saint-Jacques feminine, plural)	Scallops
Coquilles Saint-Jacques grillées	**Broiled scallops**

Crabes (masculine, plural)	Crabs
Crabes mous	Soft shell crabs
Crevettes (feminine, plural)	Shrimp
Crevettes frites	Fried shrimp
Crevettes froides	Cold shrimp
Crevettes grillées	Broiled shrimp
Crevettes sur glace	Shrimp on ice
Cocktail de crevettes	Shrimp cocktail
Ecrevisses (feminine, plural)	Crayfish, Crawfish
Ecrevisses à la nage	Boiled crayfish (culinary meaning)
Escargots (masculine, plural)	Snails
Escargots bourguignonne	Snails in garlic butter
Espadon (masculine, singular)	Swordfish
Esturgeon (masculine, singular)	Sturgeon
Esturgeon fumé	Smoked sturgeon
Grenouilles (feminine, plural)	Frogs
Cuisses de Grenouilles sautés	Frog legs sauteed
Homard (masculine, singular)	Lobster
Homard à l'Americaine	Lobster americaine
Homard froid	Cold lobster
Homard Newburgh	Lobster newburgh
Homard Parisienne	Cold garnished lobster
Homard Thermidor	Lobster Thermidor
Huîtres (feminine, plural)	Oysters
Huîtres frites	Fried oysters
Huîtres natures	Oysters on half shell
Huîtres Rockefeller	Oysters Rockefeller
Moules (feminine, plural)	Mussels
Oursin (masculine, singular)	Sea urchin
Rouget (masculine, singular)	Red snapper (culinary meaning)
Saumon (masculine, singular)	Salmon
Saumon fumé	Smoked salmon
Saumon poché	Poached salmon

Sole (feminine, singular)	Sole
Sole dorée	Golden brown sole
Sole sautée	Sauteed sole
Filets de sole	Fillets of sole
Filets de sole sautés	Fillet of sole sauteed
Thon (masculine, singular)	Tunafish
Truit (feminine, singular)	Trout
Truite au bleu	Poached blue trout
Turbot (masculine, singular)	Turbot

Vegetables

Artichaut (masculine, singular)	Artichoke
Artichauts (plural)	
Artichauts en purée	Puree of artichokes
Fond d'artichaut	Artichoke bottom
Fonds d'artichauts	Artichoke bottoms (plural)
Artichaut hollandaise	Artichoke with Hollandaise sauce
Artichauts à la vinaigrette	Marinated artichokes
Coeurs d'artichauts	Artichoke hearts
Asperges (feminine, plural)	Asparagus
Asperges froides	Cold asparagus
Asperges gratinées	Oven baked asparagus
Asperges milanaise	Asparagus sprinkled with cheese and baked
Pointes d'asperges	Asparagus tips
Pointes d'asperges au beurre	Buttered asparagus tips
Aubergine (feminine, singular)	Eggplant
Aubergines (plural)	
Aubergine farcie	Stuffed eggplant
Aubergines frites	Slices of fried eggplant (culinary meaning)
Aubergines grillées	Slices of broiled eggplant (culinary meaning)
Brocoli (masculine, singular)	Broccoli
Brocolis (plural)	

Brocoli au beurre	Buttered broccoli
Brocoli au gratin	Oven baked broccoli
Purée de brocoli	Broccoli puree
Carottes (feminine, plural)	Carrots
Carottes aux fines herbes	Carrots with herbs
Carottes glacées	Glazed carrots
Carottes nouvelles glacées	Glazed new carrots
Carottes Vichy	Vichy carrots
Céleri (masculine, singular)	Celery
Céleris (plural)	
Céleri braisé	Braised celery
Céleri en branches	Green (common) celery (culinary meaning)
Céleris à la grecque	Marinated celery
Céleri-rave	Celeriac; knob celery
Julienne de cèleri-rave	Julienne of knob celery
Purée de Cèleris	Puree of celery
Cêpes (masculine, plural)	Brown mushrooms (mostly imported)
Cêpes aux fines herbes	Mushrooms with herbs
Cêpes au jus	Brown mushrooms in meat juice
Cêpes au romarin	Rosemary-flavored mushrooms
Cêpes sautés	Mushrooms saute (Sauted Mushrooms)
Chanterelles (Girolles) (feminine, plural)	Chanterelle mushrooms
Champignon (masculine, singular)	Champignon mushrooms
Champignons (plural)	
Bouchée aux champignons	Small pattyshell with mushrooms
Champignons à la crème	Creamed mushrooms
Champignons à la Grecque	Marinated mushrooms
Champignons en croute	Mushrooms on crisp toast
Champignons grillés	Broiled mushrooms
Champignons sautés	Mushrooms sauted
Champignons en tartelettes	Mushrooms in tartlets
Champignons tournés	Turned (decoratively carved) Mushrooms (culinary meaning)

Omelette aux champignons	Mushroom omelette
Salade de champignons	Mushroom salad
Sauce aux champignons	Mushroom sauce
Têtes de champignons	Mushroom caps
Têtes de champignons farcis	Stuffed mushroom caps
Vol en vent aux champignons	Pattyshell with mushrooms
Chou (masculine, singular)	Cabbage
Choux (plural)	Cabbages
Chou braisé	Braised cabbage
Choux de Bruxelles	Brussels sprouts
Choux farcis	Stuffed cabbage (plural)
Chou-fleur (masculine, singular)	Cauliflower
Chou-fleur au beurre	Buttered cauliflower
Chou-fleur au gratin	Baked cauliflower
Chou rouge	Red cabbage
Chou rouge braisé	Braised red cabbage
Chou vert	Green cabbage
Choucroute	Sauerkraut
Salade de chou vert	Cole slaw
Concombre (masculine, singular)	Cucumber
Concombres (plural)	Cucumbers
Concombres à la dijonnaise	Cucumbers with mustard
Concombres étuves	Braised cucumbers
Concombres farcis	Stuffed cucumbers
Concombres glacés	Glazed cucumbers
Salade de concombres	Cucumber salad
Salade de concombres à l'aneth	Cucumber salad with dill
Courgette (feminine, singular)	Zucchini (summer squash)
Courgettes (plural)	
Courgettes frites	Fried zucchini
Courgettes farcies	Stuffed zucchini
Courgettes sautées aux amandines	Zucchini sautéed with almonds
Endives (feminine, plural)	Belgian endive
Endives braisées	Braised endive
Endives meuniere	Panfried endive
Salade d'endives	Endive salad

Epinards (feminine, plural)	Spinach
Epinards en branches	Leaf spinach (culinary meaning)
Epinards à la Crème	Creamed spinach
Epinards aux croutons	Spinach with croutons
Epinards aux fleurons	Spinach with fleurons (small puff paste crescents)
Epinards au gratin	Oven-browned spinach
Salade d'Epinards	Spinach salad
Fenouil (masculine, singular)	Fennel (anis)
Fenouil étuvé au beurre	Braised fennel
Fenouil au jus	Fennel with roast drippings
Fenouil à la Moelle	Braised fennel with marrow
Gombo (masculine, singular)	Gumbo, okra
Consommé aux gombo	Consomme with okra
Gombo à la creole	Okra creole (vegetable)
Gombo étuvé	Braised okra
Potage gombo creole	Gumbo (soup)
Haricots (masculine, plural)	Beans
Bouquet d'haricots verts	String beans, in bunches
Haricots blancs	Dried navy beans
Haricots panachés	Mixed beans
Haricots verts	String beans
Haricots verts sautés	String beans, sautéed
Laitue (feminine, singular)	Lettuce
Laitues (plural)	
Laitues braisées	Braised lettuce
Laitues à la crème	Creamed lettuce
Salade de laitue	Lettuce salad
Mais (masculine, singular)	Corn
Croquettes de mais	Corn croquettes
Mais à la crème	Creamed corn
Marrons (masculine, plural)	Chestnuts
Marrons étuvés	Braised chestnuts
Marrons glacés	Glazed chestnuts (sweet or salted)
Mont blanc de marrons	Chestnut dessert (sweet puree served with whipped cream and meringue)

Navets (masculine, plural)	White turnips
Navets glacés	Glazed turnips
Purée de navets	Turnip puree
Oignons (masculine, plural)	Onions
Oignons frit	Fried onions
Oignons glacés	Glazed onions
Oignons sautés	Onions sauted
Oseille (feminine, singular)	Sorrel (sour grass)
Purée d'oseille	Sorrel puree
Sauce à l'oseille	Sorrel sauce
Patates douces (feminine, plural)	Sweet Potatoes
Patates (douces) caramelisées	Candied sweet potatoes
Petits Pois (masculine, singular)	Green peas
Petits pois au beurre	Buttered peas
Petits pois à la Française	Peas with lettuce and onions (culinary meaning)
Pois mange-tout	Snow peas (chinese peas)
Pommes de Terre (feminine, plural)	Potatoes
Pommes à la créme	Creamed potatoes
Pommes duchesse	Duchess potatoes
Pommes noisettes	Noisette potatoes (tiny, oven-browned potatoes)
Pommes nature	Plain boiled potatoes
Pomme Lyonnaise	Home-fried with onions
Pommes paille	Potato straws
Pommes Parisienne	Tiny roasted potatoes
Pommes persillées	Parsley potatoes
Pommes sautées	Home-fried potatoes
Pommes soufflées	Souffle potatoes
Pomme au four	Baked Potato
Pommes vapeur	Steamed potatoes
Croquettes de pommes de terre	Potato croquettes
Purée de pommes de terre	Potato puree
Riz (masculine, singular)	Rice
Riz pilaw	Pilaff rice
Salsifis (masculine, singular)	Oyster plant (salsifis)

Salsifis au beurre	Buttered oyster plant
Salsifis frit	Fried oyster plant
Salsifis sautés	Panfried oyster plant
Tomates (feminine, plural)	Tomatoes
Tomates concassées	Chopped, stewed tomatoes
Tomates farcies	Stuffed tomatoes
Tomates grillées	Broiled tomatoes
Tomates sautées	Sauted tomatoes
Tomates aux herbes	Tomatoes with herbs
Salade de Tomate	Tomato salad
Nouilles (feminine, plural)	Noodles
Nouilles fraiches	Fresh noodles

Fruits and Berries

Abricots (masculine, plural)	Apricots
Abricots flambés	Flamed apricots
Abricots glacés	Glazed apricots
La glace à l'abricot	Apricot ice cream
La sauce à l'abricot	Apricot sauce
La tarte aux Abricots	Apricot tarts
Ananas (masculine, singular)	Pineapple
Ananas en surprise	Pineapple filled with pineapple sherbet
La glace à l'Ananas	Pineapple ice cream
Jus d'ananas	Pineapple juice
Airelles (feminine, plural)	Lingonberries (European cranberries)
Avelines (feminine, plural)	Hazelnuts, filberts
Noisettes (feminine, plural)	Hazelnuts (more elegant culinary term)
Avocat (masculine, singular)	Avocado
La Poire d'avocat	Alligator pear (more elegant culinary term)
Banane (feminine, singular)	Banana
Bananes (plural)	
Banane flambée	Flamed banana

Banane frite	Fried banana
Banane sautée	Panfried banana
Cerises (feminine, plural)	Cherries
Compôte de cerises	Stewed cherries
Cerises flambées	Flamed cherries
Cerises Jubilés	Cherries jubilee
La Sauce aux cerises	Cherry sauce
Citron (masculine, singular)	Lemon
La Glace au citron	Lemon sherbet
Sorbet de citron	Lemon sorbet
Coco (masculine, singular)	Coconut
La noix de coco (feminine, singular)	Coconut
Dattes (feminine, plural)	Dates
Dattes fourrées	Stuffed dates
Figue (feminine, singular)	Fig
Figues (plural)	
Figues sèches	Dried Figs
Framboises (feminine, plural)	Raspberries
Bavaroise aux framboises	Molded raspberry cream
Confiture de framboises	Raspberry jam
Creme aux framboises	Raspberry cream
Glace aux framboises	Raspberry sherbet
Mousse glacée aux framboises	Frozen raspberry mousse
Sauce aux framboises	Raspberry sauce
Fraises (feminine, plural)	Strawberries
Fraises au champagne	Strawberries in champagne
Fraises à la crème	Strawberries in cream
Fraises à la crème chantilly	Strawberries and whipped cream
Fraises Romanof	Strawberries Romanoff
Fraises sucrées	Sugared strawberries
Sauce aux fraises	Strawberry sauce
Groseilles (feminine, plural)	Currants
Groseilles à maquereau	Gooseberries
Groseilles noires (cassis)	Black Currants
La Gelée de groseilles	Red currant jelly

Mandarine **(feminine, singular)**	Tangerine
Melon **(masculine, singular)**	Melon
Melon glacé	Iced melon
Melon au jambon cru	Melon and prosciutto
Melon rafraichi	Chilled melon
Melon en surprise	Melon filled with fruits
Pasteque **(feminine, singular)**	Watermelon
La corbeille de pasteque	Watermelon basket
Myrtilles **(feminine, plural)**	Blueberries
Orange **(feminine, singular)**	Orange
Glace à l'orange	Orange sherbet
Jus d'orange	Orange juice
La Mousse glacée à l'orange	Frozen orange mousse
La Salade d'orange	Orange salad
Pamplemousse **(masculine, singular)**	Grapefruit
Demi pamplemousse sur glace	Half grapefruit on Ice
Demi pamplemousse aux fruits	Grapefruit half filled with assorted Fruits
Pêche **(feminine, singular)**	Peach
Pêches (plural)	Peaches
Pêches melba	Peach melba
Pêches pochées	Poached peaches
Poire **(feminine, singular)**	Pear
Poires (plural)	Pears
Poires pochées au vin rouge	Pears in red wine
Pomme **(feminine, singular)**	Apple
Pommes (plural)	Apples
La charlotte chaude de pommes	Hot apple charlotte
Crêpes fourrées aux pommes	Apple pancakes
Flan aux pommes	Open apple cake
Jus de pommes	Apple juice
Marmelade de pommes	Applesauce
Pommes bonne femme	Baked apple
Pommes glacées	Glazed apples
Prunes **(feminine, plural)**	Plums
Rhubarbe **(feminine, singular)**	Rhubarb

Desserts

Les beignets (masculine, plural)	Fritters
Beignets de pommes	Apple fritters
La charlotte à la Russe	Molded cream-lined with cake
La crème Bavaroise	Molded Bavarian cream
La crème au caramel	Caramel cream
La crème Chantilly	Whipped cream
La crème fouettée	Whipped cream
Les crêpes Suzette	Crepes suzette
La croûte dorée or pain perdu	French toast
L'omelette en surprise Norvegienne	Baked alaska (culinary meaning)
Omelette soufflée	Souffle omelette
Le soufflé	Souffle
Le soufflé au chocolat	Chocolate souffle
Le soufflé au Grand Marnier	Grand Marnier souffle
Le souffle glacé	Frozen souffle
Mont blanc aux marrons	Chestnut dessert
Oeufs à la neige	Floating island
La glace-crème	Ice cream
Glace au café	Coffee ice cream
Glace au chocolat	Chocolate ice cream
Glace aux noix	Hazelnut ice cream
Glace aux pistaches	Pistachio ice cream
Glace au pralin	Praline ice cream
Glace à la vanille	Vanilla ice cream
La bombe glacée	Ice cream bombe
Le parfait glacé	Ice cream parfait
La sauce à l'Anglaise	Vanilla sauce
Le Sorbet	Fruit sherbet
Le Granite	Fruit or brandy-flavored sherbet with ice crystals
Le Gateau	Cake
La Tarte	Open cake
Mignardises	Fancy cookies
Petits fours secs	Dry cookies
Petits fours glacés	Glazed tea cookies

Egg Dishes

Oeuf (masculine, singular)	Egg
Oeufs (plural)	
Oeufs brouillés	Scrambled eggs

Oeuf au plat	Fried egg
Oeuf poché	Poached egg
Omelette (feminine, singular)	Omelet

Phrases often used in French culinary descriptions

au beurre	In butter
au citron	In lemon
au four	Baked in oven
au gratin	Baked with cheese
au jus	In (its own) juice
au vin	In wine
aux amandes	With almonds
aux amandines	With small almonds
aux fruits	With fruits
aux legumes	With vegetables
aux pommes	With apples
aux fines herbes	With herbs
aux poivres verts	With green peppers
à la broche	On a skewer
à la carte	"On the card," on separate menu
à la crème	With cream
à la duchesse	In the duchess' style
à la gelée	Jellied
à la maison	In the house style
à la mode	"In style," with ice cream

Cheeses

Le plateau de fromages	Cheese tray with assorted cheeses

Bleu de Bresse
Brie
Brie de Meaux
Camembert
Cantal
Coulommiers
Emmenthal
Epoisse
Fromage de chevre
Gorgonzola
Gouda
Gruyere

Liederkranz
Limbourge
Neufchatel
Parmesan
Pont-l'Eveque
Port-salut
Roquefort
Saint-Marcellin
Stilton

Salads

Salade (feminine, singular)	Salad
La salade verte	Green salad
La salade de la saison	Salad of the season
La salade de betteraves	Beet salad

Frequently Misspelled Words

à l'Americaine
al dente
Arroz con pollo
Arrugola
Aspic
Avgolemono soup

Ballotine
Barquette(s)
Belle-vue
Bercy
Bernerplatte (die)
Beurre
Bratwurst (die)
Bibb lettuce
Biscuit
Bisque (soup)
Borscht
Bouillabaisse
Bouillon
Boulangère
Brunoise
Bourguignonne

Canape(s)
Chanterelles
Chasseur (sauce)
Chateaubriand
Chervil
Chicory
Choucroute
Clamart
Coupe (fruit, ice cream)
Court-bouillon
Crecy
Croquette(s)
Crudité

Dandelion
Darne
Demi-glace
Diable
Dolma
Doré(e) (golden brown)
Doria
Dubarry
Duchesse
Duxelles

Eclair
Endive
Escargots
Escarole

Feuilletage
Fines Herbes
Fleuron
Forestière

Gelée
Goujonette(s)
Grand'Mere
gratiné(e)
Gruyere
Guinea hen

Hasenpfeffer (der) (masculine, German)
Henri IV
Hors d'oeuvres

Jardinière
du Jour
Julienne

Kohlrabi

Lingonberries
Lyonnaise
Lucullus

Macaroon
Macédoine
Madeira Sauce (English)
Maître d'hôtel
Marchand de vin
Marguery
Marjoram
Marrons glacées
Meunière
Milles feuilles
Mirepoix
Moelle
Montmorency
Morilles
Mousseline (sauce)
Moutarde
Mozzarella

Navarin
Niçoise
Noisette

Paillettes au parmesan
Panache, Panachée, Panachés, Panachées
Parisienne
Pâté
Pâté à chou
Paupiette(s)

Bosc-Pear
Elberta Pear
Pfannkuchen (der)
Piemontaise
Pithiviers
au poivre
Pojarski
Polonaise
Pomegranate
Printanier
Profiterole(s)
Prosciutto Ham
Provençale
Provolone
Purée

Quenelle(s)

Ratatouille
Ricotta
Rissolé, rissolée, rissolés, rissolées
Rizotto
Rosemary
Rossini
Rutabagas

Saffron
Salpicon
Salsify
Saucisson
Sauerbraten (der)
Savoyard(e)
Scallopini
Schnecken (die)
Schnitzel
Sesame
Smitane
Sorrel
Soubise
Strasbourgeoise
Strudel

Tarragon
Tartelette(s)
Thyme
Torte (die)
Tournedos
Timbale
Truffle
Tureen

Veronique
Vichy
Vin blanc
Vin rouge
Vol au Vent

Won Ton Soup

Zephyr
Zucchini Squash

INDEX